The Chinese Language

The Chinese Language

Its History and Current Usage

by Daniel Kane

TUTTLE PUBLISHING
Tokyo • Rutland, Vermont • Singapore

Published by Tuttle Publishing, an imprint of Periplus Editions (HK) Ltd
with editorial offices at 364 Innovation Drive, North Clarendon, VT 05759 USA
and 130 Joo Seng Road #06-01 Singapore 368357.

Copyright © 2006 Daniel Kane

Library of Congress Control Number: 2005935620
ISBN 10: 0-8048-3853-4
ISBN 13: 978-0-8048-3853-5

Printed in Singapore

Distributed by

North America, Latin America & Europe
Tuttle Publishing
364 Innovation Drive
North Clarendon, VT 05759-9436, USA
Tel: 1 (802) 773 8930; Fax: 1 (802) 773 6993
info@tuttlepublishing.com
www.tuttlepublishing.com

Japan
Tuttle Publishing
Yaekari Building, 3F
5-4-12 Osaki, Shinagawa-ku
Tokyo 141 0032, Japan
Tel: (81) 3 5437 0171; Fax: (81) 3 5437 0755
tuttle-sales@gol.com

Asia Pacific
Berkeley Books Pte Ltd
130 Joo Seng Road #06-01
Singapore 368357
Tel: (65) 6280 1330; Fax: (65) 6280 6290
inquiries@periplus.com.sg
www.periplus.com

07 09 10 08
2 4 6 8 10 9 7 5 3

CONTENTS

CHAPTER ONE

Introduction

Chinese is generally considered a difficult language. It is. It is also a fascinating language, as well as an important language. It cannot be ignored.

A growing number of English speakers are learning the Chinese language, and are learning it very well, to the enrichment of their lives and the admiration of their friends.

Chinese does, however, present a number of challenges. Written Chinese looks like a random set of strokes, dots and dashes. In its handwritten form it looks like a series of undifferentiated squiggles. Spoken Chinese sounds like a rapid series of almost identical monosyllables with rising and falling intonations.

This book is a contemporary introduction to modern Chinese as it is used in China during the first few years of the twenty-first century. China has changed so much and so dramatically over the past century, and indeed over the past twenty years, and these changes are reflected in the language. Textbooks written only twenty years ago are now quaint. Much information on the actual use of *putonghua*, the use of dialects or various romanization systems is now out of date. The aim of this book is to present current realities.

China is a country with a long history, and to understand modern China we must know something of its past. The same applies to the language. Earlier stages of Chinese still have a deep influence on the current language, and we should at least be aware of such influences.

This book is not a language textbook. It does not try to teach Chinese. It is a book *about* Chinese. It has been written for people who are thinking of taking up Chinese and would like some insights into what they are letting themselves in for. As the Chinese strategist 孙子 Sunzi said,

知己知彼，百战百胜
zhī jǐ zhī bǐ, bǎi zhàn bǎi shèng
"Know yourself and know the other: a hundred battles, a hundred victories"

The same applies to learning Chinese.

1.1   What is Chinese?

For all intents and purposes, Chinese is *putonghua*, the common and official national language of China. It is virtually, but not entirely, identical with varieties of Mandarin spoken outside Mainland China. I use the term Mandarin in a general sense, and the term *putonghua* to refer to the standard language of China.

The speaker of English who takes up Chinese soon finds that little is familiar. This contrasts with most other languages he may have learned before, which at least have some words in common with English, or which are at least written in an alphabetic script. The learner discovers that practically all words in Chinese are composed of elements from within Chinese itself. These word elements are each written with an individual character. There are as many of these as the hairs on an ox, as the saying goes. Many of them are very ancient, going back to forms more than 3,000 years old, but are combined to express very modern concepts.

For example, using the basic character 电 **diàn** as a starting point in vocabulary-building:

Character	Pinyin	Meaning
电	**diàn**	originally meant "lightning"; nowadays it generally means electricity
电车	**diànchē**	"electric vehicle" is a tram
电影	**diànyǐng**	"electric shadows" means the movies
电脑	**diànnǎo**	"electric brain" is a computer
电传	**diànchuán**	"electric transmission" is a fax
电报	**diànbào**	"electric report" is a telegram
电话	**diànhuà**	"electric words" means telephone

And so on. The creation of new words by joining up existing Chinese words or word elements in new patterns stands in contrast to the practice in most languages you are likely to learn, which freely borrow words from other languages. Nowadays this is mainly English, and English itself has borrowed

huge numbers of words from other languages: *sputnik, zebra, tsunami, blitz...*
even if they are pronounced somewhat differently from the source language.
Modern Japanese accepts huge numbers of English words. Chinese does not.
There are some, which will be discussed later, but these are relatively few
in number. In Chinese you have to learn a certain number of unfamiliar
words, but once you have learned them you can combine them in ways
which produce thousands of different combinations. What seems to be a
string of monosyllables is really a string of word elements which are joined
together in various ways sanctioned by usage to form the working vocabulary
of Chinese.

1.1.1 Who speaks Chinese?

There are over a billion people in China, and almost all of them speak Chinese. Almost all the Chinese you are ever going to come in contact with
speak *putonghua,* "the common language." This was not always the case. A
hundred years ago China was a patchwork of spoken languages, with a written language based on the Confucian classics of 2,000 years earlier. One of
the aspects of nation building in the early twentieth century was the creation
of a national language, based on the colloquial language, rather than on the
traditional written one. It was based on the language of Beijing, but many of
the most influential writers of the new vernacular style were speakers of
southern dialects.

The national language reached a degree of maturity during the next few
decades, incorporating a variety of styles, northern and southern, vernacular
and literary. One of the major tasks of the new government in China in the
second half of the twentieth century was to standardize the "common language," which was still evolving from the earlier "national language." A
number of conferences during the 1950s determined the modern Chinese
script ("simplified characters"), the official romanization system (*pinyin*) and
the pronunciation, based on Beijing dialect. Linguists were not able to decide
on a standard grammatical description, and only a provisional scheme was
adopted. This is the basis of the grammatical descriptions one finds in textbooks from China.

Rapid and far-reaching social and political change meant that many terms became obsolete, and many new terms were introduced. China's "opening up to
the outside world" over the past couple of decades has had a dramatic effect
on the language, as in many other facets of life. Many older expressions have
been revived, and the traditional script is very much in vogue. Despite at-

tempts to insist on "standard characters" (the simplified script) there are now essentially two scripts in common use. Newspapers, magazines and novels are almost all in the simplified script, but many academic books and articles, new ones as well as reprints of older editions, continue to be in the traditional script. This is bad news for the learner, but such are the facts of life. The good news is that the scripts are not all that different, and after some period of adjustment most advanced students manage to learn to read, and sometimes write, both.

Mandarin spoken outside China has not necessarily followed the same stages. Simplified characters are not generally used outside China, except in Singapore. The *pinyin* romanization system is now almost universal, but the spelling of Chinese names outside China is very irregular. Usage in Taiwan, Hong Kong and Southeast Asia sometimes differs from that in China, but the differences are no greater than different usages in England, the United States and Australia.

Mandarin spoken in Chinese communities in Southeast Asia, Hong Kong and Taiwan is virtually, but not entirely, identical with the standard language of Mainland China. One might compare it with the varieties of English spoken in various countries. Many people speak it impeccably, many speak with a slight local accent, some speak with a strong local accent, but they are all basically speaking the same language.

Chinese dialects are another matter. The dialects spoken in south China differ markedly from each other, and from Mandarin. Sometimes it is asserted that linguistically they are really separate languages, but Chinese speakers all feel they are speaking Chinese, even if there are marked variations. Chinese dialects spoken in south China were brought to Southeast Asia by immigrants from the southeastern coastal areas of China.

Hong Kong is a rather special case, where English is the official language and Cantonese the most common variety of Chinese. Immigration from Mainland China and continuing integration over the next decades, however, will ensure the continued spread of *putonghua* in Hong Kong.

Chinese in Southeast Asia were avid supporters of the National Language Movement, and Chinese schools were established with Mandarin as the main language of instruction. The result is that Mandarin is very common in those countries. In Europe, the United States, Canada, Australia and New Zealand,

Mandarin is also now very commonly spoken, due to immigration from Mainland China and elsewhere over the past few decades.

Nowadays almost all Chinese speak Mandarin in varying degrees, and almost all foreigners learning Chinese learn Mandarin. The variety of Mandarin standard in Mainland China is called *putonghua*. That is the language described in this book.

1.1.2 Foreigners learning Chinese in the past

The earliest description I have found of Chinese in English was written by Bishop Wilkins in 1668. Wilkins wrote:

> As for the *China* Character and Language so much talked of in the world, if it be rightly represented by those that have lived in that Country, and pretend to understand the Language, there are many considerable faults in it...
>
> The *multitude* of Characters and Words, of which there are about 80000, others say 120000, and of these a man must have in readiness about eight or ten thousand before he is counted one that can write the Character, or judged fit to express his mind by it.
>
> These Characters are strangely complicated and difficult as the Figure of them ...
>
> Beside the difficulty and perplexedness of these Characters, there doth not seem to be any kind of Analogy (so far as I am able to judge) betwixt the shape of the Characters, and the things represented by them, as to the Affinity or Opposition betwixt them, nor any tolerable provision for necessary derivations.
>
> To this may be added the great *Æquivocalness* of the Language, every word having divers significations, some of them no less than twenty or thirty several sences; upon which account *Alvarez Semedo* affirms it to be more difficult than any other Language in the World.
>
> The *difficulty* of *pronouncing* it, every Syllable (as this of Ko) hath no less than ten several ways of pronunciation, as saith one Author, and it hath more than thirty several significations in the Anamitish Language, as *Alexander Rhodes* observes in this *Dictionary*. Such various Accents they are necessitated to make use of, as other people cannot imitate. The Syllable Ba, according to its various Accents, hath six several sences, of no kind of affinity or nearness to one another. And the most expert Men among themselves are not able so exactly distinguish in pronunciation, without using several attempts and repetitions to explain what they mean; or sometime by making the Figure of the Character they would express with their Fingers in the Air, or upon a Wall, or Table...
>
> In this is is to be acknowledged that they have a great advantage above the Latin, because their words are not declined by Terminations, but by Particles, which makes their Grammar much more easie than that of Latin.

I rather like the idea of those "who pretend to understand the language" (though "pretend" to Bishop Wilkins meant "to claim"), and also the "great aequivocalness" of the language. Some things never change.

The most famous of the early learners of Chinese, Matteo Ricci, remembered his characters by a complex scheme of imagining various parts of the characters as objects in a room. It must have worked, as he amazed Chinese mandarins by his ability to repeat long classical texts—backwards.

In 1759 James Flint was sent on a mission to Beijing. He was arrested and jailed for three years because he had entered areas off-limits to foreigners, and had illegally learned to speak Chinese!

In Giles' introduction to his *Chinese-English Dictionary* (1892), he notes "a close observer has not hesitated to declare that 'the Chinese language requires the age

TO

THE MEMBERS OF H.B.M. CONSULAR SERVICE

IN CHINA

AND OTHER STUDENTS OF THE CHINESE LANGUAGE

THIS DICTIONARY

IS SYMPATHETICALLY OFFERED

IN THE HOPE

THAT IT MAY LIGHTEN THE BURDEN

OF WHAT MUST ALWAYS BE A TOILSOME TASK

FIGURE 1 Dedication page of Giles' *Chinese-English Dictionary.*

of Methuselah to overtake it.' Yet an ordinary Chinaman practically manages to overtake it in less than an ordinary lifetime. The foreigner is of course at a disadvantage. He generally begins late in life... [but] the acquisition of Chinese need no longer be regarded as a hopeless task."

In 1907 Sir Walter Hillier reassured his readers in *The Chinese Language and How to Learn It*:

> From what has been said above it will be realized that the popular estimate of the supreme difficulty of the Chinese language is not far wide of the mark. Fluency in speaking, as it has been shown, is attainable by most people who will devote the necessary labour to its acquisition, and translation of written Chinese into a foreign language is not beyond the capacity of any diligent student... Theoretically, Chinese colloquial is not a difficult language to acquire... No traveller can pass two months in Japan without acquiring, without effort, a sufficient stock of words to make his wants easily known, whereas in China the stranger would leave the country after several months' sojourn with no idea of the language whatever beyond a few abusive epithets which had fastened themselves on his memory from their constant reiteration in his hearing.

And when the famous sinologist C.P. Fitzgerald went to China in 1924 and let it be known he wanted to learn Chinese, he was warned by long-term residents of Shanghai that "those who learn Chinese go mad."

Learning Chinese was probably restricted to missionaries, scholars, government officials and a few eccentrics until World War II, when the United States needed to train personnel quickly in basic Chinese. This led to a more streamlined and practical methodology. A number of textbooks were published in Britain and the United States, and Chinese departments were established in several universities. China began teaching Chinese to foreigners, and producing textbooks, as early as the 1950s. The various editions of their textbooks reveal the political vicissitudes of the times.

1.1.3 Foreigners learning Chinese today

From being an esoteric pastime a generation ago, the learning of Chinese has become big business. The Beijing Language Institute, for decades the major teaching institution and compiler of textbooks, has been upgraded to a university. There can be few universities throughout China which do not offer courses to foreigners. Textbooks, dictionaries, tapes, CDs, videos and other language learning aids proliferate. The Chinese government has established a

National Office for the Teaching of Chinese as a Foreign Language (NOCFL), which administers the HSK Chinese Proficiency Examination, the China Bridge Speech Competition and organizes debates in Chinese between teams from various countries. These competitions are broadcast on prime-time television, and Chinese are delighted to see foreigners learning Chinese with the same dedication their own teenagers are learning English.

The production of textbooks is now more professional, and the presentation much more elegant than ever before. The new series of textbooks published by NOCFL is likely to become mainstream for most beginners in Chinese departments at Western universities.

There is an enormous range of other books aimed at the tertiary market and at the general market. As might be expected, these vary greatly in quality and reliability. Despite the "methodology" used in the textbooks from China being somewhat different from that approved of by some applied linguists and language teachers in the West, all things being equal, if you want to learn the current language as it is actually used in China, you cannot go far wrong if you choose a recently published textbook compiled in China.

1.1.4 How long will it take me to learn Chinese?

Hearing foreigners speaking Chinese is no longer unusual in Beijing or Shanghai. Even on national television. Clearly it can be done, and done very well. But how, and how long will it take? This is one of the frequently asked questions from would-be learners. What we really need to ask is: "how long will it take to reach a particular level of competence in Chinese?" For many people, a smattering of a few words will meet their needs. University courses usually offer a three-year course, combining language study with literature and culture.

Diplomats need more specialized training. For many years these standards were set by the United States Foreign Service Institute. Five levels of competence were established for both speaking and reading for any foreign language. In rough terms, S1 was defined as basic conversational ability, S2 general conversational ability, S3 basic professional competence, S4 professional competence and S5 quasi-native speaker competence. And so on with the reading levels, R1–R5. Government personnel posted abroad were expected to have certain levels of competence, depending on the nature of their jobs. For people dealing with everyday embassy business, a level of S3 R3 was required. To reach this level of competence, an officer was given language training which differed according to the language in question. To reach S3 R3 in French, or most western European languages, required 520 hours. However, to reach a similar level of competence in Chinese, Japanese or Korean would require 2,400 hours. In other words, Chinese took five times longer to reach a certain level of competence than say, French or other western European languages. A three-year language course at university is likely to provide about 500 contact hours—about 20% of the time needed to reach the level of competence required of diplomats. The road to high levels of competence in Chinese is a long one.

1.2 HSK—The Chinese Proficiency Examination

Although the FSI scale is still used in some government departments, for most people the standard proficiency scale nowadays is the HSK, which is the abbreviated form for 汉语水平考试 *Hanyu Shuiping Kaoshi*, the Chinese Proficiency Examination. This is the examination all students studying in China are expected to sit for. It is used as a diagnostic test, to determine which aspects need to be improved: pronunciation, comprehension, the written language, and so on. If students have been studying full-time in China for one year (that is, 4 hours a day for about 40 weeks, or 1,600 hours) they are expected to reach the Basic Level. Passing this exam qualifies students to attend higher level courses, and a year later sit for the Intermediate Level examinations. If they pass this level, they are qualified to attend university courses in Chinese literature, history or other humanities subjects. The Advanced Level of the HSK is for people preparing to be interpreters, translators or professional teachers of Chinese. That requires another year of full-time study.

Experience has shown that the HSK is an excellent examination for students studying Chinese in China, but those who lack that language environment felt it a bit too challenging. There is now a Basic Level HSK which people studying Chinese overseas can aspire to. But the fact remains: if your ambition is to study Chinese history using Chinese sources, or Chinese philosophy or literature at tertiary level in China, or if you want to be a professional interpreter, translator or teacher, keeping to the various levels of the HSK is probably the right path to follow.

1.2.1 Learning "a bit of Chinese"

Of course not everyone aspires to become a professional interpreter, or even a government official who needs a knowledge of Chinese as a career skill. Many people master the minimum amount of Chinese to get along in general basic conversation without going to such lengths. There are now so many courses available, especially at the beginners level, that you will probably have quite a choice of classes. You may get hooked—many people do—and then you have a fairly major commitment on your hands. Or you may be happy with a dozen or so expressions and a couple of hundred words. It is far better than knowing nothing at all, and is sure to make your life in China or amongst Chinese far more interesting than is the fate of those to whom Chinese and the culture to which it gives access is a closed book.

1.2.2 The romanization question

When Westerners first encountered Chinese they wrote down the pronunciation of the characters in accordance with the orthographies they were familiar with in European languages. This led to French-type romanizations, German-type romanizations, and so on. Towards the end of the nineteenth century Herbert Giles modified an earlier English-based romanization, that of Thomas Wade, and this romanization became the most widely accepted form in English language publications. It is still commonly found in books on Chinese history, though it is gradually being replaced by *pinyin*. This romanization uses apostrophes to show aspiration and raised numbers to show tones (so 清 **Ch'ing**[1] for **Qīng**), though in popular publications both the apostrophes and the raised numbers are usually omitted.

The Chinese were also experimenting with a variety of phonetic scripts, of which the National Phonetic Symbols were adopted in 1918. (See Figure 2.) These symbols, which look rather like Japanese *katakana*, are printed at the right side of characters to indicate their pronunciation, rather than an inde-

---

The National Phonetic Symbols, with their equivalents in *pinyin*

ㄅ	b	ㄆ	p	ㄇ	m	ㄈ	f
ㄉ	d	ㄊ	t	ㄋ	n	ㄌ	l
ㄍ	g	ㄎ	k	ㄏ	h		
ㄐ	j	ㄑ	q	ㄒ	x		
ㄓ	zh	ㄔ	ch	ㄕ	sh	ㄖ	r
ㄗ	z	ㄘ	c	ㄙ	s		
ㄚ	a	ㄛ	e	ㄜ	o	ㄝ	ei
ㄞ	ai	ㄟ	ei	ㄠ	ao	ㄡ	ou
ㄢ	an	ㄣ	en	ㄤ	ang	ㄥ	eng
ㄧ	i	ㄨ	u	ㄩ	ü	ㄦ	-r

FIGURE 2 The National Phonetic Symbols.

pendent script. They are still occasionally used in textbooks and dictionaries published in Taiwan.

The National Phonetic Symbols were devised in the early twentieth century by a group of traditional philologists. They derive, ultimately, from the Song dynasty (960–1279) rhyme tables, which listed the initials of Middle Chinese under thirty-seven characters. All characters with readings beginning with **m-**, for example, were listed under 明 **míng**, all characters beginning with **l-** were listed under 来 **lái**. The characters from which some of the National Phonetic Symbols were derived are fairly clear in some cases: ㄅ [**b**] is from 包 **bāo** "package," ㄉ [**d**] is from 刀 **dāo** "knife," ㄋ [**n**] is from 乃 **nǎi** "then," ㄕ [**sh**] is from 尸 **shī** "corpse," ㄙ [**s**] is from 私 **sī** "selfish," ㄚ [**a**] is from ㄚ **yā** (see below), 日 [**r-**] is from 日 **rì** "sun," ㄡ [**ou**] is from 又 **yòu** "again," 一 [**i**] is from 一 **yī** "one," and ㄦ [**-r**] is from 兒 (simplified form 儿) **ér** "son." In other cases the derivation is not so clear: ㄓ [**zh**] is from the archaic form of 之 **zhī** "possessive particle"; ㄨ [**u**] is from the archaic form of 五 **wǔ** "five," and 彳 [**ch**] is from radical 60, 彳 **chì**. The old word for "maid" was ㄚ头 **yātou**, literally **ya**-head, the ㄚ being a picture of the plait down the back of a maid's head. The National Phonetic Symbols are not in common use, but the latest edition of the *Xinhua Zidian* (2004), the standard pocket dictionary of characters, lists the pronunciation of all its characters in the National Phonetic Symbols after the *pinyin* transcription.

In 1924 another scheme, 国语罗马字 **Gwoyeu Romatzyh**, or GR, was proposed. This system was characterized by using different spellings to indicate tones, examples as shown:

	1st tone	2nd tone	3rd tone	4th tone
Pinyin	郭 **guō**	国 **guó**	果 **guǒ**	过 **guò**
GR	郭 **guo**	国 **gwo**	果 **guoo**	过 **guoh**
Pinyin	贪 **tān**	谈 **tán**	毯 **tǎn**	探 **tàn**
GR	贪 **tan**	谈 **tarn**	毯 **taan**	探 **tann**
Pinyin	青 **qīng**	情 **qíng**	请 **qǐng**	庆 **qìng**
GR	青 **ching**	情 **chyng**	请 **chiing**	庆 **chinq**

The system is quite hard to learn, but distinguishes the tones more distinctly than the accent marks of *pinyin*: 买 **mae** "to buy," and 卖 **may** "to sell" are more clearly different words than 买 **mǎi** and 卖 **mài**, and this helps impress the correct tones on the memory. It used to be said that students began their studies by swearing at GR, but after a few years would swear by it. It still has its proponents and is still occasionally seen in academic papers, but it has also basically given way to *pinyin*.

It used to be said that sinologists had to be like musicians, who might compose in one key and readily transcribe into other keys. Books were published listing Chinese syllables with their romanization in a number of systems. Such books and lists are now pretty much obsolete. As recently as 1968 one author could complain "because of their large number, it would be rather tiresome to present a survey of even the very widely used transcriptions of Modern Standard Chinese." The issue is now settled once and for all.

拼音 *pinyin* has become established as *the* romanization system. Occasionally one sees other new romanization systems, such as that devised by Lin Yutang, in which GR **ching chyng chiing chinq** are written **ching**, **chirng**, **chiing** and **chingh**, or hybrids of *pinyin* which include tonal spelling (**qing, qirng, qiing, qingh**), but these are idiosyncratic.

1.2.3 The spread of *putonghua* in China

In 1982, the new constitution of the PRC specifically promoted the popularization of *putonghua* throughout the country. Standard Chinese was to be used in all Chinese schools and other institutions, on the radio, television, film and theater. The policy to make *putonghua* obligatory in all schools and other spheres of public life has been spectacularly successful. Nowadays practically everyone any foreigner is likely to meet speaks *putonghua*. And not only in the north of China. One can spend a whole day in the streets of a city like 西安 Xi'an and not hear a word of any language except standard *putonghua*.

A few years ago Shanghaiese was the main language of Shanghai, and still is. But Mandarin is extremely common everywhere. As well as the government policy, the massive expansion of *putonghua* is connected with the large numbers of non-Shanghaiese now attracted to live in this vibrant city. Shanghaiese tend to use *putonghua* for formal occasions. Participants at an academic conference will use *putonghua* in the seminars, Shanghaiese during a smoke break and revert to *putonghua* to continue the discussions. Even primary school children speak *putonghua* amongst themselves, outside school as well as in school, as any walk through a Shanghai housing estate will reveal. Many of their parents are concerned that their children are far more proficient in *putonghua* than Shanghaiese.

Cantonese is still the language of Guangzhou, of course, but Shenzhen and Zhuhai are immigrant cities, and the immigrants communicate amongst themselves and with local people in *putonghua*. Similarly, speakers of *putonghua* from the large cities who go into the provinces as administrators, teachers or simply visitors bring their language with them. A hundred years ago most Chinese spoke no language other than their own dialect, nor did they need to. Officials who had been through the official examination system could communicate amongst themselves in Mandarin, based on the language of the court in Beijing, but spoken with a very wide range of provincial accents.

That is no longer the case. There are probably few Chinese any foreigner is likely to meet who cannot speak *putonghua* reasonably well. Most will speak it fluently. *Putonghua* has become *the* language of China.

1.2.4 *Putonghua* in Hong Kong

Until recently *putonghua* was rarely heard on the streets of Hong Kong. Now it is heard everywhere. This partly reflects political reality: Hong Kong was returned to Chinese sovereignty in 1997, and the official language of China is *putonghua*. There is a large number of visitors, officials and recent arrivals from China, and many people in Hong Kong can see it is in their interests to have at least a nodding acquaintance with *putonghua*. The language of Hong Kong remains predominantly Cantonese, but the role of *putonghua* cannot but expand over the next few decades.

1.3 Mandarin in Southeast Asia

The Chinese of Southeast Asia were among the most enthusiastic supporters of the National Language Movement in the first half of the twentieth century. Wherever there were sizeable communities of Chinese, schools were established in which Mandarin was the main language of instruction. For decades movies and popular songs also spread a Mandarin consciousness throughout Southeast Asia. Under the name 华语 [華語] *Huayu*, Mandarin is one of four official languages of Singapore, and government campaigns encourage its use instead of the various Chinese dialects among the Chinese community. For the traveler in Southeast Asia—Malaysia, Vietnam, Cambodia, Indonesia— Mandarin is on par with English as a *lingua franca* with whom one can converse with practically any Chinese anywhere.

1.4 Chinese as a world language

"The sun never sets on the overseas Chinese," as Sun Yat-sen used to say, and that observation is now even truer than ever. Over the past twenty years hundreds of thousands of young educated Chinese have settled in the United States, Canada, Europe, Australia and other countries. Many commute between their new countries of residence and China. They include many Chinese intellectuals. This is a difficult term to explain because it means different things to different people. To some, it simply means an educated person. The traditional concept of intellectual was someone who had a commitment to society, history, philosophy, culture and generally the future of China. Monthly journals full of articles on such themes now circulate throughout the Chinese world—Mainland China, Hong Kong, Taiwan and the Chinese intellectual diaspora in the United States, Europe and elsewhere. The language of practically all these people is *putonghua*.

The rise of the internet has also contributed to Chinese becoming a world language, and it is said that there is more Chinese on the net than English.

1.4.1 Chinese dialects

Dialects are of great interest to linguists, and many foreigners like to pick up a few words of Shanghaiese, Cantonese or another dialect. The dialects are discussed in detail in Chapter Three. But there would be very few foreigners, if any, who did not already have a very good grasp of *putonghua* before learning even a few words of any of the dialects. The exception might be Hong Kong, where some missionaries and policemen learned Cantonese without learning Mandarin, but those days have probably come to an end.

1.4.2 How to start?

There are now thousands, tens of thousands of people learning Chinese as a second language—in high schools, universities and evening colleges. Universities and language-training centers in China are full of foreigners learning Chinese. Most of them are learning it very well. There is a huge range of textbooks and other learning aids available. It is easy to travel to China and easy to learn Chinese in China. It is also easy to begin to learn Chinese in practically any city of any size around the world. Check out evening classes at local colleges or high schools, or enroll in a university course if you are more ambitious. If you really want to learn Chinese, it is relatively easy to take the first steps.

1.4.3 The spoken language

Given that learning the written language takes a lot of time and effort, can the same be said about the spoken language? Can one learn spoken Chinese without learning the written language? The short answer is: yes and no. Research has shown that students who study only the spoken language intensively attain a level of competence in spoken Chinese far higher than those who are learning both written and spoken Chinese at the same time. In the short term. Beyond the basics, however, students who have learned characters (and associated them with the word elements, or morphemes, of which the Chinese language is basically constructed) are able to absorb and learn "higher level vocabulary" at a faster rate than those without this training in characters. In other words, you can get to a certain level of competence in spoken Chinese without learning the written language, but you cannot get much beyond that level of competence. There is practically nothing written in *pinyin* for you to increase your vocabulary, except textbooks. You can find some Chinese primary school textbooks with characters annotated in *pinyin*, but these are really to help children pronounce the characters correctly. They are a long way from "real Chinese." If you are really interested in Chinese for the long haul, you are better off learning Chinese characters right from the beginning—even if your progress is slow. If you are living in a Chinese-speaking environment, of course your knowledge of spoken Chinese will race ahead of the language of the textbooks you are using in class—but to really be able to engage in normal conversation with Chinese people (beyond bartering in the markets), you will still need the "higher level vocabulary" which comes from reading and consulting dictionaries.

The modern Chinese language has several levels, some more appropriate for the spoken language, some for the written. When China decided on the need for a national language in its first constitution, the question arose as to what sort of Chinese was going to be the national language. This was by no means obvious or uncontroversial, and a committee came up with a mixed language, which was based on northern Chinese but incorporated aspects of other varieties of Chinese, such as initial **v** and initial **ng**, and a notation to represent syllables which formerly ended in **p**, **t** or **k**, which still exist in Cantonese but which disappeared from the language of Beijing over 700 years ago. This plan was soon abandoned and "Mandarin" as spoken in Beijing was adopted as the standard language. At about the same time, a decision was made to adopt vernacular, or spoken Chinese, as the written style of the new national language, rather than the Classical Chinese of traditional China.

It took quite some time for this new style to develop, as it was still influenced by the native dialects of the writers and of course Classical Chinese, which was the language the early writers of vernacular literature had been educated in.

During the 1950s a series of conferences tried to determine a set of norms for the standard language, but this work was interrupted by the Cultural Revolution. The style adopted at this time was heavily influenced by translations of the Marxist classics, by peasant speech and by an aversion to anything "bourgeois" or "feudal." Over the past twenty years writers have developed a far more elegant style, incorporating many Classical Chinese expressions and drawing on the vast literary heritage.

1.5 Levels of Modern Chinese

The role Classical Chinese plays in Modern Chinese can be compared to the role that Latin and Greek roots, or word elements, play in English. If one goes through the parts of the human body, for example, one level of vocabulary is basic spoken English: *head, eye, nose, ear, hand, heart, liver, foot.* For each of these there is a word derived from Latin or Greek: *capital, ocular, nasal, aural, manual, cordial, hepatitis, podiatry.* The basic words are more homely, the words derived from Latin and Greek more educated. Similarly, in spoken Chinese the word for "head" is 头 **tóu**, in Classical Chinese 首 **shǒu**. The classical word is used in such expressions as 首都 **shǒudū** "capital" [head city], the vernacular word in 头疼 **tóuténg** "headache." In both Classical and vernacular Chinese "hand" is 手 **shǒu**, but "foot" is 脚 **jiǎo** in vernacular Chinese, and 足 **zú** in Classical. The Classical Chinese word for "eye" is 目 **mù** and in spoken Chinese 眼睛 **yǎnjìng**. Many classical words are still used in the modern language, many are obsolete, and many remain as word elements rather than words. "Wing" is 翅膀 **chìbǎng**, but the classical word 翼 **yì** is still found in 左翼 **zuǒyì** "left wing." "Dog" is 狗 **gǒu**, but the classical word 犬 **quǎn** is still found in 狂犬病 **kuángquǎnbìng** (mad dog disease), "rabies."

Drawing on the resources of the classical vocabulary has meant that most words of modern Chinese are made up of word elements—some classical, some vernacular. Very few words are borrowings from other languages in the sense that Japanese has many borrowings from English. Some of these word elements regularly translate a foreign suffix: 化 **huà**, for example, which originally means "to change," translates English -*ize*, so 现代化 **xiàndàihuà** [present era change] is "modernization," 国有化 **guóyǒuhuà** [country having change] is "nationalization." 化 **huà** does not always correspond to English -*ize* or -*ization*: 老年化 **lǎoniánhuà** [old years change] means "ageing" in the sense of an ageing population, and 复杂化 **fùzáhuà** means "to make something more complicated than it has to be." 化学 **huàxué**, the study of changes, is "chemistry." Other examples as follows:

The suffix 学 **xué** translates -*ology*, as in
  社会学 **shèhuìxué** "sociology," or
  人类学 **rénlèixué** [human type study] "anthropology"

The suffix 主义 **zhǔyì** translates -*ism*, so
  社会主义 **shèhuìzhǔyì** "socialism"
  资本主义 **zīběnzhǔyì** "capitalism"
  共产主义 **gòngchǎnzhǔyì** [common property -*ism*] "communism"

The classical suffix 者 **zhě** is added to these to indicate a person who practices the ideology:
  社会主义者 **shèhuìzhǔyìzhě** "socialist"
  学者 **xuézhě** "scholar"

You can build up a very large vocabulary of quite sophisticated words after you have learned a few hundred of these basic building blocks. But you have to know which combinations are acceptable in general usage, and which are not—you cannot simply combine word elements as you see fit.

1.5.1 Varieties of *putonghua*

Standard *putonghua* is based on the language of Beijing. People from all over China speak standard Chinese without any trace of a local accent. However, one also hears *putonghua* spoken with a wide variety of regional accents, which might differ as much as British English from American English. The major differences in accent (as distinct from dialect) in Chinese are:

(1)   Many speakers in south China do not distinguish their dentals from their retroflexes. They pronounce **sh** as **s**, **zh** as **z** and **ch** as **c**. So you will hear **wǒ sì Zōngguó yén** for **wǒ shi Zhōngguó rén** 我是中国人 [I am a Chinese]. This can be a bit confusing, but it is easy enough to get used to.

(2)   Many speakers do not use the characteristic final **r** of Beijing *putonghua*, and say 一点 **yīdiǎn** instead of 一点儿 **yīdiǎnr**, 这里 **zhèli** and 那里 **nàli** for 这儿 **zhèr** and 那儿 **nàr**, respectively. Many avoid the 儿 **r** ending completely.

(3)   The use of the neutral tone. Standard *putonghua* for "beautiful," for example, is 漂亮 **piàoliang** [liang is in the neutral tone]. Many speakers, however, pronounce **liàng** in the fourth tone: **piàoliàng**.

(4)   In some areas the tones tend to sound awry. The second tone sounds like the fourth tone, or the fourth tone sounds like the first tone. This can lead to some confusion, especially in words which are distinguished only by their tone, such as 买 **mǎi** "to buy," and 卖 **mài** "to sell." When **sh** is pronounced **s**, 四 **sì** "four" and 十 **shí** "ten" sound almost identical.

(5)   You hear many other minor differences in pronunciation as you move around the country. Initial **r** is pronounced in various ways: 日本 **Rìběn** "Japan" may be pronounced *Yiben, Ibben, Zippen, Nippen*, and so on. Many dialects mix up **n** and **l**, so one hears 兰 **lán** "orchid" for 男 **nán** "male," and vice versa. In Shanghai **sh** is pronounced **s**, so the city is called Sanghai or Sanghae. Final **ng** is often not distinguished from final **n**, so the surnames Chen and Cheng sound the same.

The preponderance of Shanghai officials in Beijing in recent years has made a Shanghai accent synonymous with being an important government official, which has given it a certain prestige. This accent is known as *Shang-pu*, or *Sang-pu*, short for "Shanghai *putonghua.*"

In recent times the invasion of Hong Kong and Taiwan culture in the form of pop songs, films and martial arts novels has its effect on *putonghua* with the adoption of numerous expressions from Taiwan Mandarin and Cantonese.

Generally speaking these differences do not impede comprehension, but sound more like a "lilt" or a "brogue," or perhaps like the characteristic intonation of Swedes or Irish people speaking English.

1.6 Tones

Chinese has tones. They are hard to imitate and hard to remember. Otherwise Chinese syllables are simple and seem to be easy to pronounce, though one should be careful with voiced and voiceless, aspirated and unaspirated, palatal and retroflex consonants, and try to get them right. Chinese syllables are not "hard to get your tongue around," as in some other languages.

It is in the area of grammar, however, that Chinese has it over most languages you might ever consider learning. Chinese has no declensions or conjugations. There are certain rules of word order, but they are also mostly straightforward: subject, verb, object (as in English), the adjective stands before the noun (as in English) and the adverb stands before its verb (different from

English). In Chinese "I'll come tomorrow" is 我明天来 **wǒ míngtian lái** [I tomorrow come], and "I came yesterday" is 我昨天来了 **wǒ zuótian lái le** [I yesterday come]. The verb **lái** "to come" does not change, but when the action has been completed, one has to add the particle 了 **le**. This is one of the trickier parts of Chinese grammar, on which more will be said later.

Such are the characteristics of modern standard *putonghua*. Let us now look at some of them in greater detail.

CHAPTER TWO

Chinese Characters

2.1 Origins

The invention of the Chinese script was traditionally accredited to the mythological 仓颉 Cang Jie, an official under the reign of the Yellow Emperor some 5,000 years ago. When he invented the Chinese script, it is said, ghosts and demons howled during the night. The modern learner of Chinese can empathize with this story. Cang Jie's name has been perpetuated into modern times as a type of character input method for Chinese word processors.

Symbols which some people think are ancestral to Chinese characters were found on clay pots discovered in the Yangshao culture in the village of 半坡 Banpo, near 西安 Xi'an. They are approximately 6,000 years old.

FIGURE 3 Symbols on pottery from Banpo, near Xi'an. Some scholars see a resemblance between these and early Chinese numerals.

The earliest continuous texts, however, are the oracle bone inscriptions of approximately 1300 BC. These characters are clearly ancestral to the modern script, and many can be identified with their modern descendants.

2.1.1 The traditional six categories

The traditional analysis of characters was based on the "six categories" of Xu Shen in his book 《说文解字》 **Shuō wén jiě zì** "Explanation of Simple Characters and Analysis of Compound Characters," usually called the *Shuowen*, published almost 2,000 years ago. The six categories are: (1) pictographs; (2) indicative characters; (3) associative characters; (4) characters formed from a radical and phonetic; (5) derivative characters; and (6) loan characters.

Examples of the six categories were:

(1) 指示 **zhǐshì** "indicate things" such as 上 **shàng** "above" and 下 **xià** "below";

(2) 象形 **xiàngxíng** "resemble form," such as 日 **rì** "sun" and 月 **yuè** "moon";

(3) 形声 **xíngshēng** "form and sound," such as 江 **jiāng** "river" and 河 **hé** "river";

(4) 会意 **huìyì** "combined meanings" such as 武 **wǔ** "military" and 信 **xìn** "trust";

(5) 转注 **zhuǎnzhù** "turn and derive" such as 考 **kǎo** "deceased father" [formal] and 老 **lǎo** "old," and

(6) 假借 **jiǎjiè** such as 领 **lǐng** "to lead" and 长 **zhǎng** "leader."

Groups (1) and (2) are self explanatory. Group 3 are the "radical and phonetic" characters, which in this case show 氵 "three dots of water" at the left to indicate that the character has something to do with water, while the remaining part of the character gives a clue to its pronunciation. In Group (4), 武 **wǔ** "military" is said to be made up of 止 **zhǐ** "to stop" and 戈 **gē** "halberd," a type of weapon. This character is often quoted by Chinese politicians to demonstrate the essentially pacifist nature of Chinese culture. 信 **xìn** "to trust" shows a man and "word": a man's word is his bond. Group (5) contains only a small number of characters, and there has been much debate over the last 2,000 years as to what exactly Xu Shen meant by this category. In Group (6), 令 **lìng** "order" is used to write the homophonous word 领 **lǐng** "to lead," and **cháng** "long" is used to write the (almost) homophonous word **zhǎng** "leader."

2.1.2 The modern three categories

Terms such as 象形 **xiàngxíng**, 会意 **huìyì**, 形声 **xíngshēng** and 假借 **jiǎjiè** are still commonly used technical terms in historical linguistics and paleography. The traditional six categories are traditionally listed in popular books on characters and calligraphy.

Modern Chinese paleographers have, however, proposed new ways of classifying characters. In 1935 Tang Lan published his *Introduction* to *the Study of Ancient Chinese Scripts*, in which he proposed his Three Principles theory. Tang divided characters into those depicting figures, those depicting concepts, and those depicting sounds. In 1956 Chen Mengjia pointed out some of the problems with this classification, and proposed a three principle theory of his own. Chen's three categories are pictographs, loan graphs and phonograms. This classification has been accepted by the doyen of Chinese paleography, Qiu Xigui, and now forms the basis of the classification below, rather than the venerable but dated "six categories" classification.

2.1.3 Pictographs

Many basic characters are pictographs, and can still be recognized as such in their modern form. They are even more obvious in the oracle bone script or the bronze inscription script. Traditional characters are given in square brackets. Typical examples are:

日 **rì** "sun"	牛 **niú** "ox"	目 **mù** "eye"
月 **yuè** "moon"	羊 **yáng** "sheep"	口 **kǒu** "mouth"
水 **shuǐ** "water"	马 [馬] **mǎ** "horse"	齿 [齒] **chǐ** "teeth"
山 **shān** "mountain"	鸟 [鳥] **niǎo** "bird"	舟 **zhōu** "boat"
雨 **yǔ** "rain"	鱼 [魚] **yú** "fish"	门 [門] **mén** "door"
田 **tián** "field"	人 **rén** "person"	木 **mù** "tree"

Characters such as 上 **shàng** "above," 下 **xià** "under," **yī** "one," 二 **èr** "two," 三 **sān** "three" can also be considered pictographs. Some characters are slightly modified pictures: 本 **běn** "root" from 木 **mù** "tree," and 刃 **rèn** "blade" from 刀 **dāo** "knife." Others combine characters in novel ways:

磊 **lěi** "to accumulate" from three stones;
森 **sēn** "forest" from three trees;
休 **xiū** "to rest" from 人 **rén** "person" and 木 **mù** "tree" (a person at the side of a tree);
旦 **dàn** "dawn" (showing the sun over the horizon);
明 **míng** "bright" from 日 **rì** "sun" and 月 **yuè** "moon," or
鸣 [鳴] **míng** ("to cry, of birds") from 口 **kǒu** "mouth" and 鸟 [鳥] **niǎo** "bird."

2.1.4 Loan graphs

Loans are more a way of using or adapting characters from existing characters, rather than a description of their structure. The term simply means that a character is used to write another word, or word element, in addition to that it normally does, or originally did. The principle is known in English as the "rebus" type of writing. When someone sends a text message "w8 4 me @ 7" they are using the same basic idea. "4" normally means the word "four," but here it is used to write a preposition which has the same pronunciation: "for." "@" is a symbol originally used in mathematics; here it stands for the preposition "at." "8" normally means "eight"; here it stands for part of a syllable, *ait*, so "w8" means "wait." And "7" has its usual meaning of seven, but in this context it means a particular hour of the day. Hence the message can easily be deciphered as "wait for me at 7 (o'clock)."

In the same way the character 之 **zhī** "to go" was written for the homophonous word 之 **zhī** "possessive particle." 安 **ān** "peace" was written for an interrogative pronoun 安 **ān** "where." The character 来 [來] **lái** was originally a picture of a wheat plant. The cognate form 麦 [麥] **mài** still means "wheat." Very early, however, this was borrowed to write the word for 来 [來] **lái** "to come." 舍 **shè** "a hut" could also take on the meaning for the word [捨] **shě** "to abandon," which in the simplified script has again been simplified to 舍. 能 **néng** "to be able" was originally a pictograph of a type of bear. The cognate form for "bear" 熊 **xióng** is still in use. 足 **zú** "a foot" was also used to write the word 足 **zú** "sufficient." It still is. 卒 **zú** "a soldier" was borrowed to write the word 卒 **zú** "to come to an end," meaning "to die." This is the main reason a character often has so many "meanings." It has been borrowed, at one time or another during China's long history, to write so many words, whose meanings differ vastly from one another.

This principle has been widely extended in the modern simplified script. 谷 **gǔ** "valley" is now the simplified written form for both [穀] **gǔ** "grain," and 谷 **gǔ** "valley"; 后 **hòu** "empress" for [後] **hòu** "afterwards" and 后 **hòu** "empress." 丑 **chǒu** "a clown in Beijing opera" is also written for [醜] **chǒu** "ugly"; and 面 **miàn** "side" for both [麵] **miàn** "noodles" as well as 面 **miàn** "side." There seems to be no confusion as to whether 后 **hòu** means "afterwards" or "empress" in context. In rapid handwriting, unofficial abbreviations are also common. A waiter in a restaurant might write 旦 **dàn** "dawn" for 蛋 **dàn** "egg," or 反 **fǎn** "against" for 饭 [飯] **fàn** "cooked rice," but would hardly write those forms in a school essay.

2.1.5 Phonographs

Phonographs are composed of two parts: a radical and a phonetic. The radicals are almost all pictographs, as are many of the phonetics. As these are by far the most numerous characters, we shall spend some time examining their component parts: radicals and phonetics.

2.1.6 How many radicals are there?

There were 540 radicals in the *Shuowen*. Modern dictionaries of oracle bone and bronze inscription characters still use this system, which presuppose the reader had internalized Xu Shen's radicals. The *Kangxi Dictionary*, published in 1716, adopted a simpler system from a dictionary compiled 100 years earlier, and arranged all characters under 214 radicals. (Refer to Figure 4.) The *Kangxi Dictionary*, named after a famous emperor of the Qing dynasty, under whose auspices it was compiled, became *the* standard dictionary of all China.

From the foreign learner's point of view, it was also the system used in every Chinese–English dictionary and practically any other reference work he might wish to consult.

The 214 radicals were arranged in an ascending order of stroke count, from 一 (with one stroke) to 龠 (with 17). They were in a set order, and foreign students of Chinese gave each radical a number to help remember its place in the series. So the "speech" radical 言 **yán** (written 訁 as a radical, 7 strokes) was 149; the "door" radical 门 [門, 8 strokes] **mén** 169; the "woman" radical 女 [3 strokes] **nǚ** 38; the "horse" radical 马 [馬, 10 strokes] **mǎ** 187; and so on. These were the first characters students were urged to learn, together with their numbers.

Many of the radicals are not used as characters in their own right, they are simply strokes under which other characters can be classified. For example, radical 8 亠 is little more than a symbol under which a variety of characters, such as 亡 **wáng** "to perish," 亥 **hài** "the twelfth of the earth branches," 交 **jiāo** "to hand over," 京 **jīng** "capital city," and 亭 **tíng** "pavilion" can be listed in a dictionary. It is not a character in its own right. Radical 14 冖 is the top part of 冠 **guān** "hat," 冤 **yuān** "injustice," 冥 **míng** "dark" and 冢 **zhǒng** "tomb," and this is where you will find those characters in a dictionary. Radical 40 宀 serves as a component of 安 **ān** "peace," 定 **dìng** "to settle," 官 **guān** "an official," 客 **kè** "guest," 室 **shì** "room," 害 **hài** "to harm," 家 **jiā** "family," 富 **fù** "wealthy," 察 **chá** "to investigate," 寶 **bǎo** "treasure," and 寵 **chǒng** "to love." Radical 53 广 is in 店 **diàn** "shop," 府 **fǔ** "government office," 廟 **miào** "temple," 康 **kāng** "healthy," 廠 **chǎng** "factory," 廚 **chú** "kitchen," and 廣 **guǎng** "broad." All of these radicals originally indicated various types of roofs, as is evident from the meaning of some of the characters, but certainly not obvious from the meaning of many others. Radical 27 厂, used in characters such as 厚 **hòu** "thick" and 原 **yuán** "plateau," is very similar to radical 53 广, and some characters could be found with either radical: **chú** "kitchen," for example, could be written 廚 or 厨. The standard simplified form is 厨, without the dot. In the simplified script, 广 has been adopted as the simplified form of 廣 **guǎng** "broad," while 厂 has now become the simplified form

FIGURE 4 Chart of Traditional Radicals

1 STROKE		夂	34	方	70	白	106
一	1	夊	35	无,旡	71	皮	107
丨	2	夕	36	日	72	皿	108
丶	3	大	37	曰	73	目,罒	109
丿	4	女	38	月	74	矛	110
乙	5	子	39	木	75	矢	111
亅	6	宀	40	欠	76	石	112
		寸	41	止	77	示,礻	113
2 STROKES		小	42	歹,歺	78	禸	114
二	7	尢,尣,尢	43	殳	79	禾	115
亠	8	尸	44	毋	80	穴	116
人,亻	9	屮	45	比	81	立	117
儿	10	山	46	毛	82		
入	11	巛,川,巜	47	氏	83	**6 STROKES**	
八	12	工	48	气	84	竹,⺮	118
冂	13	己	49	水,氵	85	米	119
冖	14	巾	50	火,灬	86	糸,糹	120
冫	15	干	51	爪,爫	87	缶	121
几	16	幺	52	父	88	网,罒,罓	122
凵	17	广	53	爻	89	羊	123
刀,刂	18	廴	54	爿	90	羽	124
力	19	廾	55	片	91	老	125
勹	20	弋	56	牙	92	而	126
匕	21	弓	57	牛,牜	93	耒	127
匚	22	彐,彑	58	犬,犭	94	耳	128
匸	23	彡	59			聿	129
十	24	彳	60	**5 STROKES**		肉,月	130
卜	25			玄	95	臣	131
卩,㔾	26	**4 STROKES**		玉,王,王	96	自	132
厂	27	心,忄,㣺	61	瓜	97	至	133
厶	28	戈	62	瓦	98	臼	134
又	29	戶	63	甘	99	舌	135
		手,扌	64	生	100	舛	136
3 STROKES		支	65	用	101	舟	137
口	30	攴,攵	66	田	102	艮	138
囗	31	文	67	疋	103	色	139
土	32	斗	68	疒	104	艸,艹	140
士	33	斤	69	癶	105	虍	141

FIGURE 4 *continued*

虫	142	邑,阝	163	風	182	**12 STROKES**	
血	143	酉	164	飛	183	黃	201
行	144	采	165	食	184	黍	202
衣, 衤	145	里	166	首	185	黑	203
西	146			香	186	黹	204
		8 STROKES				**13 STROKES**	
7 STROKES		金	167	**10 STROKES**		黽	205
見	147	長,镸	168	馬	187	鼎	206
角	148	門	169	骨	188	鼓	207
言	149	阜,阝	170	高	189	鼠	208
谷	150	隶	171	髟	190	**4 STROKES**	
豆	151	隹	172	鬥	191	鼻	209
豕	152	雨,⻗	173	鬯	192	齊	210
豸	153	青	174	鬲	193		
貝	154	非	175	鬼	194	**15 STROKES**	
赤	155					齒	211
走	156	**9 STROKES**		**11 STROKES**			
足	157	面	176	魚	195	**16 STROKES**	
身	158	革	177	鳥	196	龍	212
車	159	韋	178	鹵	197	龜	213
辛	160	韭	179	鹿	198		
辰	161	音	180	麥	199	**17 STROKES**	
辵, 辶	162	頁	181	麻	200	龠	214

of 廠 **chǎng** "factory." When the character for **xiě** "to write" was simplified, it also lost a dot: 寫 is now 写, without the dot. Needless to say, many of the characters in the list above have also been simplified, and are now under different radicals, and some radicals formerly used in only a few characters now have many more (simplified) characters classified under them.

Note, too, that radical 34 夂, and radical 35 夊, are almost identical: the long stroke to the right slightly protrudes through the shorter right to left stroke at the top in radical 35. They are often not distinguished in modern dictionaries of traditional characters. Strange to say, however, they are distinguished in modern dictionaries of unsimplified characters: 备 and 变 are listed under 夂, while 复 and 夏 are listed under 夊 .

Trying to find a character is sometimes straightforward enough, but at other times can be infuriating. Some dictionaries may contain a *List of Characters with Obscure Radicals* which one can consult if all other attempts at locating a particular character by radical were unsuccessful. Modern dictionaries generally have several indices, listing under pronunciation, under radicals, and under total number of strokes.

2.2 Simplified radicals

And so it was until simplified characters became official. The basic principles of the Chinese script remained much the same, but many of the details were modified. Some radicals remained the same, but many other radicals were simplified. Still, some other radicals remained unsimplified when used as characters in their own right, and simplified when used as radicals, for example: the speech radical was simplified to 讠 in 说话 **shuō huà** "say words" but remained as 言 in 语言 **yǔyán** "language."

This clearly necessitated a rethink of the radical system for classifying characters. The problem was that compilers of different dictionaries rethought the problem in different ways. The standard dictionary of characters, the *Xinhua Zidian*, and the standard dictionary of words, the *Xiandai Hanyu Zidian* [Dictionary of Modern Chinese] (1978) both used a new system of 189 radicals. The newly re-edited encyclopedic dictionary, the *Cihai* [Sea of Words] used 250, but its companion volume *Ciyuan* [Origin of Words] used the traditional 214 radicals. The 1977 edition of the standard *Chinese–English Dictionary*, which practically every student of Chinese acquires sooner or later, arranged its characters under 227 radicals. The revised edition (1995) uses 189 radicals, and adds a list of obscure ones.

In 1983, a government committee to unify the character referencing system was established, and proposed a unified system of 201 radicals. Most dictionaries published after that date, however, took no notice. The 2002 edition of the *Xiandai Hanyu Cidian*, published by the Academy of Social Sciences and the functional equivalent of the *Concise Oxford Dictionary*, still used the 189 radicals of the 1978 edition. The latest edition, however, the 5th, published in 2005, uses the new unified official system of 201 radicals. (See Figure 5.) Perhaps the situation has settled at last.

The student nowadays is faced with a number of systems, but luckily they are more or less variants of each other. Once one has mastered one system, it is not difficult to use a dictionary which uses another system.

In the simplified script, of course, the order of radicals has changed. 讠, the simplified form of 言 **yán**, was radical 10 (as it has 2 strokes instead of 7) in the *Chinese–English Dictionary*, but in the new official system it is regarded as a variant of 言, which is now number 166. In the traditional system it was radical 149. 门 **mén** the "door" radical was 46 and is now 47; 女 **nǔ** the "woman" radical was 73 and is now 56; and 马 the "horse" radical, which was 75, is now number 58. The traditional "horse" radical, [馬] **mǎ**, was radical 187.

Perhaps because of this chaos, there seems to be less emphasis nowadays on learning the number of the radicals. Chinese simply "know" where to look in a dictionary because they are so familiar with the system, much as you might look for "cat" towards the beginning of an English dictionary, for "mouse" about the middle and "snake" towards the end, without ever thinking what "number" a particular letter has in the alphabet. Foreign students also get used to their Chinese dictionaries, but it takes a long time, and has to be done step by step.

2.2.1 Notes to the Chinese Characters Unified Radical Chart (Draft)
This is now the official radical chart, used in the most recent editions of the authoritative 现代汉语词典 *Xiandai Hanyu Cidian* [Modern Chinese Dictionary] (5th edition, 2005) and the 新华字典 *Xinhua Zidian* [New China Dictionary] (10th edition, 2004). It is *not* a simplified radical index; rather, *it lists both traditional and simplified radicals in a single chart*. In this scheme there are 201 "main radicals" (主部首 **zhǔ bùshǒu**), and another 59 "subsidiary radicals" 附形部首 (**fùxíng bùshǒu**). The main radicals are either originally unsimplified radicals (such as the metal radical 金) or simplified radicals (such as the "cowry shell" radical 贝). The subsidiary radicals are then the originally simplified forms (such as for 钅) or the originally unsimplified forms (such as 貝 for 贝). All radicals are listed under the number of strokes in them; the subsidiary radicals are enclosed in round brackets, and their numbers, which are the same numbers as the main radicals they correspond to, are enclosed in square brackets. Generally speaking, the main radicals are the unsimplified forms, and the subsidiary radicals are the traditional forms, unless the unsimplified form is also common in simplified characters, when it is chosen as the main radical.

That is why this chart looks so confusing. Some examples might make the system clearer. If you are looking for a simplified character with the simplified "metal" radical 钅, you will find it under 5 strokes. However, it is enclosed in round brackets, which means it is a subsidiary radical. The number

FIGURE 5 Chinese Characters Unified Radical Chart (Draft): 汉字统一部首表（方案）

1 STROKE

一	1
丨	2
丿	3
丶	4
乛(丁乀乚乙)	5

2 STROKES

十	6
厂	7
匚	8
(卜)	[9]
(刂)	[22]
卜	9
冂	10
(亻)	[12]
(厂)	[7]
八	[11]
人	12
入	[12]
(宀)	[22]
(冂)	[10]
勹	13
(八)	[16]
儿	14
匕	15
几	16
亠	17
冫	18
(丷)	[11]
冖	19
(讠)	[166]
凵	20
卩	21
阝(在左)	[175]
阝(在右)	[159]
刀	22
力	23

又	24
厶	25
廴	26
(巴)	[21]

3 STROKES

干	27
工	28
土	29
(士)	[29]
(扌)	[80]
艹	30
寸	31
廾	32
大	33
(尢)	[34]
尢	34
弋	35
小	36
(⺌)	[36]
口	37
囗	38
山	39
巾	40
彳	41
彡	42
(犭)	[66]
夕	43
夂	44
(饣)	[185]
⺽	45
广	46
门	47
(氵)	[77]
(忄)	[98]
宀	48
辶	49
(彐)	[50]

(彑)	50
尸	51
己	52
(己)	[52]
(巳)	[52]
弓	53
子	54
屮	55
(屮)	[55]
女	56
飞	57
马	58
(纟)	50
(纟)	[148]
幺	59
巛	60

4 STROKES

王	61
无	62
韦	63
(歺)	[123]
木	64
(朩)	[64]
支	65
犬	66
歹	67
车(车)	68
牙	69
戈	70
(旡)	[62]
比	71
瓦	72
止	73
攴	74
(小)	[98]
(曰)	[75]
日(日)	75

(月)	[88]
贝	76
水	77
见	78
(牛)	[79]
牛(牛)	79
手	80
(龵)	[80]
气	81
毛	82
(攵)	[74]
长	83
片	84
斤	85
爪	86
父	87
(爫)	[34]
(⺼)	[86]
月	88
氏	89
欠	90
风	91
殳	92
文	93
方	94
火	95
斗	96
(灬)	[95]
户	97
(礻)	[100]
心	98
(聿)	[145]
(⺺)	[45]
毋	99

5 STROKES

(玉)	[61]
示	100
甘	101

FIGURE 5 *continued*

石	102	虍	130	里	157	香	183
龙	103	虫	131	(⻊)	[158]	鬼	184
(少)	[67]	肉	132	足	158	食	185
业	104	缶	133	邑	159	(風)	[91]
(氺)	[77]	舌	134	(臼)	[136]	音	186
目	105	竹(⺮)	135	身	160	首	187
田	106	臼	136	辵	[49]	(韋)	[63]
罒	107	自	137	采	161	(飛)	[57]
皿	108	血	138	谷	162		
(钅)	[176]	舟	139	豸	163	**10 STROKES**	
生	109	色	140	龟	164	髟	188
矢	110	齐	141	角	165	(馬)	[58]
禾	111	衣	142	言	166	髙	189
白	112	羊	143	辛	167	鬥	190
瓜	113	(⺶)	[143]			高	191
鸟	114	(⺷)	[143]	**8 STROKES**			
疒	115	米	144	青	168	**11 STROKES**	
立	116	聿	145	(長)	[83]	黄	192
穴	117	(⺺)	[145]	卓	169	(麥)	[149]
(礻)	[142]	艮	146	雨(⻗)	170	(鹵)	[156]
(聿)	[145]	(艸)	[30]	非	171	(鳥)	[114]
(艮)	[146]	羽	147	齿	172	(魚)	[177]
(疋)	[118]	糸	148	(虎)	[130]	麻	193
疋	118	(纟)	[148]	(門)	[47]	鹿	194
皮	119			黾	173		
癶	120	**7 STROKES**		隹	174	**12 STROKES**	
矛	121	麦	149	阜	175	鼎	195
(母)	[99]	(镸)	[83]	金	176	黑	196
		走	150	(飠)	[185]	黍	197
6 STROKES		赤	151	鱼	177		
耒	122	(車)	[68]	隶	178	**13 STROKES**	
老	123	豆	152			鼓	198
耳	124	酉	153	**9 STROKES**		(黽)	[173]
臣	125	辰	154	革	179	鼠	199
覀(西)	126	豕	155	(頁)	[128]		
而	127	卤	155	面	180	**14 STROKES**	
页	128	(貝)	[76]	韭	181	鼻	200
至	129	(見)	[78]	骨	182	(齊)	[141]

FIGURE 5 *continued*

15 STROKES (齒)	[172]	16 STROKES (龍)	[103]	17 STROKES (龜)	[164]
				龠	201

in square brackets next to it [176] indicates that the main radical corresponding to it is 金, number 176. Characters with both the main radical and the subsidiary radical are listed together, those with the main radical under 176, and those with the subsidiary radical under [176], immediately following. If, however, you are looking for an unsimplified character with the "cowry shell" radical 貝, you will find this under 7 strokes. However, this time the traditional (unsimplified) radical is the *subsidiary* radical, and so is enclosed in round brackets. The number next to it is [76], meaning it is the subsidiary form of the *main* radical 贝, the simplified form, which is number 76. Again, characters with main radical 76 and subsidiary radical [76] are listed together, 76 first, followed by [76]. The distinction between main radicals and subsidiary radicals is not necessarily one between traditional and simplified. The main radical form of the "knife" radical is 22 刀, and the subsidiary radical form is [22] 刂, but these were considered variants in the traditional system. Similarly, the main radical form of the "fire" radical is 95 火 and the subsidiary radical form is [95] 灬, which were also regarded as variants in the traditional system. Now 土, the traditional "earth" radical, is now main radical 29, and the traditional "scholar" radical 士 is now subsidiary radical [29], though semantically and historically they have nothing in common.

The first five radicals in this system are the single strokes 一 丨 丿 丶 一. Having located the radical, you look under the number of additional strokes, as in earlier systems. However now, if there are a number of characters with the same number of strokes, they are listed according to their first stroke, in accordance with the first five single-stroke radicals. This is an improvement on the traditional system, where the arrangement was arbitrary, and much time was spent looking up and down columns of characters until you located the one you were looking for.

All of this suggests several things. There does not seem to be a straightforward way of classifying characters under radicals, but that is the only accepted way there is—such schemes as the four corner system have not really caught on. The fact that both simplified and unsimplified characters are in common use has led to the complications of Figure 5. A dictionary is a tool of trade to the language learner. You have to get used to how it works, as you have to get used to a new DVD recorder or digital camera. As your new car or your new computer will probably not work the same as an older model, so your new Chinese dictionaries will very likely not work the same as the older ones either.

There is probably still much to be said for the old practice of learning the numbers of the (traditional) radicals by heart, or at least being familiar with their general order. Knowing the 214 traditional radicals at one's fingertips at least gives the serious student a firm foundation by which any number of variants can be absorbed, and easy access to older reference material can also be made.

The following list gives an idea of the role of radicals in the construction of characters:

RADICAL: 贝 [貝] **bèi** — "cowry shell"
EXAMPLES

财 [財] **cái** "wealth"	赌 [賭] **dǔ** "to gamble"
贫 [貧] **pín** "poor"	贿 [賄] **huì** "bribe"
贪 [貪] **tān** "greedy"	购 [購] **gòu** "to purchase"
贵 [貴] **guì** "expensive, honorable"	贸 [貿] **mào** "trade"
赠 [贈] **zèng** "to present"	赎 [贖] **shú** "to redeem"

This radical was also in [買] **mǎi** "to buy" and [賣] **mài** "to sell," but has disappeared from the simplified forms 买 **mǎi** and 卖 **mài**, respectively.

RADICAL: 艹 **cǎo** — "grass"
EXAMPLES

花 **huā** "flower"	茶 **chá** "tea"	药 [藥] **yào** "medicine"
芍 **sháo** "peony"	蘑菇 **mógu** "mushroom"	蒜 **suàn** "garlic"
芥末 **jièmò** "mustard"	葡萄 **pútáo** "grape"	莲 [蓮] **lián** "lotus"
芝 **zhī** "sesame"	菜 **cài** "vegetable"	蕊 **ruǐ** "stamen"
苦 **kǔ** "bitter"	葵 **kuí** "sunflower"	藕 **ǒu** "lotus root"
苗 **miáo** "sprouts"	葱 **cōng** "spring onion"	兰 [蘭] **lán** "orchid"

RADICAL: 虫 [蟲] **chóng** — "insect"
EXAMPLES

虱 **shī** "louse"	蚊子 **wénzi** "mosquito"	蜂 **fēng** "bee"
蝌蚪 **kēdǒu** "tadpole"	蚯蚓 **qiūyǐn** "earthworm"	蜻蜓 **qíngtíng** "dragonfly"
蜈蚣 **wúgōng** "centipede"	蛇 **shé** "snake"	蜜 **mì** "honey"

蝴蝶 **húdié** "butterfly"	蜡 [蠟] **là** "wax"	蛊 [蠱]* **gǔ** "a sort of poison"
蝙蝠 **biānfú** "bat"	蚂蚁 [螞蟻] **mǎyǐ** "ant"	
蜘蛛 **zhízhū** "spider"	蛮 [蠻] **mán** "southern	
蟋蟀 **xīshuài** "cricket"	barbarian"	

According to Matthews, 蛊 **gǔ** means "to put all sorts of poisonous insects into a vessel, cover it up and leave it for a year; the insects devour each other until only one is left, this is **gǔ**." The concept may seem weird but it is still around: the saying 蛊惑人心 **gǔhuò rénxīn** "to poison people's minds" was common during the Cultural Revolution.

RADICAL: 刀 **dāo** — "knife"
EXAMPLES

刃 **rèn** "blade"	刎 **wěn** "to cut one's	剐 [剮] **guǎ** "to cut a criminal into pieces"
切 **qiē** "cut"	throat"	
刻 **kè** "to carve"	割 **gē** "to cut"	
剃 **tì** "to shave"	剑 [劍] **jiàn** "sword"	

RADICAL: 耳 **ěr** — "ear"
EXAMPLES

闻 [聞] **wén** "to hear"
聪 [聰] **cōng** "acuity of hearing" (in 聪明 [聰明] **cōngmíng** "intelligent")

耳 was also in the traditional forms for 聽 **tīng** "listen" and 聲 **shēng** "voice," which have now been simplified to 听 and 声 respectively.

RADICAL: 火 **huǒ** — "fire"
EXAMPLES

炒 **chǎo** "stir fry"	煤 **méi** "coal"	爆 **bào** "to explode"
烤 **kǎo** "roast"	灯 [燈] **dēng** "lamp"	

In some characters 火 **huǒ** appears as four dots (灬) along the bottom:

煮 **zhǔ** "to cook"	热 [熱] **rè** "hot"	点 [點] **diǎn** "a little, a bit, a dot"
煎 **jiān** "to fry"	熟 **shóu** "cooked"	

热 [熱] **rè** "hot" can also be used as a verb: 热饭 **rè fàn**, 热菜 **rè cài** "to heat up rice, to heat food." 点 originally meant to light a lamp (点灯 [點燈] **diǎn dēng**), thus the four dots.

When in this position, this radical is sometimes called 四点火 **sì diǎn huǒ** "four dots of fire."

RADICAL: 巾 **jīn** — "cloth"
EXAMPLES

帆 **fān** "sail"	席 **xí** "mat"	帘 [簾] **lián** "curtain"
帛 **bó** "silk"	帽 **mào** "hat"	

Note: The traditional form of 帘 [簾] shows the "bamboo" radical.

RADICAL: 钅[金] **jīn** — "metal"
EXAMPLES

钉 [釘] **dīng** "nail"	铅 [鉛] **qiān** "lead"	钱 [錢] **qián** "money"
针 [針] **zhēn** "needle"	铀 [鈾] **yóu** "uranium"	钢 [鋼] **gāng** "steel"
钏 [釧] **chuàn** "bracelet"	铜 [銅] **tóng** "bronze"	锡 [錫] **xī** "tin"
钓 [釣] **diào** "fish hook"	银 [銀] **yín** "silver"	锅 [鍋] **guō** "cooking pot"
钙 [鈣] **gài** "calcium"	锈 [銹] **xiù** "rust"	锚 [錨] **máo** "anchor"
钩 [鈎] **gōu** "hook"	锤 [錘] **chuí** "hammer"	铁 [鐵] **tiě** "iron"

RADICAL: 目 **mù** — "eye"
EXAMPLES

盲 **máng** "blind"	眼 **yǎn** "eye"	瞪 **dèng** "to stare"
看 **kàn** "look at"	睡 **shuì** "go to sleep"	瞳 **tóng** "pupil of the eye"
眉 **méi** "eyebrow"	瞄 **miáo** "aim at"	
眠 **mián** "sleep"	瞎 **xiā** "blind"	

In traditional dictionaries the character 相 **xiàng**—of which one of its meanings is "to look at, to examine,"—was listed under the 目 **mù** "eye" radical, not under the 木 **mù** "wood" radical, it is currently listed.

RADICAL: 木 **mù** — "tree"
EXAMPLES

本 **běn** "root"	桃 **táo** "peach"	橡 **xiàng** "oak"
杯 **bēi** "cup"	梁 **liáng** "beam"	树 [樹] **shù** "tree"
松 **sōng** "pine tree"	森 **sēn** "forest"	楼 [樓] **lóu** "building"
柴 **chái** "firewood"	枫 [楓] **fēng** "maple"	
桑 **sāng** "mulberry tree"	桥 [橋] **qiáo** "bridge"	

The unofficial character 柚 for 楼 appears on buildings, but not in print. The character 柚 is officially read **yòu**, and means "pomelo" (a tropical citrus fruit).

RADICAL: 鸟 [鳥] **niǎo** — "bird"

EXAMPLES

鸭 [鴨] **yā** "duck"	鸽子 [鴿子] **gēzi** "pigeon"
鸳鸯 [鴛鴦] **yuānyāng** "Mandarin duck"	鹅 [鵝] **é** "goose"
鸵鸟 [鴕鳥] **tuóniǎo** "ostrich"	鹌鹑 [鵪鶉] **ānchún** "quail"

RADICAL: 女 **nǚ** — "woman"

EXAMPLES

奶 **nǎi** "breast"	娘 **niáng** "girl"	婚 **hūn** "marriage"
妻 **qī** "wife"	姐 **jiě** "elder sister"	
姑 **gū** "girl"	妹 **mèi** "younger sister"	

The "woman" radical is also in a number of terms indicating something unpleasant, such as 奴 **nú** "slave," 奸 **jiān** "wicked, evil, treacherous" (written with three 女 in the traditional script: 姦), 妒 **dù** "jealous" and 佞 **nìng** "given to flattery," the female version of 仁 **rén**, the Confucian virtue of benevolence and kindness. Ample proof, say the feminists, of the inherent Confucian patriarchal hegemony in the Chinese writing system. However, it is easy enough to find characters with quite pleasant meanings with this radical: 妙 **miào** "wonderful, excellent, fine," 婷 **tíng** "graceful," 嫩 **nèn** "tender, delicate," 娇 **jiāo** "tender, lovely, charming," and of course 好 **hǎo** "good." Whatever the case, there has been no attempt in the various reforms of the Chinese script to deal with this perceived bias.

RADICAL: 犭 [犬] **quǎn** — "dog"

EXAMPLES

狗 **gǒu** "dog"	狼 **láng** "wolf"	獾 **huān** "badger"
狐 **hú** "fox"	猴 **hóu** "monkey"	猪 [豬] **zhū** "pig"
狮 [獅] **shī** "lion"	猿 **yuán** "ape"	

In the traditional form the character for 猪 **zhū** "pig" had the "pig" radical 豕, but the simplified form has a "dog" radical instead.

RADICAL: 日 **rì** — "sun"

EXAMPLES

旦 **dàn** "dawn"	星 **xīng** "star"	晚 **wǎn** "evening"
早 **zǎo** "early"	晨 **chén** "morning"	暑 **shǔ** "summer"

This radical should be distinguished from 曰 **yuē** "to say." In the simplified script 曰 is only used in a few characters: 旨 **zhǐ**, 曲 **qǔ**, 冒 **mào**. In the traditional script it was also used for 最 **zuì**, 會 **huì**, 曾 **zēng** and some others. Now 會 **huì** has been simplified to 会 **huì** and is under the 人/入 radical, while 最 **zuì** and 曾 **zēng** are listed under the 日 radical.

RADICAL: 月 [肉] **ròu** — "meat"
EXAMPLES

肌 **jī** "muscle"	胖 **pàng** "fat"	脑 [腦] **nǎo** "brain"
肚 **dù** "stomach"	背 **bèi** "back"	腮 **sāi** "cheek"
肝 **gān** "liver"	胆 **dǎn** "gall bladder"	腿 **tuǐ** "leg"
肘 **zhǒu** "elbow"	肺 **fèi** "lung"	肤 [膚] **fū** "skin"
肛 **gāng** "anus"	脚 **jiǎo** "foot"	脸 [臉] **liǎn** "face"
肥 **féi** "fat"	肠 [腸] **cháng** "intestines"	臀 **tún** "buttocks"
肩膀 **jiānbǎng** "shoulder"	腰 **yāo** "waist"	脐 [臍] **qí** "navel"

When used as a radical, 肉 **ròu** is written 月, and is indistinguishable from 月 **yuè** "moon." This was, in the traditional script, a separate radical (number 74), but not a common one. It can still be seen in the characters 期 **qī** "period of time," and 朔 **shuò** "first day of the new moon," which clearly have nothing to do with meat. In the simplified script, the characters with the former "moon" radical are included under the "meat" radical.

RADICAL: 饣 [食] **shí** — "food"
EXAMPLES

饭 [飯] **fàn** "cooked rice"	饱 [飽] **bǎo** "to have eaten enough"	饼 [餅] **bǐng** "griddle cake"
饥 [饑] **jī** "famine"	餐 **cān** "meal"	馒头 [饅頭] **mántou**
饮 [飲] **yǐn** "to drink"		"steamed bread"

The character 食 **shí** is slightly modified when it is used as a radical in the traditional script, and is written 飠. The simplified form is based on the cursive form 饣. In a few characters the slightly modified character 飠 is written at the bottom, as in 餐 **cān**. In the simplified script 食 is considered an independent character, different from 饣.

RADICAL: 扌 **shǒu** — "hand"
EXAMPLES

打 **dǎ** "hit"	拉 **lā** "pull"	捏 **niē** "to knead"
抓 **zhuā** "grasp"	按 **àn** "push down"	摇 **yáo** "to shake"
投 **tóu** "throw"	捆 **kǔn** "tie up"	摸 **mō** "to grope"
扶 **fú** "support"	捉 **zhuō** "catch"	择 [擇] **zé** "to choose"
招 **zhāo** "beckon"	插 **chā** "insert"	

In some characters, the radical is written at the bottom of the character and retains its original form: 掌 **zhǎng** "palm of the hand."

RADICAL: 氵 **shuǐ** — "water"
EXAMPLES

汁 **zhī** "juice"	泳 **yǒng** "swim"	渴 **kě** "thirsty"
池 **chí** "pond"	洋 **yáng** "ocean"	汤 [湯] **tāng** "soup" (formerly: "hot water")
汗 **hàn** "sweat"	海 **hǎi** "sea"	
江 **jiāng** "river"	浪 **làng** "wave"	湿 [濕] **shī** "wet"
泣 **qì** "weep"	泪 [淚] **lèi** "tears"	滴 **dī** "drip"
河 **hé** "river"	深 **shēn** "deep"	潮 **cháo** "tide"
泥 **ní** "mud"	浅 [淺] **qiǎn** "shallow"	泽 [澤] **zé** "marsh"
泡 **pào** "bubble"	液 **yè** "liquid"	浊 [濁] **zhuó** "muddy"
油 **yóu** "oil"	港 **gǎng** "harbor"	

In some characters 水 is written at the bottom, and retains its original form: 泉 **quán** "spring [of water]." 氵 is known as 三点水 **sān diǎn shuǐ** "three dots of water"—to distinguish it from 冫 the "ice" radical, also known as 两点水 **liǎng diǎn shuǐ** "two dots of water." 冫 only appears in a few words, such as 冰 **bīng** "ice," 冻 **dòng** "to freeze," 凉 **liáng** "cool," and, for obscure reasons, 冲 **chōng** "to pour boiling water on." It also appears as two dots in 冬 **dōng** "winter" and 寒 **hán** "cold" (although now 冬 **dōng** is listed under 夂 **zhì** "to follow," and 寒 **hán** is listed under 宀 the "roof" radical). Some of these words were listed under 冫 in the traditional script: 凉 **liáng** "cool" as [涼] and 冲 **chōng** "to pour boiling water on" as [沖].

RADICAL: 纟 **sī** — "silk"
EXAMPLES

红 [紅] **hóng** "red" (originally red silk)	绢 [絹] **juàn** "thin silk"
纱 [紗] **shā** "gauze"	绸 [綢] **chóu** "silk"
素 **sù** "plain, undecorated"	绿 [綠] **lǜ** "green"
绛 [絳] **jiàng** "deep red"	缩 [縮] **suō** "to shrink"
绒 [絨] **róng** "velvet"	

RADICAL: 疒 **bìng** — "sickness"
EXAMPLES

病 **bìng** "sick"	痘 **dòu** "smallpox"	瘦 **shòu** "thin"
疼 **téng** "pain"	痰 **tán** "phlegm"	瘟 **wēn** "epidemic"
痕 **hén** "scar"	疯 [瘋] **fēng** "madness"	
痔 **zhì** "piles"	瘤 **liú** "tumor"	

RADICAL: 土 **tū** 十 "earth"

EXAMPLES

地 **dì** "place"	城 **chéng** "city wall"	堤 **dī** "dyke"
坑 **kēng** "pit"	埋 **mái** "bury"	

RADICAL: 訟 **xīn** — "heart"

EXAMPLES

忍 **rěn** "patience"	忠 **zhōng** "loyal"	怒 **nù** "angry"

When the "heart" radical is written at the side of a character, it takes the form 忄: 怕 **pà** "fear." In the character 恕 **shù** "forgive," it is written in its original form, but at the bottom. In the traditional form of 爱 **ài** "love," namely [愛], the "heart" radical appears in the middle of the character. The simplified form of 爱 shows only 友 **yǒu** "friend"—the "heart" has disappeared.

RADICAL: 讠[言] **yán** — "speech"

EXAMPLES

记 [記] **jì** "to record"	请 [請] **qǐng** "to invite"
讨论 [討論] **tǎolùn** "to discuss"	谅 [諒] **liàng** "forgive"
许 [許] **xǔ** "to promise"	谈 [談] **tán** "chat"
讼 [訟] **sòng** "to accuse"	谋 [謀] **móu** "to plot"
诈 [詐] **zhà** "to deceive"	诺 [諾] **nuò** "to promise"
评 [評] **píng** "to criticize"	谓 [謂] **wèi** "to say"
诉 [訴] **sù** "to tell"	谎 [謊] **huǎng** "lies"
话 [話] **huà** "speech"	讲 [講] **jiǎng** "to speak"
诗 [詩] **shī** "poem"	谢 [謝] **xiè** "to thank"
说 [說] **shuō** "to speak"	译 [譯] **yì** "to translate"
误 [誤] **wù** "mistake"	读 [讀] **dú** "to read"
语言 [語言] **yǔyán** "language"	

RADICAL: 鱼 [魚] / 鱼 **yú** — "fish"

EXAMPLES

鲤 [鯉] **lǐ** "carp"	鳗鱼 [鰻魚] **mányǔ** "eel"
鲨鱼 [鯊魚] **shāyú** "shark"	鳄鱼 [鱷魚] **èyú** "crocodile"
鲸鱼 [鯨魚] **jīngyú** "whale"	

RADICAL: 雨 **yǔ** — "rain"

EXAMPLES

雪 **xuě** "snow"	雷 **léi** "thunder"
雹 **báo** "hail"	震 **zhèn** "earthquake"

| 霉 **méi** "mildew" | 雾 [霧] **wù** "fog" |
| 霜 **shuāng** "frost" | 露 **lù** "dew" |

In the traditional script [雲] **yún** "cloud" also had this radical. The simplified script 云 has revived the earliest form, which appears on the oracle bones. It is a picture of a swirling cloud. 云 is now under the radical 厶.

RADICAL: ⺮ **zhú** — "bamboo"

EXAMPLES

竿 **gān** "pole"	箱 **xiāng** "chest, box"	笼 **lóng** "bamboo basket"
笋 **sǔn** "bamboo shoots"	篙 **gāo** "boat pole"	符 **fú** "mark"
笛子 **dízi** "flute"	筑 [築] **zhù** "building"	第 **dì** "position"

The character 简 [簡] **jiǎn** "simple" originally referred to bamboo strips used to make books in ancient China. They were tied together with string. The ancient books can still be seen in the character 册 **cè** "book."

[書]**shǔ** originally meant "to write" and is a picture of a hand holding a brush over a table. The simplified form derives from the running stroke form of this character: 书, and now means "book." The traditional character for [筆] **bǐ** "writing brush" shows the same element. The simplified form 笔 shows bamboo at the top and hair at the bottom, a drawing of a Chinese writing brush.

2.3 The phonetics

In older textbooks more than 1,600 "phonetics" were listed. The phonetics were supposed to indicate the pronunciation of the character, and many of them did—more or less. Historical changes, however, meant that the system of phonetics, even in the traditional script, was so irregular as to be thoroughly misleading. It made more sense to regard the phonetic as the residual part of the character, besides the radical. Pages 51–52 list a few common phonetics. This will give you a general idea on how much the phonetic is relevant to the present pronunciation of the character. As you can see, some of the phonetics have been changed in their simplified forms.

In forms like [體] **tǐ** "body" and [禮] **lǐ** "ceremony," or [麗] **lì** "beautiful" and [曬] **shài** "to expose to the sun" the common "phonetics" of the traditional forms have disappeared in the simplified variants: 体 for [體], 礼 for [禮], 丽 for [麗] and 晒 for [曬].

包 **bāo** "package"

部 **bù** "section"

采 **cǎi** "pluck, gather"

才 **cái** "talent"

成 **chéng** "to become"

冬 **dōng** "winter"

多 **duō** "much"

反 **fǎn** "against"

分 **fēn** "divide"

富 **fù** "rich"

告 **gào** "report"

各 **gè** "each"

哥 **gē** "elder brother"

古 **gǔ** "ancient"

广 [廣] **guǎng** "broad"

果 **guǒ** "fruit"

害 **hài** "harm"

侯 **hóu** "lord"

或 **huò** "someone"

甲 **jiǎ** "armor"

交 **jiāo** "hand over"

今 **jīn** "now"

京 **jīng** "capital city"

九 **jiǔ** "nine"

可 **kě** "able"

孔 **kǒng** "surname of Confucius"

良 **liáng** "good"

跑 **pǎo** "to run"

陪 **péi** "accompany"

菜 **cài** "vegetable"

财 [財] **cái** "wealth"

城 **chéng** "city wall"

终 [終] **zhōng** "end"

侈 **chǐ** "extravagant"

饭 [飯] **fàn** "rice"

盆 **pén** "bowl"
粉 **fěn** "powder"

福 **fú** "good fortune"

造 **zào** "create"

略 **lüè** "plan"
路 **lù** "road"

歌 **gē** "song"

苦 **kǔ** "bitter"

扩 [擴] **kuò** "to broaden"

课 [課] **kè** "lesson"

瞎 **xiā** "blind"

喉 **hóu** "throat"

域 **yù** "territory"

押 **yā** "press down"

校 **xiào** "school"

念 **niàn** "to read"

凉 **liáng** "cool"

仇 **chóu** "enemy"

河 **hé** "river"

娘 **niáng** "woman"

材 **cái** "timber"

诚 [誠] **chéng** "sincere"

移 **yí** "to move"

板 **bǎn** "plank"

贫 [貧] **pín** "poor"

逼 **bī** "force"

靠 **kào** "rely on"

客 **kè** "guest"

姑 **gū** "girl"

割 **gē** "cut off"

猴 **hóu** "monkey"

鸭 [鴨] **yā** "duck"

贪 [貪] **tān** "corrupt, greedy"

景 **jǐng** "scene"
影 **yǐng** "shadow"

何 **hé** "what"

吼 **hǒu** "to roar"

每 **měi** "each"   海 **hǎi** "sea"   悔 **huǐ** "regret"
                                                        侮 **wǔ** "insult"

莫 **mò** "no one; do not"   模 **mó** "model"   漠 **mò** "desert"
                            暮 **mù** "evening"   墓 **mù** "grave"

前 **qián** "in front of"   剪 **jiǎn** "scissors"

且 **qiě** "moreover"   姐 **jiě** "elder sister"   祖 **zǔ** "ancestor"

秋 **qiū** "autumn, fall"   愁 **chóu** "worried"

少 **shǎo** "few"   纱 [紗] **shā** "gauze"   妙 **miào** "wonderful"

深 **shēn** "deep"   探 **tàn** "investigate"

市 **shì** "city"   肺 **fèi** "lung"

蜀 **shǔ** "ancient state"   浊 [濁] **zhuó** "muddy"   独 [獨] **dú** "alone"
                            烛 [燭] **zhú** "candle"

寺 **sì** "temple"   时 [時] **shí** "time"   等 **děng** "wait"
                            持 **chí** "hold"   特 **tè** "special"

台 [臺] **tái** "terrace"   治 **zhì** "control"   始 **shǐ** "beginning"

同 **tóng** "same"   筒 **tǒng** "tube"   铜 [銅] **tóng** "bronze"
                            洞 **dòng** "cave"

通 **tōng** "through"   痛 **tòng** "pain"   桶 **tǒng** "bucket"

忘 **wàng** "forget"   忙 **máng** "busy"

我 **wǒ** "I"   饿 **è** "hungry   俄 **è** "Russia"
                            鹅 [鵝] **é** "goose"

昔 **xī** "long ago"   借 **jiè** "borrow"   错 [錯] **cuò** "mistake"
                            惜 **xī** "pity"

先 **xiān** "first"   洗 **xǐ** "to wash"

译 [譯] **yì** "translate"   泽 [澤] **zé** "marsh"   择 [擇] **zé** "to choose"

由 **yóu** "from"   油 **yóu** "oil"   抽 **chōu** "extract"
                            轴 [軸] **zhóu** "axle"

余 **yú** "I"   除 **chú** "except,   徐 **xú** "go slowly"
                                get rid of"

早 **zǎo** "morning"   草 **cǎo** "grass"

争 **zhēng** "struggle"   净 **jìng** "clean"   静 **jìng** "quiet"

重 **zhòng** "heavy"   种 [種] **zhǒng** "type"   懂 **dǒng** "understand"

The reasons for the regularity and irregularity of the phonetics lay in the long history of Chinese. It is precisely such irregularities as 各 **gè** in 洛 **luò**, and 俞 **yú** in 偷 **tōu** that have given scholars some insight into the language of the Zhou dynasty, when these characters were formed. Others come from the simplification of the 540 radicals of the *Shuowen* to the 214 of the *Kangxi Dictionary*. Words like 市 **shì** "market" and 肺 **fèi** "lung" originally had nothing to do with each other. Even the simplified script has not regularized the number of different sounds represented by one phonetic. For example the element 又, in isolation pronounced **yòu**, is used as the "phonetic" in 汉 [漢] **hàn** "Chinese," 权 [權] **quán** "power," 难 [難] **nán** "difficult," 叹 [嘆] **tàn** "sigh" and even 戏 [戲] **xì** "drama," or 双 [雙] **shuāng** "double." In some cases the simplified script has regularized some phonetics, writing 肤 **fū** for [膚], for example, where 夫 **fū** is a closer indicator of the present pronunciation than 虍 **hǔ**, or 艺 **yì** for [藝] **yì**, using the phonetic 乙 **yǐ** instead of the more complex phonetic, pronounced **zhì**.

问 **wèn** "to ask" and 闻 **wén** "to hear" are often explained as "a mouth 口 at a door 门" and "an ear 耳 at a door 门" respectively, but etymologically they are derived from **mén** 门 as the phonetic element. Middle Chinese words beginning with **m-** and followed by **-iu-** are now pronounced with initial **w-**. This explains, by the way, the alternation between **m-** and **w-** in such words as 忘 **wàng** "to forget" and 忙 **máng** "busy." The same applies to Middle Chinese words beginning with **p-** and **b-**, followed by **-iu-**; they are now pronounced with initial **f-**. This explains the alternation between **b**, **p** and **f** in such words as **bēi** 悲 "sad," **pái** 排 "to arrange," and 非 **fēi** "not."

2.4 How many Chinese characters are there?

The perennial question. One of the traditional Chinese answers was "as numerous as the hairs on an ox." Chinese dictionaries certainly contain a lot of characters, often exceeding 10,000 and beyond, depending on the level of readership for each dictionary. The *Kangxi Dictionary* contains 47,035. The most recent large dictionary of Chinese characters, the *Hanyu Da Zidian*, published in 1986, contains 56,000.

But what is a more realistic figure for everyday purposes? Let us look at some statistics. For a start, the five volumes of *The Collected Works of Mao Zedong* contain more than 900,000 characters, but only 3,136 different characters are used.

Statistics based on a large sampling of modern material reveal the following picture: 28 characters make up 20% of a typical text; 163 characters 50%;

243 characters 60%; 363 characters 70%; 560 characters 80%; and 950 characters 90%. That is to say, with 950 characters you will know 90% of the characters in practically any modern text. That looks much more attainable. To cover 99% of a text, you will need just 2,400 characters.

That is not quite the whole story, because knowing the characters of a particular compound does not mean that you know what they mean when they are put together. Many expressions made up of very simple characters are by no means obvious. In addition, if you are reading very specialized material you will need the characters and vocabulary relevant to that discipline. But at least you can be reassured that the problem is of a finite nature.

There have been many discussions about what a basic list of frequently used characters should contain. In 1952 a list of 2,000 characters was issued by the Chinese Ministry of Education. In 1988 a list was published containing the 3,500 most frequently used characters. The first 2,500 were required to be taught in primary schools, and the remaining 1,000 at secondary level.

The *Xinhua Zidian* and the *Xiandai Hanyu Cidian*, mentioned above and meant for general use, contain 7,668 and 8,373 characters respectively. The most recent official *List of Generally Used Characters in Modern Chinese* lists 7,000 characters, or twice as many as the basic high school level of literacy. The standard *Chinese-English Dictionary* contains over 6,000 single character entries.

Whatever way you analyze these figures, you are dealing with a large number of characters. The first hundred or so characters you learn are in many ways the hardest to remember. After that, patterns begin to emerge, and you can remember characters by their component radicals and phonetics. It is still a lot of work, and there are many pitfalls, but it is something to latch onto! When you first start learning characters you count them—each one is an achievement. After a while you lose track of the number of characters you have learned—they just accumulate. Alas, they also fade away if you do not use them constantly. Keeping on top of characters is a constant task, and requires a lot of practice. The Chinese say it is like 逆水行舟 **nì shuǐ xíng zhōu** "rowing a boat against the tide." If you ease off your efforts you go backwards.

2.4.1 How to learn characters

Some people might hope that the characters might one day be replaced by some form of phonetic script, but that is not the present reality. Japanese uses the phonetic syllabaries, *hiragana* and *katakana*, along with characters (*kanji*), and one can start to read and write genuine Japanese more or less from Lesson One. The same applies for Korean, which from that point of view is even easier: you will learn your Korean in the native Korean phonetic script, *Hangul*, and you will probably not have to start learning characters until at quite an advanced state in your studies. With Chinese, however, characters start at Lesson One, and have to be (painstakingly) learned, one by one, lesson by lesson, until you have accumulated enough of them to begin seeing patterns, which help to remember and internalize them.

The maximum rate for the absorption of characters, especially at the beginning, is about 30 a week. It is going to take you quite some time before you have mastered the 2,400 characters needed to recognize 99% of a modern text, or any of the other benchmarks listed above.

Long before you reach that stage, however, you will be able to read some modified and simplified stories, perhaps with extensive vocabulary lists. It will take at least three years before you can expect to even begin to decipher a newspaper, or start to read a simple novel.

Faced with such a task, one can easily despair. Remember, however, that many people have done this. Perseverance brings rewards.

Nowadays there are many books available which make learning characters easier. Most of these analyze characters into their component radicals and phonetics, and give you the stroke order of the character. This is very important in learning to write characters which actually look (more or less) like the real thing. If you write the strokes in the wrong order, or the wrong direction, they are likely to look grotesque.

Many textbooks for learning characters go further, giving the ancient form of the pictographs, together with some explanation for why the character is written as it is. These hints are very important—the more one can latch onto, the better. Many Chinese characters were indeed "pictures" of everyday items: 鱼 [魚] **yú** "fish," 马 [馬] **mǎ** "horse," 象 **xiàng** "elephant," 龟 [龜] **guī** "turtle"—even if the modern forms, unsimplified or simplified, do not look much like fish, horses, elephants or turtles. For other characters, learning the structure can be made easier by seeing how the character was put together during the period in which the script developed. You can also learn about the principle of "borrowing"—when a character was used to write an unrelated word with the same (or similar) pronunciation. An early example was

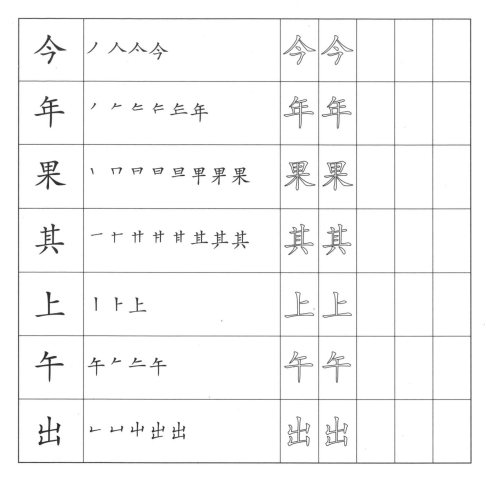

FIGURE 6 A modern character workbook indicating the correct order for writing the strokes of all characters in the accompanying textbook.

足 **zú** "foot," used to write the word 足 **zú** "enough." A later example was the classical word 没 **mò** "to sink" being "borrowed" to write the vernacular Chinese word 没 **méi**, as in 没有 **méiyǒu** "to be without, not to be there, to have none." This explains why 没 **méi** has the "water" radical.

The traditional way to start learning characters was to learn by heart a relatively short text containing several hundred common characters in context. This was the 《三字经》 *San Zi Jing* [The Three Character Classic], which was not only a primer for learning characters, but also a summary of Confucian morality. It is still available in most Chinese bookshops, and in various modern editions. A common Chinese saying is 孔子门前卖三字经 **Kǒngzǐ ménqián mài sān zì jīng** "to sell the *Three Character Classic* in front of the

FIGURE 7 An extract from the *Three Character Classic*. This was the first primer for children in China many decades ago.

door of Confucius," meaning to show off your meager knowledge in front of an expert. At some stage in your studies you might like to try learning characters in the traditional way. But preferably only after you have learned a lot of them from your modern textbook!

Referring to Figure 7: The first two lines of the text (starting from the right and reading downwards) are in modern, simplified characters and they read:

人之初，性本善　**rén zhī chū, xìng běn shàn**

性相近，习相远　**xìng xiāng jìn, xí xiāng yuǎn**

苟不教，性乃迁　**gǒu bù jiào, xìng nǎi qiān**

教之道，贵以专　**jiào zhī dào, guì yǐ zhuān**

In the beginning, man's nature is originally good. Their natures are close to each other, but their habits make them distant from each other. If not taught, his nature will then change [for the worse]. The most valuable principle of education lies in concentration.

2.4.2 Characters and *pinyin*

When you are beginning the study of Chinese, you will probably find the characters and the "basic sentences" in your textbook enough to keep you occupied. Learning the characters by transcribing *pinyin* texts into them, or transcribing characters into *pinyin*, will help remember them—though you should try to wean yourself off *pinyin* as your familiarity with characters increases. As you move on to "real Chinese," (that is, not "textbook Chinese") you will spend a great amount of time looking up characters. There is no point scribbling the meaning or the pronunciation in *pinyin* in the margins of a text you are reading. It will be more helpful, in the long run, to write your new characters in a spiral bound exercise book, leaving plenty of space to note down a few compounds you think might be useful, or add other comments that help you to remember the character better. This will help you recognize the characters out of the context in which you have learned them.

2.5 Simplification

In 1956 the Chinese Government published the *Scheme for Simplifying Chinese Characters*, and in 1964 the *Complete List of Simplified Characters* was put into common use. The 1964 list contained a total of 2,236 simplified characters, eliminating 2,264 complex characters—mainly through the simplifying of complex radicals and phonetics. This list was reissued in 1986, with some minor amendments.

第二次汉字简化方案（草案）
第一表（248个）

一、不作简化偏旁用的简化字.

本表共收简化字 172 个。按读音的拼音字母顺序 排列。
本表的简化字都不得作简化偏旁使用。

A
忕〔憾〕

B
巴〔芭笆粑〕
邦〔帮〕
苊〔蓖篦蔽〕
毕〔弊〕
毕几〔哔叽〕
扁〔蒱蒱褊〕
屏〔摒〕
广〔病〕
捗〔播〕
卩〔部〕

C
采〔彩〕
芽〔菜蔡〕
少〔餐〕
仓〔舱〕
芷〔藏〕
叉〔权权权汉〕
抐〔撤〕
眍〔眍〕
蒭〔葱〕

D
荅〔答〕
旦〔蛋〕
弨〔弹〕
跀〔蹈〕

E
式〔贰〕

F
忿〔愤〕
孚〔孵〕

和〔稻〕
辺〔道〕
屟〔殿〕
付〔副〕

G
杆〔秆竿〕
苓〔董〕
叙〔罐〕
桂〔鳜〕
果〔裹〕
炖〔燉〕

H
荮〔薅〕
合〔盒〕
胡〔葫猢蝴糊〕

夫〔伕〕
实〔富〕

丁〔叮盯钉钉〕
勾〔钩〕
斗拱〔枓栱〕
朴〔短〕

殳〔毁〕

J
笈〔籍〕
迠〔建〕
江〔豇〕
各〔酱〕
交〔胶〕
芡〔椒〕
亍〔街〕
井〔阱〕
埘〔境〕
铕〔镜〕
芫〔韭〕①
氿〔酒〕
桔〔橘〕②
钬〔镢钁〕

K
卡几〔咔叽〕
忼〔慷〕
滀〔溜溜熘馏〕
倍〔靠〕
科斗〔蝌蚪〕
牧〔款〕

L
兰〔蓝篮〕
泞〔澜滥〕
讠〔阑〕
忏〔懒〕
纟〔缆〕
轰〔磊〕
芀〔荔〕
功〔璃〕
昻〔量〕
了〔潦〕③
仃〔僚〕
灯〔燎〕
宁〔寮寥〕
庁〔廖〕
矹〔磷〕
令〔龄〕
淄〔瀦〕
房〔掳〕

M
忙〔慢〕

耗〔帽〕
皃〔貌〕
灮〔煤〕
芑龙〔矇眬〕
〔朦胧〕
〔蒙眬〕

N
酕〔酿〕
吂〔虐〕

P
辟历〔霹雳〕

Q
沏〔漆〕
岐〔歧〕
口〔器〕
讦〔谦〕
汗〔潜〕
欠〔歉〕
垟〔墙〕
劥〔勤〕
丘引〔蚯蚓〕

距〔渠〕

R
吐〔嚷〕
坴〔壤〕
亻〔儒〕

S
宷〔赛〕
扇〔煽搧〕
丄〔绅紳〕
勺〔杓〕
纵〔输〕
夹〔爽〕
厶〔私〕
祘〔算〕

T
太〔泰〕
杬〔檀〕
扩〔糖〕
套〔套〕
卷〔腾〕
仃〔停〕④

W

秋〔稳〕
午〔舞〕

X
希〔稀〕
息〔熄〕
盰〔瞎〕
钍〔镶〕
梄〔橡〕
肖〔萧〕
跬〔鞋〕
仪〔信〕

厷〔雄〕
多〔修〕
宀〔宣〕
疣〔癣〕
虺〔靴〕
彐〔雪〕
忄〔愉〕
闫〔阎〕
汃〔演〕
忔〔意〕

肊〔臆〕
羽〔翼〕
辺〔迎〕
彡〔影〕
朋〔腾〕
沈〔游〕
忦〔愉〕
迀〔遇〕①
予〔预像〕
元〔圆〕
屍〔原〕

沅〔源〕
纺〔缘〕

Z
赞〔赞〕
宲〔寨〕
帐〔账〕
轫〔辙〕
夿〔整〕
孑〔籽〕
咀〔嘴〕②
坐〔座〕

① 迂回的迂仍读 yū。　② 咀嚼的咀仍读 jǔ。

二、可作简化偏旁用的简化字

本表共收简化字 21 个。按读音的拼音字母顺序排列。

B
鼻〔鼻〕

C
宊〔察嚓〕

G
志〔感〕

J
北〔冀〕
贝〔具〕

L
峀〔留〕

M
匸〔眉嵋〕
芐〔蒙〕
百〔面〕

N
申〔囊曩〕
专〔青〕

柔〔桑〕
屈〔属〕

T
坐〔堂〕

Y
勿〔易〕
妛〔婴〕

Z
巳〔展辗〕
真〔真〕
直〔直〕
卆〔卒〕
专〔尊〕

三、应用 21 个可作简化偏旁用的简化字
类推简化得出来的简化字

本表共收类推出来的简化字 55 个。按 21 个可作简化偏旁用的简化字的顺序排列。同一部首中的简化字，按笔数排列。

鼻	蚨〔蟒〕	喙〔嗓〕	慎〔慎〕
鼾〔鼾〕	百	屡	演〔滇〕
宊	绐〔缅〕	喎〔喎〕	镇〔镇〕
按〔擦〕	申	暆〔瞤〕	颠〔颠〕
忈	抻〔攘〕	坐	直
扺〔撼〕	专	蛭〔蟥〕	值〔值〕
忦〔憾〕	诗〔请〕	剐〔剐〕	植〔植〕
北	芌〔菁〕	伤〔伤〕	殖〔殖〕
驰〔骥〕	狫〔猜〕	肠〔肠〕	罝〔置〕
贝	忮〔情〕	赐〔赐〕	卆
俱〔俱〕	泫〔清〕	钖〔锡〕	晬〔晬〕
怳〔惧〕	暒〔晴〕	踼〔踢〕	怊〔悴〕
枧〔枧〕	暒〔睛〕	妛	碎〔碎〕
峀	请〔静〕	绠〔绥〕	痒〔痒〕
榴〔榴〕	桜〔樱〕	怊〔悴〕	粹〔粹〕
瑠〔瘤〕	精〔精〕	巳	翠〔翠〕
尸	靛〔靛〕	矴〔碇〕	醉〔醉〕
妠〔媚〕	柔	真	专
芐	揉〔揉〕	填〔填〕	挼〔搏〕

FIGURES 8 & 9 The second installment of simplified characters issued in 1979. They were used in the newspapers but withdrawn three weeks later.

In December 1979 a second list of character simplification was released by the Chinese Government, and daily newspapers were published with these new characters. There was a public outcry, however, and the list was withdrawn after three weeks, to "allow the masses to decide" which were acceptable and which were not. (See Figures 8 and 9.)

Some of these characters have caught on. In Beijing one often sees 柚 for 楼 [樓] **lóu** "building," and 丁 for 街 **jiē** "street." 桔 has been commonly written for 橘 **jú** "orange, tangerine" for a long time, although it is still regarded as a "vulgar character," and not an official simplified character. Some of the newly invented characters were 仃 for 停 **tíng** "to stop," 氿 for **jiǔ** "wine," 百 for 面 [麵] **miàn** "noodles," 忪 for 懂 **dóng** "to understand," 忈 for 德 **dé** "virtue" (the character is made up of 一 **yī** "one" and 心 **xīn** "heart") and ヨ for 雪 **xué** "snow." Most of these used the same principles as earlier simplifications, with simpler phonetics replacing more complex ones (冬 for 董), or only parts of characters written (ヨ for 雪 **xué** "snow" shows the same principle as 电 for 電 **diàn** "electricity"). For a discussion on these principles, see pages 62–63.

Australia is often written 沃大利亚 **Aòdàlìyà** instead of 澳大利亚, the official form. [澳洲 **Aòzhōu** "Ao-continent," the usual term in Taiwan and Hong Kong, is now also very common in *putonghua*.] The character 沃 is usually pronounced **wò** as in 肥沃 **féiwò** "fertile." Many others are used in handwritten signs and letters, but none have been officialized. One occasionally sees, for example, 付主席 **fùzhǔxí** "vice chairman" written instead of the correct 副主席, which was one of the suggested simplifications. Some are local conventions: shop signs in the beach resort 北戴河 Beidaihe are often written 北代河, writing 代 instead of 戴 for convenience. During the 1980s, the situation became chaotic, with the revival of the traditional script, especially for shop signs and name cards, and many cases of people simply making up their own characters. Campaigns were launched to write "standard characters" (that is, the simplified script) alongside campaigns to speak the "standard language" (that is, *putonghua*).

The second list of simplified characters was formally abolished in 1986, and few of the suggested simplifications seem to have caught on. Traditional characters have made a major comeback, but the official script is still the standard simplified script. Little seems to have happened on the issue of further simplification since the chaos of the eighties.

2.5.1 Simplified characters and unsimplified characters

For the practical person, the choice is easy: the simplified script is the official script of China, and all textbooks and most dictionaries from China are in this script, as are newspapers, novels, official documents and practically anything else you might want to read.

However, even the most practical-minded person will see unsimplified characters everywhere—particularly in Hong Kong and Taiwan of course, but also in Mainland China. All the daily Chinese newspapers in Australia, for example, are printed in the traditional script. If you want to read material from Hong Kong or Taiwan, or reprints of books written before the 1950s, you will need to learn to read the traditional script. And if you want to do scholarly work in Chinese history, literature or philosophy, most of your reading material will be in the traditional script.

So you certainly need to learn to read the traditional script sooner or later in your Chinese studies, if you intend going beyond the basics. But there would seem to be little need to learn to write it, unless you want to take up Chinese calligraphy as an art form.

Pedagogically, it probably makes more sense to learn the traditional script properly first before moving on to the simplified script. As we will see below, the simplified script can be easily derived from the traditional script, but it is not so easy to guess the traditional characters from the simplified forms. Pedagogy, however, is not the only factor. Most people will be better off, in the real world, learning to read and write the standard simplified script first. Those who need it can learn the traditional script later. Probably the easiest way to do this is by using intermediate and advanced level language texts from Taiwan, or by reading texts in traditional characters for those you had previously read in simplified characters.

When you first start to read texts in traditional characters, after having learned 1,000 or so simplified characters, many characters are instantly recognizable. Many are identical in both scripts, and many others have only minor changes: [謝謝] **xièxie** "thanks" for 谢谢, for example. However, it will take some time to get used to characters that underwent major changes for simplification, for example [飛機] **fēijī** "airplane" for 飞机, or 中國歷史 **Zhōngguó lìshǐ** for 中国历史. The high frequency of such terms makes them easier to assimilate. The logo for the Hong Kong and Shanghai Banking Corporation is written in Hong Kong as 匯豐 but 汇丰 in Shanghai. Such forms as [體] **tǐ** "body" for 体, or [麗] **lì** "beauty" for 丽 will take longer to learn, but one usually sees them in context, such as [身體] 身体 **shēntǐ** "body" and [美 麗] 美丽 **měilì** "beautiful." It is not as hard as it might seem on first sight. Most advanced students read material in either simplified or unsimplified scripts without realizing what script they are reading, until they have to look up a dictionary or identify an unfamiliar character.

2.5.2 The simplified and traditional scripts—a comparison

In comparing the simplified and unsimplified scripts, one can make some general observations. In one type, simpler components (radicals or phonetics) replace more complex ones. For example the phonetic 侖 **yuè** in the word 鑰匙 **yàoshi** "key" has been replaced by 月 **yuè** "moon," so the new form is 钥 匙. The following (and those on page 63) are examples of the same principle.

2.5.3 Simplification by changing the phonetic element to a graphically simpler one, or to a handwritten form

Examples of these are shown as follows:

笔 [筆] **bǐ** "pen"	疗 [療] **liáo** "cure"
边 [邊] **biān** "side"	刘 [劉] **Liú** "a surname"
迟 [遲] **chí** "late"	乱 [亂] **luàn** "disorder"
达 [達] **dá** "to reach"	苹 [蘋] **píng** "apple"
担 [擔] **dàn** "load"	权 [權] **quán** "power"
灯 [燈] **dēng** "lamp"	晒 [曬] **shài** "to sunbake"
递 [遞] **dì** "to hand over"	胜 [勝] **shèng** "victory"
对 [對] **duì** "column"	属 [屬] **shǔ** "to belong"
凤 [鳳] **fèng** "phoenix"	态 [態] **tài** "attitude"
风 [風] **fēng** "wind"	铁 [鐵] **tiě** "iron"
沟 [溝] **gōu** "ditch"	图 [圖] **tú** "chart"
观 [觀] **guān** "to look at"	团 [團] **tuán** "group"
国 [國] **guó** "country"	戏 [戲] **xì** "drama"
汉 [漢] **Hàn** "Chinese"	牺 [犧] **xī** "sacrifice"
价 [價] **jià** "value"	虾 [蝦] **xiā** "prawn"
进 [進] **jìn** "to enter"	献 [獻] **xiàn** "to contribute"
剧 [劇] **jù** "opera"	药 [藥] **yào** "medicine"
块 [塊] **kuài** "piece"	邮 [郵] **yóu** "post office"
蜡 [蠟] **là** "wax"	远 [遠] **yuǎn** "far"
礼 [禮] **lǐ** "ceremony"	运 [運] **yùn** "transport"
历 [歷] **lì** "history"	战 [戰] **zhàn** "war"

赵 [趙] **Zhào** "a surname"　　证 [證] **zhèng** "to prove"
这 [這] **zhè** "this"　　种 [種] **zhǒng** "type"

2.5.4 Simplification by retaining part of a traditional character

In another type of simplification, only parts of the traditional characters were used to form the simplified character:

产 [産] **chǎn** "to produce"　　灭 [滅] **miè** "to extinguish"
电 [電] **diàn** "electricity"　　亲 [親] **qīn** "relative"
飞 [飛] **fēi** "to fly"　　伞 [傘] **sǎn** "umbrella"
丰 [豐] **fēng** "rich"　　杀 [殺] **shā** "to kill"
号 [號] **hào** "number"　　声 [聲] **shēng** "voice, sound"
开 [開] **kāi** "to open"　　术 [術] **shù** "skill"
亏 [虧] **kuī** "to lack"　　虽 [雖] **suī** "although"
类 [類] **lèi** "category"　　务 [務] **wù** "service"
丽 [麗] **lì** "beautiful"　　乡 [鄉] **xiāng** "village"
离 [離] **lí** "to leave"　　医 [醫] **yī** "doctor"

The unsimplified character 開 **kāi** shows two hands lifting the bar across a traditional Chinese door, made up of two wings. The character 闩 **shuān** means "a door latch." 廾 indicates two hands. In the simplified character, only the door latch and the hands remain: 开; the door itself (门 [門]) has disappeared.

2.5.5 Simplification based on the handwritten forms of characters

In others, the simplified form is based on the "running script" handwritten form.

车 [車] **chē** "vehicle"　　农 [農] **nóng** "peasant"
发 [發] **fā** "to emit"　　寿 [壽] **shòu** "longevity"
马 [馬] **mǎ** "horse"　　书 [書] **shū** "book"
门 [門] **mén** "door"

In other cases, totally new characters were invented along standard construction methods: 惊 [驚] **jīng** "startled" is a new combination of the "heart" radical 忄 with the 京 **jīng** phonetic; 尘 [塵] **chén** "dust" is a new character combining the characters **xiāo** 小 "small" and **tǔ** 土 "earth, soil." Some simplifications were drastic: [纔] **cái** was simplified to 才 "only then" (才 **cái** also means "talent"); [豐] **fēng** "rich, abundant" was simplified to 丰. In [餐廳] **cāntīng** "dining room [in a dormitory, etc.]," [廳] **tīng** was simplified to 厅 but **cān** "meal" remained 餐. Foreign students in China often call the **cāntīng** "the canteen," but any resemblance is coincidental!

2.6 Learning characters

So now that we have a clear idea of how many characters primary school children, or high school children are expected to know, and how many are generally agreed to be "in common use." But just "learning" a character is not the end of your problems. Many characters have more than one pronunciation, and many characters have more than one meaning.

If we take some characters at random from Liang Shih-chiu's *A New Practical Chinese Dictionary* (1971), for example:

- Character number 2615 检 [檢] **jiǎn** can mean (1) a book label; (2) to collate, to arrange; (3) to sort, to gather; (4) to inspect, to examine, to watch; (5) a form, a pattern; (6) to restrict, to regulate.

- Character number 2911 涵 **hán** can mean (1) wet, damp and marshy; (2) to contain; (3) to show nothing; (4) lenient and broad-minded.

- Character 4750 腊 [臘] **là** can mean (1) a sacrifice at the end of the lunar year; (2) the end of the lunar year; (3) salted and smoked meat, fish and chicken; (4) the age of a Buddhist monk (this latter meaning is so rare most educated Chinese would not know it, but it is listed in the dictionary).

If we check the standard *Chinese-English Dictionary*, published in Beijing in 1979, we find:

- The character 局 **jú** to mean (1) chessboard; (2) game, set, innings; (3) situation; (4) largeness or smallness of mind; (5) gathering, a dinner party, a banquet; (6) ruse, trap; (7) limit, confine; (8) part, portion; (9) office, bureau; (10) shop.

- The character 相 **xiàng** to mean (1) looks, appearance; (2) bearing, posture; (3) to look at and appraise; (4) to assist; (5) prime minister; (6) ministers in a Japanese government; (7) photograph; (8) marine facies; (9) phase, as in phase modulation; (10) elephant, one of the pieces in Chinese chess.

- The same character 相 is also pronounced **xiāng**, when it means (1) each other, one another, mutually; (2) action in the direction of another, as in 实不相瞒 **shí bù xiāng mǎn** "to tell you the truth"; (3) to see for oneself if somebody or something is to one's liking, as in 相女婿 **xiāng nǚ xù** "to take a look at one's prospective son-in-law"; (4) a surname.

• The character 冒 **mào** to mean (1) to emit, send out; (2) risk, brave; (3) boldly, rashly; (4) to claim falsely; (5) a surname.

Some of my favorites are from Matthews' *Chinese-English Dictionary*, where we find that 私 **sī** means "private, personal, selfish, partial, unfair, secret, contraband, underhand, illicit; the private parts; a deprecatory term used by a woman for the husband of her sister."

This even applies to very common characters. As well as meaning "to thank" 谢 **xiè** can mean "to apologize," "to decline an invitation," or "to wither, to wilt." You can amuse yourself for hours investigating the multiple meanings and readings of Chinese characters by browsing through any reasonably sized dictionary.

2.7 Characters with more than one pronunciation

This is also a common phenomenon, sometimes involving a slight semantic change, sometimes with an entirely different meaning. 长 **cháng** means "long," 长大 **zhǎng dà** means "to grow up (of a child)." In the word 曾祖 **zēngzǔ**, "great grandfather," 曾 is pronounced **zēng**. In 曾经 **céngjīng** "already, at some time in the past" it is pronounced **céng**. 行 is pronounced **xíng** "to go, to be alright," but in the word 银行 **yínháng** "bank" it is pronounced **háng**. Many such characters are surnames. 华 [華] is usually pronounced **huá**, but when used as a surname, it is pronounced **huà**. 单 [單] is usually pronounced **dān**, but when it is a surname, it is pronounced **Shàn**. And 单于, an ancient title of the leader of the 匈奴 **Xiōngnú**, an ethnic group in North China perhaps related to the Huns, is pronounced **chányú**. 石 **dàn** "a measure for grain" is written exactly the same as 石 **shí** "stone," but has no connection, phonetically or semantically. There are many such characters, and it is easy to misread them, thus revealing one's ignorance. They are known as 破音字 **pò yīn zì** "broken sound characters," and there are whole dictionaries of them. The standard dictionaries always refer to other possible readings, so if something does not make sense with one pronunciation, it might with another. There is a story of a foreign learner of Chinese going to China for the first time. He is utterly amazed at a perceived lack of Chinese humility. Everywhere he can see signs 中国很行 **Zhōngguó hěn xíng** "China is really great," 中国人民很行 **Zhōngguó rénmín hěn xíng** "the Chinese people are just fantastic," and so on. What he was really seeing was 中国银行 **Zhōngguó yínháng** "The Bank of China," and 中国人民银行 **Zhōngguó rénmín yínháng** "The People's Bank of China."

2.8 How can I learn characters more efficiently?

The fact that such a multiplicity of meanings is attached to practically every character (not all by any means, but certainly very many of them) means that such meanings must occur in some texts somewhere. Even putting the obsolete curiosities of Matthews to one side, the modern, everyday dictionaries mentioned above also teem with such characters. One can well ask oneself how one could possibly get one's head around all these peculiarities.

2.8.1 Learning words rather than characters

A generation ago most textbooks were based on teaching a certain number of characters, usually thirty, a lesson. Once you get the hang of radicals and phonetics, and the general principles of how to write characters in the correct stroke order, progress is faster. The texts were then limited to what could be written with the characters learned. This was (and is) a perfectly legitimate way of going about learning Chinese, but it does tend to an obsession with "how many characters you know," rather than "how many words you know." More recent textbooks are mainly based on everyday conversations using high frequency words. So 谢谢 **xièxie** is taught in the first lesson, even though the characters for it are comparatively difficult, but 三七 **sānqī** "a type of Chinese medicine" will probably not get mentioned at all, despite the individual characters being written with high frequency and are easily written characters.

This is the approach taken by the 汉语水平考试 *Hanyu Shuiping Kaoshi*, the Chinese Proficiency Examination. The emphasis is on the number of words you know, not the number of characters, though of course the words are written in characters. So this places a different complexion on the issue: the question is not so much how many *characters* you need to know to be "proficient" in Chinese, it is how many *words* you need to know. And that is another question.

2.8.2 How many words do I need to know?

A recent textbook from China lists about 1,000 words in the introductory text, and a further 1,000 words in a supplementary reader. They are meant to be covered in one semester of full time study. The prescribed word list for the Basic HSK examination contains 1,033 words for Level One, 2,018 for Level Two, and 3,051 for Level Three. The HSK exam is meant to be the Chinese equivalent of English language proficiency examinations such as TOEFL or IELTS. So the Basic Level (required for admission to more advanced language courses) requires about 3,000 words. These are written with 1,604 different characters.

For the Advanced HSK examination, for people planning to be professional interpreters or translators, an additional 1,033 words are required at Level One, 2,018 at Level Two, 2,202 at Level Three, and 3,568 at Level Four—a total of an additional 8,821 words. The *Guide to the Usage of HSK Vocabulary* translates this basic list and gives the words in context. It also lists idioms and set phrases the student is expected to know at this stage. Students wishing to sit for the HSK examinations can now consult an *HSK Dictionary*, published by the Beijing Language University, in which the headwords in the dictionary give information on the HSK level, the nature of the characters (e.g. parts of speech, whether the term can be used in repetitions such as 快 快乐乐 **kuàikuàilèlè** "happily" etc.) This sort of information is very useful in knowing what characters should be learned first, and which can be left to a later stage. As in other languages, most native speakers would use about 10,000–12,000 words for everyday use, and this is the level foreigners are expected to attain at the higher levels of the HSK examination.

At the upper end of the scale, the standard *Chinese-English Dictionary* contains about 6,000 single-character entries, 50,000 compound character entries, and about 70,000 compound words, set phrases and examples. This more or less sets the upper limits on whatever anyone could reasonably be expected to know, but if you are reading specialized works, you will need additional specialized dictionaries. The same, of course, applies to English.

2.8.3 Character cards

Many students find it very useful to use character cards. These are often available with your textbooks, or you can make your own. People typically prepare cards the size of name cards, or perhaps playing cards, and write the character on one side, and its pronunciation and perhaps some other information (radical number, number of extra strokes, stroke order, other words that particular character is used in) on the other. You can flip through them on the bus or while waiting for a train. As you master the hundred or so you have started with, you can make up cards for another hundred or more, storing away the first group for future reference.

2.8.4 Character writing as a motor skill

Learning to write Chinese characters is to a large extent a motor skill. The more you do it the easier it becomes, and the more you practice your characters the more they look like they are supposed to look. When you have finished the daily newspaper you can cover it with rapidly written Chinese characters you are trying to learn. You can use a thick whiteboard marker or something similar to write the characters over and over and over, until the newspaper is covered in your doodles and you can write them automatically, without pausing to think what stroke to write next or where to put the dot. Some people prefer a pencil, others a fountain pen. If you have some artistic talent you may like to try writing characters with a Chinese writing brush— the tool for the traditional way of writing characters and a major element of their beauty—but this will require a teacher showing you how to hold the brush and how to make the basic strokes. You can buy brushes rather like Western fountain pens, with synthetic fibers (instead of the traditional rabbit fur), which are certainly easier to manipulate. Most learners (and most Chinese nowadays) are content to use a pen or pencil—though the whiteboard markers do give a rough impression, at least, of characters written with a brush. At the initial stages, however, aesthetics will probably play a secondary role to the more basic skills of writing the strokes in the right place, of the right size and in the right order. Calligraphy can come later.

2.9 The revival of traditional characters in modern China

During the 1980s many things from before the cultural revolution, and even before liberation, resurfaced. These included traditional characters. This development was also encouraged by the influx of "Hong Kong and Taiwan culture"—romances and martial arts novels, written of course in traditional characters, and also by reprints of scholarly works written in the old script. Shop signs and name cards in traditional characters became more and more common. The older characters were regarded as more elegant, more stylish.

From time to time the authorities would start a campaign to encourage the use of the "standard" script (that is, simplified characters), and sometimes teams of school children would "correct" shop signs by pasting the simplified character over the unsimplified one. The situation has now more or less stabilized, with simplified characters still being the "official script," but no further attempt is made to try to restrict the traditional script. Traditional characters are now very commonly seen, and apparently most people have no problem with them.

2.10 How to use a Chinese dictionary

Modern dictionaries are more user-friendly than the *Kangxi Dictionary*, but finding a character in any of them still presents a formidable challenge until you get used to the system or systems used in your dictionary. Even after

many years of advanced study you will still be looking up characters in dictionaries, and quite often not finding them. Let us start with basic principles.

The first task is to acquaint yourself with the 201 radicals of the Unified Radical Chart (or the set of radicals in the dictionary you are using), and later
with the 214 traditional radicals. This will save a lot of time in identifying
the radical. It will also help you to avoid trying to find a character like, for
example 音 **yīn** "sound," under 立 **lì** "stand" or under 日 **rì** "sun," when it is
a radical in its own right.

When you want to look up a character, you take the following steps:

1. Identify the radical, count its strokes, check its number in the radical list
   in the selected dictionary.

2. Turn to the list of all characters under that radical.

3. Count the number of strokes in the rest of the character (i.e. you do not
   count the strokes for the radical itself).

4. Look under the list of characters with the same number of strokes you had
   obtained under step 3, until you find the character you are looking for.

5. This will refer you to a page in the main part of the dictionary, or to the
   pronunciation of a character arranged alphabetically.

6. With a bit of luck, you find the character you are looking for without any
   further trouble.

All this seems to be a very difficult way of going about things, and some
other methods have been devised, such as the four-corner system and various
computer input systems. But the "radical and phonetic" method remains the
standard way of arranging Chinese characters, and you will have no choice
but to get used to this system. Students were encouraged to learn the numbers of the radicals, which saved a certain amount of time. 木 **mù** the "wood"
radical is number 75, 水 **shuǐ** the "water" radical is radical 85, and so on.
Mnemonic schemes can be found in some older dictionaries, such as 羊 **yáng**,
the "sheep" radical, number 123, which you can remember by associating
counting sheep (1, 2, 3) with trying to go to sleep. Such mnemonics are no
longer fashionable, but they must have had their uses in the past.

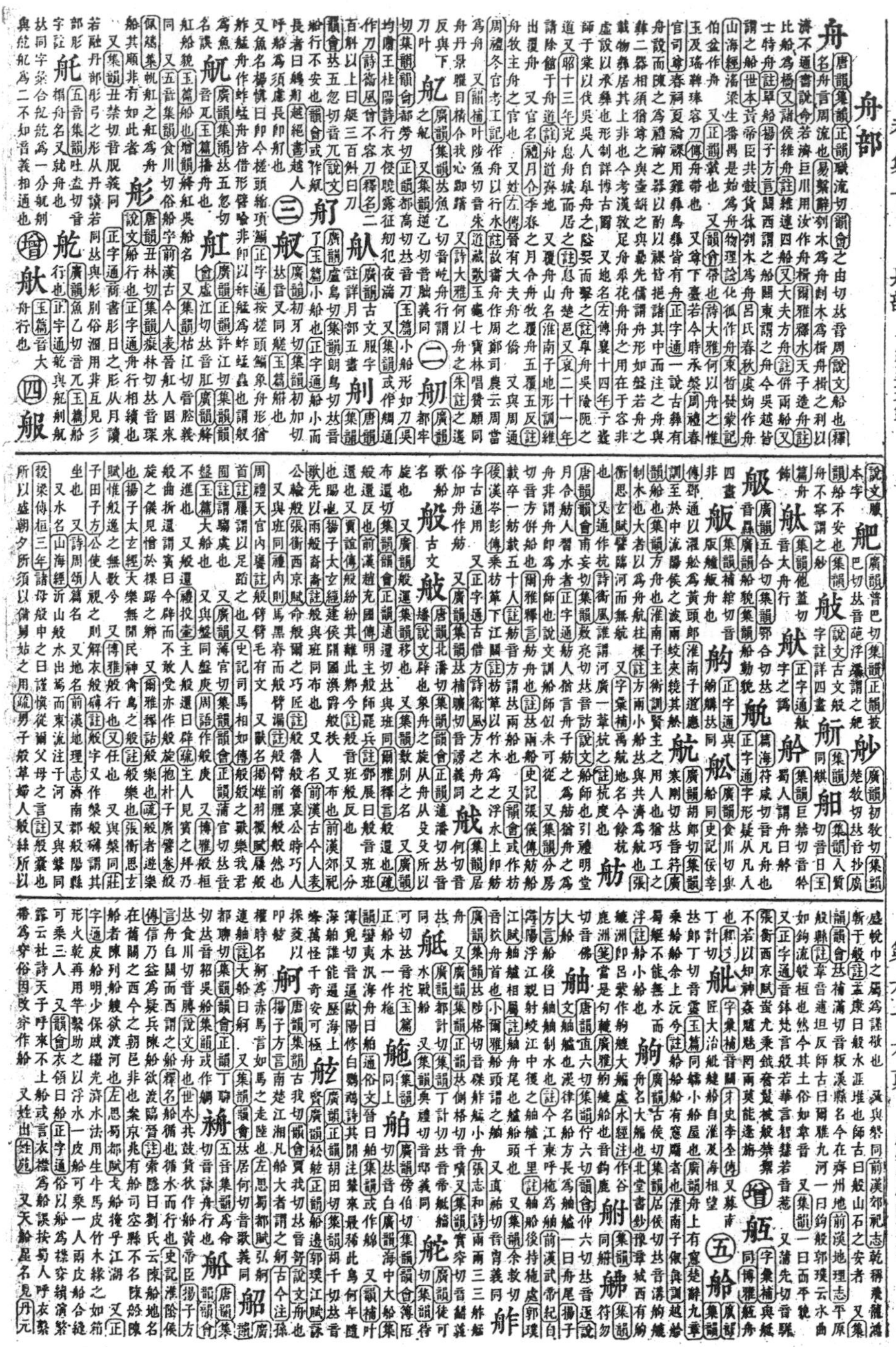
未集下 舟部 一畫至五畫

舟部

第六十六頁

FIGURE 10 A page from the *Kangxi Dictionary* showing entries under the radical **zhōu** "boat." Modern dictionaries are somewhat more "user-friendly."

To give a concrete example of the process, let us say you are looking for the character [講], in the traditional script.

First you identify the radical (言 **yán**, radical 149, the "speech" radical), and turn to the Radical Index of the dictionary. You locate radical 149, where you will find all the characters in the dictionary with this radical. Then you count the additional strokes. For [講], this comes to 10 strokes. There are 18 characters having 10 strokes under radical 149; you eventually find [講], and the character list will refer you to a number, or perhaps a page in the main part of the dictionary. It may or may not tell you how the character is pronounced. When you find the character in the main part of the dictionary, you will find about 40 compounds of which [講] is the first element, and with a bit of luck you will find the word you are looking for. The entry will also tell you the pronunciation of the character (if this is not in the index), which in the case is **jiǎng**. If the character has another pronunciation or meaning, the main entry should also give this information.

In dictionaries of simplified characters, the same procedure is followed, but the radicals and their sequence, and the number of extra strokes, will be different. If you are looking up **jiǎng** 讲, the simplified version of [講], the radical is now 讠 with 2 strokes instead of 言 with 7 strokes. It is radical 10 in the standard *Chinese-English Dictionary*. The number of additional strokes is now 4. There are 15 characters with 4 strokes under radical 10. This particular dictionary will give you the pronunciation of the word in *pinyin*. Others may refer you to a character number, or a page number. There are only 6 characters pronounced **jiǎng**, and so we can find it quite easily. Under **jiǎng** you find over 20 compounds with **jiǎng** as the first element, and hopefully you can find the word you are looking for. In many cases, however, you will not. You sometimes have to consult several dictionaries, especially if you are reading material beyond the purely contemporary.

This of course is a time-consuming process, and all students of Chinese spend an inordinate amount of time with their dictionaries. Looking up a character is sometimes straightforward. Often it is not. Sometimes you miscount the number of extra strokes, so you have to look under 6 strokes or 8 strokes as well as 7, for example. Often what appears to be the radical is not. You may try to look up 慕 **mù** "to admire," or 墓 **mù** "grave" under the "grass" radical 艹, but the radical of 慕 **mù** is 心 **xīn** "heart," and the radical of 墓 **mù** is 土 **tǔ** "earth." This is logical enough when you know what the character means, but if you don't know what it means, then you may go on a wild chase before you finally locate the character in the dictionary.

In many other cases, the radical is not easy to identify. Many dictionaries have a list of characters with obscure radicals, which can be consulted in cases of desperation. Others list all the characters in their dictionary by the total number of strokes, rather than by radicals and residual strokes. The problem is that a character like **jiǎng** [講] is one of about 400 characters with a total number of 17 strokes, and that can take some time to locate.

Some dictionaries list characters according to the number of strokes, but subdivide them according to the shape of the first stroke, in the order 一 丨 丿 丶. There are several variants of this scheme. Some reference works use the four-corner system, in which each character is given a number according to the shape of each of the four corners: 1 is a horizontal stroke, 2 a vertical stroke, 3 a dot, 4 a cross and so on. Not many people use the four-corner system nowadays, but there are some valuable reference works which still use it.

Almost all dictionaries are arranged according to the radical and phonetic system, either simplified or unsimplified, and occasionally both. It is just another one of those facts of life the student of Chinese has to cope with, and eventually takes for granted.

2.11 How to write Chinese characters

The strokes in Chinese characters are written in a prescribed order. There are eight basic strokes in Chinese characters: the dot, the dash, the downstroke, the downstroke to the left, the downstroke to the right, hook, the upstroke to the right, and the bend. (See Figure 11.) Generally speaking, the stroke order is from left to right, top to bottom. If the character is divided into top and bottom parts, such as 雪 **xuě**, write the top part first, then the bottom part. If the character has a left hand part and a right hand part, such as **xiāng** 相, write the left part first, from top to bottom, then the right hand part. For characters that are "framed," for example **guó** 国 "country," the outside strokes are written first, then the inside part, and finally the bottom stroke. Horizontal strokes precede vertical strokes, as in **wáng** 王. These simple rules cover almost all characters, though in 小 **xiǎo** "small" for example, the middle stroke is written first. The order of strokes is important, partly for aesthetic reasons, and partly because they can be joined together rapidly when written in the right order to produce a recognizable "running" character.

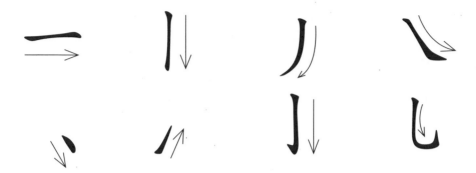

FIGURE 11 Some of the basic strokes used in writing characters, showing the direction the strokes should be written in. These strokes refer to the basic strokes in any part of a character. They are not the same as the first five single stroke radicals, under which characters are classified in dictionaries. These strokes refer to handwriting, not the order they are listed in dictionaries.

FIGURE 12 The character 永 **yǒng** "eternal," which was traditionally said to contain all the strokes needed to write any Chinese character.

Traditionally it was said that all the strokes needed to write Chinese characters were in the character 永 **yǒng** "eternal." Although this is not entirely so, it is still a favorite character for beginning calligraphers.

Characters can be written slowly or quickly, linked together or kept separate. These result in different calligraphic styles. Some calligraphic styles are modeled on early forms of the script, such as the oracle bones script and the bronze inscription script, often with innovations. For most people who write the script everyday, but who are not calligraphers, the most important forms are the regular script, 楷书 **kǎishū**, and the running script 行书 **xíngshū**, or its

FIGURE 13 Characters written in different styles, from ornamental through standard to cursive. The text is the beginning of the *Thousand Character Classic*, traditionally the second book to be studied by children learning to read and write, after the *Three Character Classic* mentioned earlier.

more rapid form 草书 **cǎoshū**, the grass script (also called the draft script). See Figure 13.

Printed Chinese characters are based on the 楷书 **kǎishū** forms. Simplified characters are also written in the same type of standard form, though their details, and sometimes structure, differ.

There are now many computer programs readily available, which show learners the correct sequence of strokes on the screen for all the characters in its databank; they also commonly give the pronunciation of the character, in male and female voices, and some compounds using the character. Most textbooks now come with character practice workbooks, and you can buy special exercise books and paper from any Chinese stationery shop for practicing your calligraphy.

Characters can range in complexity from one stroke: 一 **yī** "one" to 36 strokes, the largest number of strokes in any character actually used: 齉 **nàng** "to speak with a blocked up nose." Learning them is full of pitfalls, and not only the more complicated ones. Some of the simple ones are so simple they can be mistaken for each other. For example:

人 **rén** "person"	入 **rù** "to enter"	
大 **dà** "big"	太 **tài** "too much"	犬 **quǎn** "dog"
天 **tiān** "heaven"	夫 **fū** "male"	失 **shī** "to lose"
	矢 **shǐ** "arrow"	
士 **shì** "gentleman"	土 **tǔ** "earth"	
王 **wáng** "king"	玉 **yù** "jade"	
往 **wǎng** "to go towards"	住 **zhù** "to reside"	佳 **jiā** "fine, beautiful"
主 **zhǔ** "master"	任 **rèn** "responsibility"	
木 **mù** "wood"	本 **běn** "root"	
未 **wèi** "not yet"	末 **mò** "end"	
来 **lái** "to come"	米 **mǐ** "rice"	
十 **shí** "ten"	千 **qiān** "thousand"	
小 **xiǎo** "small"	少 **shǎo** "few"	
口 **kǒu** "mouth"	田 **tián** "field"	甲 **jiǎ** "first of the heavenly stems"

	由 **yóu** "from"	申 **shēn** "ninth of the earthly branches"
日 **rì** "sun"	旧 **jiù** "old"	曰 **yuē** "to say"
中 **zhōng** "middle"	古 **gǔ** "old"	右 **yòu** "right [direction]"
	石 **shí** "stone"	
合 **hé** "to join together"	舌 **shé** "tongue"	舍 **shè** "hut"
又 **yòu** "also"	叉 **chā** "fork"	义 **yì** "significance"
上 **shàng** "on"	止 **zhǐ** "to stop"	正 **zhèng** "correct"
下 **xià** "under"	卞 **biàn** "a surname"	

A dot here, a dash there—it makes the world of difference. Most of these are among the first characters you learn, and are easily confused until you get used to them.

Later in your studies you have to distinguish:

庄 [莊] **zhuāng** "village" from 压 [壓] **yā** "to press down"
乌 [烏] **wū** "black" from 鸟 [鳥] **niǎo** "bird"
厂 [廠] **chǎng** "factory" from 广 [廣] **guǎng** "broad"

and in the traditional script,

[鬥] **dòu** "struggle" from [門] **mén** "door"
[書] **shū** "book" from [畫] **huà** "painting" and [晝] **zhòu** "morning," or
[茶] **chá** "tea" and [荼] **tú** "a bitter edible plant."

And many others. These characters are more easily distinguished in their simplified form: 斗 **dòu**, 门 **mén**, 书 **shū**, 画 **huà**, 昼 **zhòu**.

But then you have to remember that 斗 **dǒu** (in the third tone) means "a unit of measure for grain, a pipe, a funnel, the Big Dipper," and, by extention, many other things. 斗筲 **dǒushāo** "rice bag" was Confucius' description of the officials of his time. 斗方 **dǒufāng** is a square sheet of paper used to write calligraphy, so 斗方名士 **dǒufāng míng shì** is a pretender to refinement and elegance. And 阿斗 A Dou was the idiot son of 刘备 Liu Bei, the last emperor of the Han dynasty. So after the Cultural Revolution a common popular slogan was 群众不是阿斗 **qúnzhòng bùshi Ā Dǒu** "the masses are not imbeciles," meaning they should not be treated as such, as they were during the so-called 愚民政策 **yúmín zhèngcè** "keep the people stupid policy." Which is all very well if you know who the unfortunate A Dou was, but very obscure if you don't. The same sort of concatenation of ideas and associations can be applied to practically any character.

The learning of Chinese is a life sentence. To quote the philosopher Xun Zi, 学不可已矣 **xué bù kě yǐ yǐ** "study never comes to an end." It just goes on and on.

CHAPTER THREE

History and Dialects

3.1 A brief history of the Chinese language

The earliest records of the Chinese language are the inscriptions on tortoise shells and animal bones known as the "oracle bone inscriptions," which record the questions put by the last seven or eight kings of the Shang dynasty to spirits and ancestors on a wide variety of issues. They date from about 1300 BC.

Many of these texts can be read with a fair degree of accuracy, but there are still many characters which cannot be deciphered. Some texts from the oracle bones are given—refer to Figures 14 and 15.

FIGURE 14 "Will there be a disaster within the next ten days?"

癸未卜，争贞：旬无祸？三日乙酉夕，月有食。闻。八月。

Guǐ wèi bǔ, Zhēng zhēn: xún wú huò? Sān rì yǐ yǒu xī, yuè yǒu shí. Wén. Bā yuè.

On the day *guiwei* Zheng asked: "Will any disasters occur during the next ten day period?" On the third day, *yiyou*, in the evening, there was an eclipse of the moon. Reported. Eighth month.

The terms 癸未 **guǐ wèi** and 乙酉 **yǐ yǒu** refer to day 20 and day 22 respectively in a sixty-day cycle. The same terms are still used, and can be found on paintings and even the daily newspapers, but now refer to years.

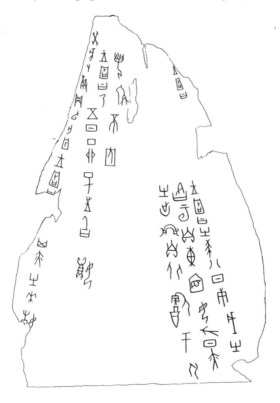

FIGURE 15 A dragon drinks at the Yellow River.

王占曰：有祟. 八日庚戌，有各云自东，贯母。昃亦有出虹自北，饮于河。

Wáng zhàn yuē: yǒu suì. Bā yuè gēng xù, yǒu gè yún zì dōng, guànmǔ. Zè yì yǒu chū hóng zì běi, yǐn yú hé.

The king inspected the bone and said: "A disaster will happen." Eight days later, on the day *gengxu*, clouds came in from the east, and the sky became overcast. As the sun was setting, a dragon in the form of a rainbow appeared in the north, and drank from the Yellow River.

FIGURE 16 The character for "drink" in the oracle bone script.

In these texts we have the basic vocabulary of Classical Chinese: numerals, directions, animal names, verbs and the names of a large number of sacrifices to the ancestors. The question "Will there be a disaster in the next ten days?" was particularly common, which suggests that things have not changed very much over the past couple of millennia.

The structure of many characters can be more clearly seen from their earlier forms. If you are interested in this aspect of Chinese, there are now many books available which give genuine etymological information on Chinese characters. These are very useful in impressing the characters on your memory. The more links you can make with the familiar, the more mnemonics you can use, the easier it will be to remember the characters. You also have the added thrill of actually learning to read characters and texts well over 3,000 years old.

Note the character in Figure 17 for "father" 父, **fù** is a hand holding a stick, 育 **yù** "to give birth" is a pictograph of a child under a woman, 年 **nián** shows a hand grasping wheat. "Harvest" is the original meaning of **nián**, which in later times came to mean "year." 友 **yǒu** "friend" is two hands joined together, 教 **jiào** "to teach" shows a hand holding a stick next to a child, and 生 **shēng** "to be born" shows a growing plant. Learning the early forms of characters is an excellent way of memorizing them, as well as reflecting on notions such as father, birth, education and friend.

FIGURE 17 The oracle bone script adapted by modern calligraphers.

The characters read (from right to left, top to bottom):
父母乳育我二十年，师友教我足一生。
Fùmǔ rǔyù wǒ èrshínián, shī yǒu jiào wǒ zú yī shēng.
"My parents nourish me for twenty years, my teachers and friends teach me all my lifetime."

The next stage in our knowledge of the history of Chinese is represented by the inscriptions on Zhou dynasty bronzes. These were inscribed on ceremonial bronze vessels presented to a general or someone of similar rank for outstanding services. Following are some examples of texts from the bronze inscriptions. (These read from right to left, top to bottom):

FIGURE 18 The inscription on the Greater Yu Tripod.

The text reads:

隹 [唯] 九月，王在宗周，令盂。王若曰：盂，丕顯文王受天佑大命。在武王嗣文作邦。闢厥慝，敷佑四方，畯政厥民… 酒無敢酣。有柴烝祀，無敢擾。故天翼臨…

Wéi jiǔ yuè, Wáng zài Zōng-Zhōu. Mìng Yú. Wáng ruò yuē: Yú, pī-xiǎn Wén-Wáng shòu Tiānyòu dà mìng. Zài Wǔ Wáng sì Wén zuò bāng. Pì jué tè, fù yǒu sì fāng. Jùn zhèng jué mín ... jiǔ wú gǎn hān. Yòu chái zhēng-sì, wú gǎn rǎo. Gù Tiān yì lín ...

It was in the ninth month. The king was at Zong Zhou [the Zhou capital]. He ordered Yu. The king spoke thus: "Yu, the glorious King Wen received the great mandate with the assistance of Heaven. Then King Wu inherited this from King Wen and established the state. He expelled the evil [last king of the Shang dynasty] and took possession of the four quarters. He governed its people well. None dared to over-indulge in wine. During the sacrifices, none dared to behave in an unseemly fashion. So Heaven extended its wings of protection..."

The most famous inscribed bronze is the 毛公鼎 **Máo Gōng Dǐng**, the tripod belonging to Duke Mao (Figure 19). The first few lines are reproduced.

FIGURE 19 Inscription on the Tripod of Duke Mao.

The text reads:

王若曰: 父音! 丕显 [丕顯] 文武，皇天弘厭氒 [= 厥] 德，配我有周，
膺受大命，率懷不廷方。

Wáng ruò yuē: "Fù Yīn! Pī xiǎn Wén Wǔ, huáng Tiān hóng yàn jué dé. Pèi wǒ yǒu Zhōu, yīng shòu dà mìng, shuài huái bù-tíng fāng."

The king spoke thus: "As for the glorious kings Wen and Wu, Great Heaven is profoundly satisfied with their virtue. This entitles us, the rulers of Zhou, to receive the Mandate. We cherish all, even those who do not come to our court bearing gifts."

Some of the characters in the transcription are slightly different from those in the original inscription. This is because the modern Chinese script essentially derives from the unification of the Chinese script by the first Qin Emperor (of entombed warrior's fame) in about 200 BC. The inscriptions were written many centuries before that, when the script had far more variants. Scholars generally quote the texts in modern transcriptions, unless they are epigraphers especially interested in the actual form of the ancient characters.

3.1.1 The earliest transmitted texts

The earliest transmitted texts we have are the *Book of Documents*, the *Book of Odes* and the *Book of Changes*. The latter is a book of divination used in fortune telling, and several versions and translations can be found in any suburban bookshop. The other two are less well known but can be found in any reasonably sized library. The *Book of Documents* contains a number of texts from the early Zhou era, which Confucius regarded as the "golden age" of civilization. (See Figure 20.) The *Book of Odes* is a collection of early folk poetry.

3.2 Old Chinese

From a careful analysis of the structure of early Chinese characters, and the rhyming patterns of the *Book of Odes*, linguists have been able to get some insight into what Chinese was like over 2,000 years ago. It is generally accepted the spoken language had compound initial consonants: 来 [來] **lái** "to come" was probably something like *mleh*, and 江 **jiāng** "river" was probably pronounced something like *krong*. It also had final consonants: in addition to the final **n** and **ng** which survive in Mandarin and the **m**, **p**, **t**, **k** which are still found in Cantonese, it probably had final consonants like **b**, **d**, **r** and **h** or **g**.

So when Confucius said "四海之内皆兄弟也" **sì hǎi zhī nèi jiē xiōng dì yě** "within the four seas, all men are brothers," it might have sounded something like *sied xmeh' tieh nueb krir xiuang deid riah'*. The later falling tone is thought to be derived from a lost voiced final (**b**, **d** or **g**, here written **h**) and the rising tone from glottalization of the vowel, shown here by an apostrophe.

Elaborate schemes have been proposed for the reconstruction of the rhymes of the *Book of Odes*, but it is still not really possible to reconstruct whole texts. The word for "inside," in *putonghua* pronounced 内 **nèi**, may have been pronounced *nueb* by Confucius, or perhaps by that stage it was pronounced *nued* or *nuèt*. Some scholars think it may have been pronounced *nuts* or *nups*. We are indeed looking through a glass darkly.

FIGURE 20 The beginning of the *Analects of Confucius,* in the small script seal of the Qin and Han.

The text reads:

子曰：学而时习之，不亦说乎？有朋自远方来，不亦乐乎？人不知，而不愠，不亦君子乎？

Zǐ yuē: "Xué ér shí xí zhī, bù yì yuè hū? Yǒu péng zì yuǎn fāng lái, bù yì lè hū? Rén bù zhī, ér bù yùn, bù yì jūnzǐ hū?"

The Master said: "to study and constantly revise, is this not a pleasure? To have friends come from far away places, is this not a joy? If people do not recognize your worth, but this does not worry you, are you not a true gentleman?"

3.3 Classical Chinese

The language of the late Zhou was regularized during the Han dynasty and from then on became the literary language of China for the next 2,000 years. It is generally known as Classical Chinese, or sometimes Literary Chinese. It is still occasionally used, in prefaces to scholarly works for example. Most of the poetry written nowadays is still mainly in Classical Chinese.

What strikes the modern reader about Classical Chinese is that most words are monosyllabic (except for a few insects and onomatopoeic words). In modern Chinese most words are not monosyllabic, though word elements are. We can learn a lot from a single sentence:

> 楚人有涉江者，其剑自舟中坠于水，遽契其舟，曰：是吾剑之所从坠。舟止，从其所契者入水求之。舟已行矣，而剑不行。求剑若此，不亦惑乎！
>
> **Chǔ rén yǒu shè jiāng zhě, qí jiàn zì zhōu zhōng zhuì yú shuǐ, jù qiè qí zhōu, yuē: "Shì wú jiàn zhī suǒ cóng zhuì." Zhōu zhǐ, cóng qí suǒ qiè zhě rù shuǐ qiú zhī. Zhōu yǐ xíng yǐ, ér jiàn bù xíng. Qiú jiàn ruò cǐ, bù yì huò hū?**

In modern Chinese this would be:

> 在楚国人中有过江者，他的宝剑从船上掉到水里去了。他就急忙用刀在船上刻了个记号，说：这里是我的宝剑掉下去的地方。船停了以后，楚国人就从他刻着记号的那个地方下去寻找宝剑。船已经走动了，但是宝剑没有移动。象这样寻找宝剑不也是太糊涂了吗？
>
> **Zài Chǔguórén zhōng yǒu guò jiāng zhě, tāde bǎojiàn cóng chuánshang diàodao shuǐlī qùle. Tā jiù jímáng yòng dāo zài chuánshang kèle ge jìhào, shuō: zhèli shì wǒ de bǎojiàn diàoxiaqu de dìfāng. Chuán tíngle yǐ hou, Chǔguórén jiù cóng tā kèzhe jìhào de nèige dìfāng xiàqu xúnzhǎo bǎojiàn. Chuán yǐjīng zǒudòngle, dànshi bǎojiàn méiyou yídòng. Xiàng zhèyang xúnzhǎo bǎojiàn bù yě shi tài hútu le ma?**

Here we can see many of the characteristics of Classical Chinese: the use of 者 **zhě** to make a noun from a verb, the possessive pronouns 吾 **wú** "mine" and 其 **qí** "his," the particle 矣 **yǐ** to indicate that an action is complete, 曰 **yuē** to introduce direct speech, 若 **ruò** meaning "like," 此 **cǐ** meaning "this," 乎 **hū** as an interrogative particle, and the use of typical Classical Chinese words like 舟 **zhōu** for "boat," 止 **zhǐ** "to stop," 入 **rù** "to enter," for which the modern equivalents would be 船 **chuán**, 停 **tíng** and 进 **jìn** respectively.

The written language remained fixed while the spoken language evolved, and occasionally the spoken language was written down. The sermons of Buddhist monks during the Tang dynasty, of Song ambassadors to the northern non-Chinese states, and of the dialogs in the Yuan dramas provide historical linguists with evidence for the gradual evolution of Chinese, such as the development of classifiers (not used in Classical Chinese) and such terms as 这个 **zhège** for "this," 那个 **nàge** for "that," 怎么 **zěnme** for "how," and such particles as 着 **zhe**, 吗 **ma** and 了 **le**.

3.4 Middle Chinese

The pronunciation of Chinese was also changing. In 601 the 切韵 *Qieyun* was compiled, and this later became the official dictionary for the writing of poetry during the Tang dynasty. This language of the *Qieyun* is known as Middle Chinese, and is generally believed to be very similar to the spoken language common throughout China during the Tang dynasty, though perhaps incorporating some features of earlier stages of Chinese and different areas of China. The phonetic values of the phonological categories in this dictionary have been reconstructed from the readings in the modern dialects, the pronunciation of Tang Chinese loanwords in Korean, Japanese and Vietnamese, transcriptions in various central Asian languages and other sources.

If we look at the following transcription of the preface to the *Qieyun*, reconstructed in the way the compiler, Lu Fayan, probably pronounced it, we can see the general characteristics of the phonology of Middle Chinese:

昔，开皇初，有刘仪同臻等八人，同诣法言门宿。
Siek, Khei-huang chrio, hiéu Lieu ngi-dung Crin déng peat nyin, dung ngeei Piop Ngion men siuk.

夜永酒澜，论及音韵。
Yàe hiuóng ciéu lan, luèn gip 'im hiùn.

以今声调，既自有别。
Yí kim syeng deèu, kièi jìi hiéu biet.

诸家取舍，亦复不同。
Cyo kae chiú syáe, yeek piuk pet dung.

吴楚则时伤轻浅。
Ngu Chrió cek jyi syang khyeng chin.

燕赵则多伤重浊。
'Een Driéu cek ta syang driòng draok.

秦陇则去声为入。
Jin Lióng cek khiò syeng hiue nyip.

梁益则平声似去
Liang 'yek cek biong syeng zí khió ...

南北是非，古今通塞
Nem pek jyé piei, kú kim thung sèi ...

曰：向来论难疑处悉尽。
Hiuet: xiàng lei luèn nan ngi chiò sit jìn.

何不随口记之。
Ha pet ziue khéu kì cyi.

我辈数人定则定矣。
Ngá pèi sriú nyin deèng cek deèng hí.

法言即烛下握笔略记钢纪。
Piop Ngion cik cyok háe aok pit liat kì kang kí.

于十岁次辛酉大隋仁寿元年。
Hiu jyi siuèi chìi sin-yéu Dà Ziue Nyin-jyèu ngiuon neen.

Some time ago, at the beginning of the Kaihuang period, eight people, including the Minister of State Liu Zhen, came to visit me, Lu Fayan, and stayed the night. We drank wine deep into the night, and discussed sounds and rhymes. Modern sounds and tones differ among themselves. Various writers have chosen this one and rejected that one, and they also disagree with each other. In Chu and Wu the sounds are light and shallow. In Yan and Zhao, they are heavy and muddy. In Qin and Long the going tone sounds like the entering tone. In Liang and Yi the level tone is like the going tone... The North and the South have their rights and their wrongs, the ancient and the modern have much in common, but much cannot be understood... [Wei] said, "we have discussed the difficult points and they have all been resolved. Why don't you write down what we have said?" So I, Fayan, under the light of a candle took up my brush and made a general outline... The time was the year *yinyou*, the first year of the Renshou reign period of the Great Sui Dynasty [601 CE].

From this passage we can see many of the phonological characteristics of Middle Chinese:

(1) voiced initials: **b, d, g, j**
(2) palatal initials, indicated by **-y-**
(3) retroflex initials, indicated by **-r-**
(4) initial velars **k, kh, g, x, h**
(5) finals **p, t, k**
(6) finals **m, n, ng**
(7) initial **p-** in many words which, when followed by **iu**, became **f-** in Mandarin
(8) Mandarin **r** was Middle Chinese **ny** (palatalized **n**)
(9) four tones: *level* (not marked), *rising* **á**, *going* **à**, and *entering* (**p t k**).
(10) MC had a more complex vowel system than modern *putonghua*, or any other modern dialect. In this transcription **a**, **e**, **i**, **o**, and **u** were as in modern *pinyin*. **ae**, **ea**, **ao**, and **ee** were (more or less) like the vowels in English *man*, *men*, *morn*, *mane* respectively.
(11) Middle Chinese (MC) had a three way contrast between **p**, **ph**, **b**; **t**, **th**, **d** and so on. MC **p** was like *pinyin* **b**, MC **ph** was like *pinyin* **p**, and MC **b** was voiced, like English **b**. Similarly, MC **t** was like *pinyin* **d**, MC **th** was like *pinyin* **t**, and MC **d** was voiced like English **d**.
(12) Vowels preceded by **-i-** were modified, and regarded as separate rhymes. This *could* be specifically marked, such as **tan** but **tiän**, but in general there is no need to do this. In *putonghua*, too, the vowel in 谈 **tán** "to speak" is acoustically quite different from the vowel in 田 **tián** "field."

The Middle Chinese phonological system was reconstructed by Bernhard Karlgren in the 1920s, and although many amendments have been proposed, it has, generally speaking, stood the test of time. People nowadays prefer a less complex phonetic notation than that used by Karlgren, knowing it is impossible to know *exactly* how Middle Chinese was pronounced. But the reconstructions give us a very good idea of what Chinese probably sounded like 1,400 years ago.

3.5 Chinese during the Yuan dynasty

There are many texts which help us follow the evolution of northern Chinese. During the Yuan dynasty, Kublai Khan commissioned a Tibetan *lama*, hP'ags-pa, to devise a writing system which could be used to write Tibetan, Mongol and Chinese. (Refer to Figure 21.) This script was officially adopted but never really caught on. It did not survive the dynasty. It does, however,

FIGURE 21 The first page of the *Hundred Surnames* in the Yuan dynasty hP'ags-pa script, based on Tibetan.

give us important information as to how the language was pronounced during the thirteenth and fourteenth centuries.

赵	Tšėw **Zhào**	钱	Džěn **Qián**	孙	Sun **Sūn**
李	Li **Lǐ**	周	Džiw **Zhōu**	吴	U **Wú**
郑	Tšiŋ **Zhèng**	王	'Ŭaŋ **Wáng**	冯	Hŭuŋ **Féng**
陈	Tšin **Chén**	褚	Tš'eu **Chǔ**	卫	Uė **Wèi**
蒋	Džĭaŋ **Jiǎng**	沈	Šim **Shěn**	韩	Ĥan **Hán**
杨	Yaŋ **Yáng**	朱	Džeu **Zhū**	秦	Tsin **Qín**

The hP'ags-pa forms are given in conventional romanization; tones were not indicated in this script. Another source is the 中原音韵 *Zhongyuan Yinyun*, the "Sounds and Rhymes of the Central Plains," which lists the rhymes used in popular drama. This language is phonologically much simpler, and closer to modern Northern Mandarin.

The arrival of the Jesuits during the Ming dynasty, and other Westerners later, resulted in Chinese being written in a roman script. This makes it much easier to understand how the language was pronounced during those times.

The following passage is from the preface of *Materials for the Eyes* and *Ears of Western Scholars*, by the Jesuit priest Nicolas Trigault, published in 1625.

幸至中华朝夕讲求欲以言字通相同之理，但初闻新言耳鼓则不聪，观新字目镜则不明。恐不能触理动之内意。欲救聋瞽舍此药法，其道无由。

Him chi chūm hoâ chāo siě kiàm 'kiêu iǒ ì iên çú 'tūm siām 'tûm chì lì, tán 'chū vên sin iên, ùi kù çě pǒ çūm, kuōn sīn çū, mô kim çě pǒ mîm, 'kùm pǒ nêm 'chǒ li tùm chī núi i iǒ kiéu lûm kù xě 'çù iǒ fǎ 'kî táo vû iêu.

In this romanization, Trigault used **-m** to indicate the final we now write as **-ng**.

After arriving in China, day and night they say they seek a principle to unite the spoken words and the written characters. When they first hear a language, their ears are not acute, when they first see a new type of writing, their eyes are not sharp. They fear they cannot attain the inner meaning. If we want to save the deaf and dumb, if they do not adopt this medicine, there will be no path to follow.

The study of the history of the Chinese language is a highly specialized one, combining traditional phonology and modern linguistics. Like the history of the script, it is better left alone until much later in your studies. A few general ideas, however, even at this stage, make fascinating and hopefully tantalizing reading, and perhaps will inspire you to get interested in this aspect of the study of Chinese.

3.6 Mandarin or Cantonese?

When people hear you are learning Chinese, they frequently ask if you are learning Mandarin or Cantonese. This question is understandable, as most people are aware that there are at least two common varieties of spoken Chinese. For practical purposes, however, there is really only one answer.

There are hundreds of different forms of speech spoken in local communities in China, and many of these are difficult for outsiders to follow. In the past this was a problem, but the spread of *putonghua* in recent years had made it less so.

The dialects are used purely locally, though some have been taken to other areas by migrants. Fujian dialect is widely spoken throughout Malaysia and Singapore, for example, where it is known as Hokkien. Other dialects from South China, such as Fuzhou (Foochow), Chaozhou (Teochew), Kejia (Hakka), and Cantonese are also widespread throughout Southeast Asia.

Cantonese is the dialect of Chinese spoken around Canton (ie. present Guangzhou) and is widespread in Guangdong and Guangxi provinces in south China. Migrants from those areas brought Cantonese to Hong Kong and parts of Southeast Asia over several centuries. The earliest Chinese migrants to Australia, the United States and Canada were also from these regions. Until fairly recently, Cantonese was the main form of Chinese spoken in Chinese migrant communities. Until recently, very few speakers of Mandarin, or Shanghaiese, migrated overseas.

This is no longer the case. Mandarin is now widely taught and spoken in Hong Kong, and has been so in Southeast Asia for many decades. Recent migrants from Mainland China and Taiwan have boosted the numbers of Mandarin speakers in Australia, the United States and Canada, and these trends seem likely to continue.

For all intents and purposes, Standard Chinese under its different names and slightly different varieties— 华语 *Huayu* in Singapore, 国语 *Guoyu* in Taiwan, 普通话 *putonghua* in Mainland China and Mandarin in English—is the only form of Chinese you need worry about.

3.7 Chinese Dialects

Chinese dialects are classified into the following nine groups:

(1) Northern dialects (Beijing and other Mandarin areas)
(2) 吴 Wu dialects (Shanghai, Suzhou, Ningbo)
(3) 湘 Xiang dialects (Hunan)
(4) 赣 Gan dialects (Jiangxi)
(5) 晋 Jin dialects (Shanxi, Hebei)
(6) 客家 Kejia (Hakka)
(7) 粤 Yue dialects (Cantonese and related forms)
(8) 闽北 Northern Min (Foochow)
(9) 闽南 Southern Min (Hokkien, Teochew)

It is sometimes said that Chinese dialects are more like different languages than dialects. The northern dialects are relatively similar, but a great diversity is found in the south. A hundred years ago, few Chinese spoke anything but their home dialect. Now there are probably few Chinese you might meet who cannot speak at least some *putonghua* in addition to their home dialect. The older rural masses may well be unable to speak *putonghua* well, but most foreigners are unlikely to have much contact with such people. Younger generations in rural areas, who have at least had some primary if not secondary schooling, would have learned *putonghua* at school. And television programs, all in *putonghua*, have made it very accessible, and hence familiar, even in the most remote areas. Minority areas, such as Xinjiang and Tibet, are another matter, but even there, *putonghua* has become very common.

Nevertheless, Chinese dialects are part of the Chinese linguistic scene. As you travel around China, you will hear *putonghua* spoken with a wide variety of accents. You will also hear forms of Chinese which you will not understand at all.

Although many dialects are incomprehensible at first acquaintance, it does not usually take Chinese people who migrate to a new area very long to pick up a particular dialect (to a greater or lesser degree) if they put their minds to it. Mainland Chinese who go to live in Hong Kong tend to pick up Cantonese quite quickly if they want to. Similarly, many Cantonese speakers in Hong Kong have found it in their interests in recent times to learn at least enough *putonghua* to get around in China. Some dialects are notoriously difficult for outsiders to understand. Foochow is well known for being particularly impenetrable. On the other hand, many Chinese in Southeast Asia are comfort-

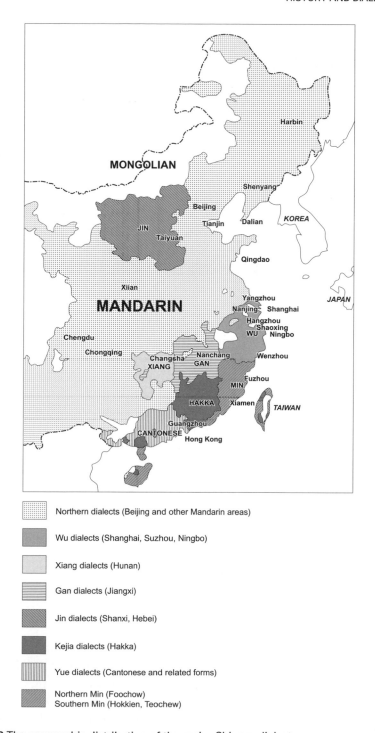

FIGURE 22 The geographic distribution of the major Chinese dialects.

able with a number of dialects. It is not uncommon for many people to be able to converse in Mandarin, Cantonese, Hakka, Hokkien, and perhaps some other Chinese dialects, as well as English, Malay, Indonesian, Vietnamese, Thai or other regional languages.

The following comments put the matter of Chinese dialects in perspective, so that when you travel around China, or meet people with accents you might find a bit hard to follow, you have some idea of the dialectal influence behind such accents or tonal patterns.

The language of Beijing is itself one of many dialects collectively called the Northern group or the Mandarin group. These dialects are spoken by about 70% of the Chinese population, mainly north of the Yangzi river, and throughout the northeast, northwest and southwest of China.

They are divided into four groups:

(1) Northern Mandarin—spoken in Hebei, Henan, Shandong, northern Anhui, Jilin, Liaoning, Heilongjiang and Inner Mongolia
(2) Northwestern Mandarin—spoken in Shanxi, Shaanxi, Gansu, Qinghai, Ningxia and parts of Inner Mongolia
(3) Southwestern Mandarin—spoken in Hubei, Sichuan, Yunnan, Guizhou, northwestern Guangxi and parts of Hunan
(4) Eastern Mandarin—spoken in central Anhui, northern Jiangsu and Nan-jing

These dialects differ to the degree that the languages spoken in Manchester, New York, Dublin or South Africa differ from each other. Someone from Harbin or Liaoning would have little difficulty communicating with someone from Kunming or Chengdu even if each used their own home dialect—though nowadays, of course, all of them would speak more or less standard *putonghua*.

In the northern dialects, the Middle Chinese voiced initials have become de-voiced. MC *deu* "head" has become Mandarin **tóu**. The velars have been palatalized: *ki* > **ji**, *khi* > **qi**, *hi* > **xi**. The MC final consonants **p**, **t**, **k** have disappeared from the language of Beijing, but are preserved as a glottal stop in some dialects. Tonal classes remain much the same across dialects, but tonal values vary greatly. The first tone, the high level tone of Mandarin 55, is pronounced 31 in Xi'an, 44 in Chengdu, and 11 in Taiyuan. The fourth tone, the falling tone of Mandarin 51, is 55 in Xi'an, 13 in Chengdu, and 55 in Taiyuan. The figures refer to a scale on which 5 is the highest pitch and 1 the lowest, so the *putonghua* tones are 55, 35, 214 and 51 respectively.

These different tonal values give the characteristic "lilt" of dialect speakers, which can sound charming or irritating depending on the circumstances, but such tonal vagaries rarely impede comprehension.

3.7.1 The Wu dialects

When you travel to Shanghai and Jiangnan, the area around Shanghai, you will hear the Wu dialects. These dialects preserve the full set of voiced Middle Chinese stops **b**, **d**, **g**, and **j** which have disappeared from other dialects. These dialects have a comparatively large number of vowels. Shanghaiese, for example, has twelve: i y e ø ɛ ï ə ɵ a u o ɔ. Syllables can end in one of these vowels, final **ng** or final ʔ, a glottal stop.

Shanghaiese has three tones with open syllables or **ng**, and two with syllables which end in ʔ. Tones are modified when preceding other tones in a complex way. The Nanjing dialect is a form of Mandarin; the Hangzhou dialect has a phonological system like that of other Wu dialects, but its vocabulary is similar to Mandarin. There are historical reasons for these anomalies.

A Conversation in Shanghaiese

ˈlɔʔ-gəʔ ˈɦiyʔ-gəʔ xø-ɲy ˈɦɔʔ-ʑiɪʔ ˈʑiɤ-iɔ tɕiʟ-sɔʔ-ləʔ.
"Six months' study of Chinese will soon end."

ˈzɨ-gəʔ, ˈzəŋ-kuaŋ ku-təʔ ˋtsəŋ kʰua, ˈnoŋ ˈgəʔ-tʰaŋ ˈləʔ ˋtsoŋ-kɔʔ xø-ɲy ˈɦɔʔ-təʔ ˈna-nəŋ ˈɦiaŋ-tsz?
"Yes, the time's gone really fast. During the time you've been in China, how have you found learning Chinese?"

ˈɲu ˈləʔ ˈgəʔ-taʔ ˈzəŋ-kuaŋ ˋse-zø ˋmɛ tø, ˈdɛ-z ˈhɔʔ-tɔ vəʔ-sɔ-gəʔ ˈməʔ-z
"Although I've been here for a very short time, I've learned quite a few things."

noŋ ˋkaŋ-kaŋ ˈlɛ-gəʔ ˈzəŋ-kuaŋ, ˈli·iɪʔ-tɕy ˋtsoŋ-kɔʔ-ɦio ˈɦia vəʔ-ɦiuɛ-təʔ kaŋ.
"When you first came here, you couldn't speak a word of Chinese."

ˈzɨ-gəʔ, ˈɦi-zɛ ˈɲu vəʔ-tɛ ˈɦuɛ-təʔ ˋtʰin ˈɦiuɛ-təʔ kʰø tɕi-tɛ-gəʔ ˈməʔ-z.
"Yes, now I not only can listen and speak, I can also read simple words."

In this short passage, many of the main characteristics of the Shanghai dialect can be seen: the voiced initials, like **v**, **z**, **g** and ɦ (a voiced **h**), the glottal stop ʔ from Middle Chinese **p t k**, the complex vowels corresponding to *putonghua* diphthongs, such as lɛ for **lái** "come" or to the *putonghua* final **-an**, such as tø for **duǎn** "short," k'ø for **kàn** "see." The basic vocabulary is similar, but often obscured by the pronunciation: 现在 **xiànzài** "now," for example, is pronounced ɦi-zɛ.

3.7.2 Central Chinese dialects

When you travel in central China, you might hear the 赣 Gan, 湘 Xiang and 晋 Jin dialects. The 赣 Gan dialect is spoken in Jiangxi and parts of Hunan, Hubei, Anhui and Fujian. The 湘 Xiang dialect is spoken in Hunan. The 晋 Jin group has only recently (1987) been recognized as a separate dialect group. It is spoken in Shanxi, Hebei, northern Henan, northern Shanxi and central and west Inner Mongolia. These dialects are spoken by millions of people, and preserve many interesting aspects of earlier forms of Chinese. Foreigners are unlikely to have much contact with these dialects unless they are linguists, or are spending a fair amount of time in the areas mentioned.

3.7.3 The southern dialects

The southern dialects are another matter. They are spoken in the southeastern provinces—those areas of China most open to foreign tourism, travel, investment and long-term residence. It was precisely these areas from which most Chinese emigrated over the past couple of centuries, mainly to Southeast Asia.

Travelers to Singapore, Malaysia or the Chinese communities of Indonesia, Vietnam, Thailand and Cambodia will hear these dialects spoken all around them. In Hong Kong the language spoken just about everywhere is Cantonese, and Taiwanese is much the same the language of Xiamen, the capital of Fujian. In Taiwan, of course, Mandarin or *Guoyu* has also been used as the official language for decades.

The linguistic names for these dialects are 粤 Yue, 客家 Kejia and 闽 Min, but here we can use the popular terms: Cantonese, Hakka, Fuchow and Hokkien. Min is divided into two groups: northern or Minbei 闽北 (Foochow), and southern or Minnan 闽南 (Hokkien). The southern dialects have lost voiced initials, like Mandarin, but in their final consonants they are very conservative: Cantonese possesses the full set of final consonants: **p t k m n** and **ng**.

Cantonese

Cantonese is the main language of Hong Kong, and is also spoken throughout Guangdong and Guangxi, often coexisting with dialects of Hakka and varieties of southern Min, such as Teochew. There are probably about 60 million speakers of Cantonese in China, six million in Hong Kong and another two million in Southeast Asia. It is also very widespread among Chinese communities in the United States, Australia and elsewhere.

Cantonese has nine tones, more than any other dialect. They are 53 21 35 24 44 33 for syllables ending in vowels or nasals, and 55 44 33 for syllables in final **p**, **t** or **k**. The vocalic system is quite complicated, with a larger number of vowels than Mandarin, and distinctions between long and short vowels. Cantonese does not have medials like the **i** in Mandarin 天 **tiān**, which in Cantonese is [thiːn]. Cantonese is probably the closest living dialect to the Middle Chinese of the Tang dynasty (618-907 CE), and the Cantonese often refer to themselves as 唐人 *tong yan*, "people of the Tang." One might compare this with the official term for the Chinese language: 汉语 *Hanyu* "the language of the Han," referring of course to the Han dynasty (206 BCE–220 CE).

A Conversation in Cantonese

hɔŋ³³ jy²³ nan¹¹ m¹¹ nan¹¹·hɔk² a⁵³?
"Is it difficult to learn Chinese?"

m¹¹ hɐi²² ke³⁵ nan¹¹, hɔŋ³³·tʃi²² pei³⁵ kau³³ nan¹¹ ʃɛ³⁵.
"It's not too hard. Chinese characters are quite hard to learn."

nei²³ wui²³ m¹¹ wui²³ kɔŋ³⁵ kwɔŋ³⁵ tʃɐu⁵³ wa³⁵ a³³?
"Can you speak Cantonese?"

wui²³ kɔŋ³⁵ kei³⁵ køy³³ la⁵⁵.
"I can speak a little."

ŋɔ²³ kɔŋ³⁵ p'ou³⁵ t'uŋ⁵⁵ wa³⁵ nei²³ t'ɛŋ⁵³ m¹¹ t'ɛŋ⁵³ tɐk⁵ tuŋ³⁵?
"When I speak Mandarin, can you understand?"

kɔŋ³⁵ man²² ti⁵⁵ tʃɐu³³ t'ɛŋ⁵³ tɐk⁵ tuŋ³⁵.
"If you speak slowly then I can understand."

In this passage we can see the complex tonal system of Cantonese, its characteristic **-p -t -k** endings, the negative 唔 *m* (*putonghua* 不 **bù**), the lack of initial **h-** in **wa³⁵** "speak," (*putonghua* 话 **huà** "words") and **wui²³** "to be able" (*putonghua* 会 **huì**). There are no words in *-m*, such as 三 **sam** "three" or 林 **lam** "forest" in this passage, but they are quite common in Cantonese.

Hakka

The Hakka traditionally claim that their ancestors came from North China. Standard Hakka is that spoken in the Meixian district of Guangdong, but varieties of Hakka are spoken over a wide area in Guangdong, Fujian, Taiwan, and to a lesser degree elsewhere in China, and of course by many Chinese in Southeast Asia. Standard Hakka distinguishes seven tones. It has lost the voiced initials of Middle Chinese, but has an initial **v** corresponding to Mandarin **w** and a palatal initial **gn**, as in English *new*. Hakka has final **p**, **t** and **k**, but they do not necessarily correspond to their equivalents in Cantonese.

A Conversation in Hakka

Vông hsīn-sāng nĝ túk ê gìt-dō gnīen Dzūng-vûn?
"Mr Wong, for how many years have you studied Chinese?"

Tsōi gō-dzūng gní-gnīen gé ŝz-jièt, ngâi chíu kōi-sz túk Dzūng-vûn.
"I began in the second year of high school to study Chinese."

Nĝ túk ā-mân-ê dō gé Dzūng-vûn.
"You've studied quite a bit of Chinese."

Ngâi túk Dzūng-vûn tsā-mĝ-dō yū ng ngîen é.
"I've studied Chinese for about five years."

Hokkien and Foochow

The Min dialects are spoken in Fujian, where the mountainous terrain has made communication between areas difficult, and where the dialects differ greatly from each other and from those described above. The dialects spoken in villages, separated by a few hours' travel from each other, can be incomprehensible. There are also Min speakers in Zhejiang, Guangxi and Sichuan, and of course Southeast Asia.

There are many archaic aspects to the Min dialects, not preserved elsewhere. *Putonghua* words beginning with **zh** are pronounced with initial *t*, reflecting a pronunciation which became extinct in the rest of China before the sixth century. An example is *putonghua* 竹 **zhú** "bamboo" = Foochow **tøiq**, Hokkien **tek**. Initial *p* when followed by *iu* became **f** in the rest of China by the Song dynasty, but remains in Min: *putonghua* 饭 **fàn** "rice" = Foochow puɔng, Hokkien png. Some words are very ancient: Foochow tiang and Hokkien **tiã** "cooking pot" are related to the word 鼎 **dǐng** "tripod," the ancient cooking pots of the Shang dynasty. The pronunciation of the word for "I," Fuchow 我 ŋuai, also dates back to the Han. The word for "tooth," in both Hokkien and Foochow 齿 khi, also reflects a pronunciation prior to the sixth century. The word for "child," Foochow 囝 kiang and Hokkien 囝 kĩa, is a very distinctive and particular Min word not found elsewhere.

Hokkien has six vowels and four nasalized vowels. The old final consonants have been preserved in varying degrees. Foochow *m*, *n*, and *ng* have all merged as *ng*; and *p*, *t*, *k* have all merged as ʔ. In Hokkien nasals have become denasalized before oral vowels: the *m* of other dialects is pronounced *b*; the *ng* of other dialects is pronounced *g*. One can see characteristic Hokkien readings in the romanized forms of Chinese names from Southeast Asia: 陈 [陳] Tan for Chen, 张 [張] Teoh or Teo for Zhang, 吴 [吳] Go or Goh for Wu.

A Conversation in Hokkien
Lí uēhiáu kóng Hokkiàn uē bô?
"Can you speak Hokkien?"

Bô símmìh uē hiáu.
"Not very well."

Nāsī lì kóng khah bān, guá khiám chhai uē thiã tāmpòh.
"If you speak slowly, perhaps I can understand a little."

Guá uēhiáu thàk, chóngsī bô símmìh hiáu kóng.
"I can read, but I can't speak very well."

Chhíã lí koh kóng chit pái.
"Please say it again one more time."

A Conversation in Fuzhou (Foochow)
Ny^{31} ts'uɔ^{213} ou^{242} kui^{44} ʒiɛ^{223} nøyŋ^{53}?
"How many people are in your family?"

Suo^{25}, laŋ^{242}, saŋ^{44} sɛi^{213}, ŋou^{242}, løyʔ^{242}, ts'ɛiʔ^{223}.
"One, two, three, four, five, six, seven."

ŋuai³¹ ts'uɔ²¹³ kuŋ⁵³ ʒuŋ³¹ ou²⁴² ts'i³⁵ tsiɛ²²³ nøyŋ⁵³.
"In my family altogether there are seven people."

I³³ tie²⁴², i⁵³ nɛ³¹, i⁴⁴ ko⁴⁴, i⁵² tsia³¹, i³³ tiɛ²⁴² køyŋ²¹ i⁵³ muoi²¹³.
"Dad, Mum, elder brother, elder sister, younger brother and younger sister."

Suo²⁵, laŋ²⁴², saŋ⁴⁴, sɛi²¹³, ŋou²⁴², løyʔ²⁵ ... tsuoŋ³¹ ŋouŋ³¹ tsiu³¹ so²²¹ tsiɛ²²¹ nøyŋ⁵³?
"One, two, three, four, five, six ... how can you explain there is one fewer [than seven]?"

Tai²¹ a⁴⁴ nøyŋ⁵³ ts'iu²¹ lɛ kouŋ³¹: tsiu³¹ ny³¹ tsi⁴⁴ a⁴⁴ sou²²¹ tsiɛ²²³ nøyŋ⁵³!
"Everyone laughed and said: The one that is missing is yourself!"

This short sample shows many characteristics of the Fuzhou dialect. The **m n ng** endings of other dialects are all ŋ, and the **p t k** endings are all glottal stops. Note the characteristic assimilation: 属只侬 suo tsiɛ nøyŋ "one person" but 几只侬 kui ʒiɛ nøyŋ "how many people," 大家 tai a "everybody," and 自家 tsi a "yourself" for tai ka and tsi ka (if spoken slowly); in 怎讲 tsuoŋ ŋuoŋ "how to say" (Mandarin **zěn jiǎng**), the **k-** of kouŋ "to speak" is assimilated to the final ŋ of tsuoŋ, but in 小礼讲 ts'iu lɛ kouŋ "laughed and said," it remains kouŋ. 六 løyʔ "six" and 七 ts'ɛiʔ "seven" have glottal stops when read individually, but they are assimilated to the following initial consonants. Other examples of the liaison and assimilation of final and initial consonants are "motor car" (Mandarin **qìchē**), which is 汽车 k'ei ts'ia when pronounced slowly, but k'i-ia when pronounced normally; "postcard" (Mandarin **míngxìnpiàn**), is 明信片 miŋ seiŋ p'ieŋ when the characters are read individually, but when put together they are pronounced miŋ niŋ mieŋ. 水仙 **shuǐxiān** "narcissus" is pronounced tsuei sieŋ slowly but tsuei lieŋ quickly.

Other characteristics are the use of the classifier 只 [隻] tsiɛ (Mandarin **zhī**) for humans; in Mandarin it is only used for animals; 属 **suo** "one"; the diphthong -ai in 我 ŋuai "I," which might derive from well before the sixth century, and the affricates (ts-) in words like 少 tsiu "few" (Mandarin **shǎo**), 笑 ts'iu "laugh" (Mandarin **xiào**) and 水 tsuei "water" (Mandarin **shuǐ**). Fuzhou preserves many archaic words, such as 汝 ny "you," 厝 ts'uo "house, family," 犬 keiŋ "dog" (Mandarin **quǎn**) and 鼎 tiaŋ "cooking pot" (Mandarin **dǐng** "bronze sacrificial vessel").

The assimilation which permeates the language and not only affects initial and final consonants—the vowels and tones also change, depending on what words precede or follow them. All this makes Foochow notoriously difficult for anyone else to follow.

The Chaozhou dialect, also known as Teochew, is a Southern Min dialect spoken in Guangdong, and widely throughout Southeast Asia, especially in Cambodia and Thailand. Chaozhou speakers and Fujian speakers can understand each other much more than either can understand Fuzhou.

A Conversation in Chaozhou (Teochew)

A: Le^2 ho^2! Le^2 sing^1 ti^2 ho^2 mê?
"How are you? How is your health?"

B: Bhoi^6 mo^2, zoi^7 sia^7. Le^2 nê?
"Not bad, thank you. And you?"

A: Wa^2 a^2 bhoi^6 mo^2. Le^2 gang^1 zak^4 m^6 oin^5 a^1 bhoi^6?
"I'm not bad, too. Your work, are you busy (have no leisure) or not?"

B: M^6 oin^5 si^2. Nang^2 ho^2 gu^2 bho^5 gin^3 ming^7 lou^3!
"Dead busy! We have not seen each other for a long time."

A: Si^6 a. Gê^1 lai^6 coh^4 nang^5 ho^2 mê?
"That's so. Are the people in your family all right?"

B: Toh^4 le^2 gai^7 hok^4. Cuang^5 bou^6 guê^3 lai^5 bhoi^6 mo^2.
"Thanks for your kindness. All of them are getting along just fine."

A: Guê^3 dui^3 m^6 zu^6. Ua^2 gao^2 diam^2 huan^1 u^6 gai^7 huê^6.
"I'm really sorry. At nine o'clock I have a meeting."

B: Hia^2 zu^6 mai^6 dam^1 ghou^7 le^2 liao^7. Zai^3 giang^3!
"Then I will not delay you. Goodbye!"

Note here the characteristic Chaozhou words **nang^5** (人) for "man, person" (Fuzhou nøyŋ, Fujian lang), **ua^2** "I" (我), **le^2** "you" (你) (which sounds like English *ler*), and **mo^2** "bad" (written 孬).

3.8 Comparative tables

The following lists give a comparison of the readings of some common characters in various dialects. Tones have been omitted from this list.

Table of comparative listings

Character	Pinyin	Cantonese	Hakka	Suzhou	Foochow	Hokkien
八	**bā**	pat	pat	pɯʔ	paiʔ	puɛʔ
白	**bái**	paːk	phak	pɒʔ	paʔ	pɛʔ
百	**bǎi**	paːk	phak	pɒʔ	paʔ	pɛʔ
北	**běi**	pak	pɛt	pɯʔ	paəʔ	pak
车	**chē**	tʂhɛ	tʃha	tshɔ	tʃhia	tʃhia
虫	**chóng**	tʂhuŋ	tʃhuŋ	zuŋ	təŋ	taŋ
帝	**dì**	tai	ti	ti	tœ	tɛ
弟	**dì**	tai	thi	di	tiɛ	ti
东	**dōng**	tuŋ	tuŋ	tɯŋ	təŋ	taŋ
读	**dú**	tuk	thuk	dɯʔ	təʔ	thak
耳	**ěr**	ji	ɲi	ɲi	ŋe	hi
飞	**fēi**	feːi	fui	fi	puɪ	pi
蜂	**fēng**	fuŋ	fuŋ	fɯŋ	phuŋ	phaŋ
改	**gǎi**	kɔi	kɔi	kœ	kuɪ	kwɛ
国	**guó**	kuək	kwɛt	kwɒʔ	kuoʔ	kok
火	**huǒ**	fɔ	fɔ	hɒu	huɪ	hɛ
加	**jiā**	ka	ka	ka	ka	ke
姐	**jiě**	tʂe	tsia	tsia	tʃia	tʃi
井	**jǐng**	tʂɛŋ	tsiaŋ	tsin	tʃaŋ	--
旧	**jiù**	kau	khiu	dʒy	ko	ku
苦	**kǔ**	fu	khu	khɒu	khu	kho
六	**liù**	luk	luk	lɯʔ	ləʔ	lak
马	**mǎ**	ma	ma	mɔ	ma	bɛ
面	**miàn**	miːn	mɛn	mi	məŋ	bin
南	**nán**	naːm	lam	nɯ	naŋ	lam
年	**nián**	niːn	nɛn	ɲɛ	ɲieŋ	ni
女	**nǚ**	nœy	ŋi	ɲy	ny	lu
七	**qī**	tʂhat	tshit	tshiʔ	tʃhɛʔ	tʃhit
穷	**qióng**	khuŋ	khiuŋ	dʒuŋ	khŋ	kioŋ
去	**qù**	hœy	khi	khɔ	khɔ	khi
日	**rì**	jɐt	ɲit	--	niʔ	dʒit
肉	**ròu**	juk	ɲuk	niɤʔ	nyʔ	dʒiok
三	**sān**	saːm	sam	sæ	saŋ	sã
蛇	**shé**	ʂɛ	ʃa	zɔ	siɛ	tʃua

Table of comparative listings (*continued*)

Character	Pinyin	Cantonese	Hakka	Suzhou	Foochow	Hokkien
十	shí	ʂap	ʃip	zəʔ	seʔ	tʃap
体	tǐ	thai	thi	thi	thœ	thui
天	tiān	thiːn	thɛn	thi	thiɛŋ	thĩ
外	wài	ŋɔi	ŋoi	ŋa	ŋiɛ	kwa
问	wèn	man	mun	--	oŋ	mŋ
五	wǔ	ŋ	ŋ	ŋ	ŋo	ko
喜	xǐ	heːi	hi	ʃi	hi	he
下	xià	ha	ha	ɔ	a	ɛ
香	xiāng	hœŋ	hioŋ	ʃiã	hioŋ	hiũ
心	xīn	ʂam	sim	sin	siŋ	sim
学	xué	hɔk	hɔk	ɔʔ	ɔʔ	ɔʔ
牙	yá	ŋa	ŋa	ŋa	ŋa	kɛ
雨	yǔ	jy	ji	jy	y	ho
鱼	yú	jy	ŋ	ŋ	ŋy	hu
月	yuè	jyt	jɛt	ŋœʔ	ŋuoʔ	kɛʔ
知	zhī	tʂi	tʃi	tsz	tʃai	tʃai
主	zhǔ	tʂy	tʃu	tsɯ	tʃio	tʃu
猪	zhū	tʂy	tʃu	tsɯ	ty	ti
足	zú	tʂuk	tsiuk	--	tʃɛyʔ	tʃiok

Chinese dialects have always been spoken languages; they have not generally developed individual written forms. In earlier times children learned to read characters in a local dialect, but this is no longer the case, except in Hong Kong. Elsewhere, whatever language is spoken at home, children learn to read and write in *putonghua*. Sometimes dialects are written in specially created characters, as in Hong Kong newspapers. In earlier decades some novels were written in the Shanghai dialect, but not nowadays. Missionaries translated many passages from the Bible into Chinese dialects in their romanized form, and one can still find them in some countries in Southeast Asia. More recent translations have been into standard *putonghua* and in standard characters.

Dialects will remain a lively aspect of Chinese for a long time to come. Most of the rural millions speak their own dialects daily and *putonghua* rarely, if at all. Unless you are a missionary or a linguist, however, it is unlikely you will ever need to learn any of the dialects.

However, it certainly does no harm to know a few words—a sure way to impress the locals! You have to be a bit careful, though. Things are easy enough to get wrong in standard *putonghua*, let alone dialects. The word for "very interesting" in Shanghaiese (蛮有意思 mɛ ɦiɤ isɨ) sounds like "really boring" (没有意思 **méiyǒu yìsi**) in *putonghua*. The word for "idiot" in Shanghaiese (憨大 gãdɤ) sounds almost the same as *putonghua* 港督 **gǎngdū** "Governor of Hong Kong." The word **yī** means "one" in *putonghua* but "two" (with a different tone) in Cantonese. 归功 **guī gōng**, which in *putonghua* means "to give credit for one's achievements" sounds like "pimp for a prostitute" in Cantonese.

Some years ago a very famous professor of Chinese was having dinner in a Chinese restaurant. He asked where the waiter was from. A few mental notes: in that dialect the first tone goes up, the second tone goes down. Initial *n* is pronounced as *l*, *ch* as *ts*, *r* as *y*. So he continued the discussion in what he thought was the waiter's dialect. His son, who was learning Chinese, could not match this erudition, and spoke simple *putonghua*. Some time later the son visited the restaurant by himself. The waiter was effusive: "You speak much better Chinese than your father ..."

CHAPTER FOUR

Grammar

Chinese has little of the "grammar," of European languages, or Japanese and Korean, in that it has little need for different endings for verbs depending on person or tense, or cases or particles for nouns and adjectives. Chinese word order is basically very simple: subject–verb–object, as in English. It is often easier to analyze a Chinese sentence as "topic-comment." First one mentions a topic ("the weather today"), and then makes a comment ("is hotter than yesterday"). There are some other constructions with a different order, and these can be a bit tricky until you get used to them. You needn't worry about these now, as they tend to belong to the more advanced sections of a textbook.

4.1 Nouns, pronouns and titles

Nouns are treated much the same as English nouns—they are the names of things, and can be both the subjects and objects of verbs. Many words can be nouns in some sentences, and verbs in others, as shown by this example: 学习很吃力 **xuéxí hěn chī lì** "study(ing) is very demanding"; 学习汉语 **xuéxí Hànyǔ** "to study Chinese." This dual role is also common in English.

The personal pronouns are: 我 **wǒ** "I," 你 **nǐ** "you," 他 **tā** "he," 她 **tā** "she," 它 **tā** "it." During the first half of the twentieth century some attempts were made to introduce words 伊 **yī** for "she" or the pronunciation of 它 **tuō** for "it," but they were not successful. One occasionally sees forms such as 牠 for "it" when referring to animals, and 祂 for "He" when referring to God, or 妳 for "you" when referring to a woman, but these forms are not official.

The plural forms have the suffix 们 **men**: 我们 **wǒmen** "we, us," 你们 **nǐmen** "you (plural)," 他们 **tāmen** "they." There is also a polite form 您 **nín** "you." In Beijing the "inclusive we" (*you* and *I*, as distinct from *others*) is common: 咱们 **zánmen**, pronounced **zámen**. "Who?" is 谁 **shéi** (also pronounced **shuí**) and "what' is 什么 **shénme**, pronounced **shémme**.

People are often addressed by their titles rather than their names: 李老师 **Lǐ lǎoshī** "teacher Li," 张局长 **Zhāng júzhǎng** "division chief Zhang," or simple by their title: 主任 **zhǔrèn** "head of academic department, dean." Other common titles are 先生 **xiānsheng** "Mister," also used politely for "husband"; 太太 **tàitai** "Mrs/Madam," also used politely for "wife"; and 小姐 **xiǎojie** (literally "little elder sister") for "Miss." Amongst friends, or people who have worked together for a long time, people are often addressed as 小李 **Xiǎo Lǐ** "Little Li" for a relatively young person, and 老李 **Lǎo Lǐ** "Old Li" for a relatively older person, though women are usually called 小 **xiǎo** whatever their age. In southern China the prefix 阿 **ā**, as in 阿王 **Ā Wáng**, is very common in this sense. Members of a family can be addressed and referred to by their order: 张三 **Zhāng Sān** "Zhang number three," 李四 **Lǐ Sì** "Li number four." The expression 张三李四 **Zhāng Sān Lǐ Sì** means "any Tom, Dick or Harry." Another way of saying this is 阿狗阿猫 **Ā gǒu Ā māo** (Ah Dog and Ah Cat) "any damn fool."

Occasionally one sees such forms as 郭老 **Guō Lǎo**, "the venerable Guo," used only of famous and senior statesmen. Guo Lao was 郭沫若 Guo Moruo, the President of the Academy of Sciences.

The Chinese differentiate between 哥哥 **gēge** "elder brother" and 弟弟 **dìdi** "younger brother"; 姐姐 **jiějie** "elder sister" and 妹妹 **mèimei** "younger sister." Occasionally the classical word 兄 **xiōng** is used for "elder brother," as in 兄弟 **xiōngdì** "brothers," and 姊 **zǐ** for "elder sister," as in 姊妹 **zǐ mèi** (for 姐妹 **jiěmèi** "sisters").

Titles for other relatives—grandparents, uncles, aunts and cousins, etc.—can be extremely complicated, depending on whether they are paternal (on your father's side) or maternal (on your mother's). The age of the person relative to your parent's, and to yourself, is also a deciding factor as to how to address him or her. People married to your close relatives also have appropriate titles. Examples of the different terms used for each group of relatives, based on the above factors, are as below. When two forms are given, the first is the more formal, the second used when talking to someone.

GRANDPARENTS

祖父、爷爷	**zǔfù, yéye**	paternal grandfather
祖母, 奶奶	**zǔmǔ, nǎinai**	paternal grandmother
外祖父、老爷 or 姥爷	**waì zǔfù, lǎoye**	maternal grandfather
外祖母、姥姥	**waì zǔmǔ, lǎolao**	maternal grandmother
曾祖父	**zēngzǔfù**	paternal great-grandfather
曾祖母	**zēngzǔmǔ**	paternal great-grandmother
高祖父	**gāozǔfù**	great-great-grandfather
高祖母	**gāozǔmǔ**	great-great-grandmother

老爷爷 **láoyéye** can mean great-grandfather, but is also used by small children to address their grandfather. 老爷 **lǎoye** was also a respectful term of address used by a servant to a master, now used sarcastically.

PARENTS

父亲, 爸爸	**fùqin, bàba**	father, dad
母亲, 妈妈	**mǔqin, māma**	mother, mum
后娘	**hòuniáng**	stepmother
干妈	**gānmā**	adopted mother/godmother
干爸	**gānbà**	adopted father

干爸爸 **gānbàba** also means "sugar daddy," so many people avoid it and say 干爹 **gāndiē** instead, 爹 **diē** being a dialect word for "father." Other dialect words (sometimes used in the standard language) include 娘 **niáng** for "mother," but 娘娘 **niángniáng** means "empress or imperial concubine of the first rank." The general word for "parents" is 父母 **fùmǔ**; "head of a family" (so parent or guardian) is 家长 **jiāzhǎng**. A man might refer to his wife as 娘子 **niángzi**, as might a teenage daughter referring to her mother (but not to her face), but to refer to oneself as 老娘 **lǎoniáng** is considered vulgar. When it was alleged that Jiang Qing (Mao Zedong's wife/widow) habitually referred to herself as 老娘 **lǎoniáng**, this only confirmed her general image as being evil beyond redemption. Young men occasionally use the term 老子 **lǎozi** to mean "I" when they are trying to sound tough, or when being funny. 老妈子 **lǎomāzi** is an old maidservant, an amah.

BROTHERS AND SISTERS

哥哥	**gēge**	elder brother
大哥	**dàgē**	eldest brother
姐姐	**jiějie**	elder sister
大姐	**dàjiě**	eldest sister
弟弟	**dìdi**	younger brother
二弟弟	**èrdìdi**	second younger brother
妹妹	**mèimei**	younger sister

兄 **xiōng** is the classical word for "elder brother," also used in 兄弟(们) **xiōngdì(men)** or 弟兄(们) **dìxiōng(men)** "brothers," also referring to members of the same gang. A man might address a friend about his own age or older as 老兄 **lǎoxiōng**, but would use 老弟 **lǎodì** to address a man much younger than himself.

子弟 **zǐdì** means "sons and younger brothers," and is commonly used in the expression 高干子弟 **gāogàn zǐdì** "the offspring of important government officials," the aristocratic set of modern China. In earlier times the corresponding term (still used occasionally) was 纨裤子弟 **wánkù zǐdì** "the silk pants set," the profligate sons of the rich. The normal word for "playboy," then and now, is 花花公子 **huāhuāgōngzǐ** "flowery flowery lordly fellow."

GRANDCHILDREN

孙子	**sūnzi**	grandson
孙女	**sūnnǚ**	granddaughter
外孙	**wàisūn**	daughter's son
外孙女	**wàisūnnǚ**	daughter's daughter
曾孙	**zēngsūn**	great-grandson
曾孙女	**zēngsūnnǚ**	great-granddaughter
玄孙	**xuānsūn**	great-great-grandson
孙媳妇	**sūnxífu**	grandson's wife

UNCLES AND AUNTS

伯父、伯伯	**bófù, bóbo**	father's eldest brother
伯母、大娘	**bómǔ, dàniáng**	father's eldest brother's wife
叔叔、大叔	**shūshu, dàshū**	father's younger brother
婶母、婶子	**shěnmǔ, shěnzi**	father's younger brother's wife
姑姑	**gūgu**	father's elder/younger sister
姑父	**gūfù**	father's elder/younger sister's husband
姑母	**gūmǔ**	father's sister (married)
舅舅	**jiùjiu**	mother's elder/younger brother, maternal uncle
舅母	**jiùmǔ**	maternal uncle's wife
姨母, 阿姨	**yímǔ, āyí**	mother's elder sister, maternal aunt
姨父	**yífù**	maternal aunt's husband

The terms 叔叔 **shūshu** and 阿姨 **āyí** are used by children to address adults of their parent's generation, especially family friends. 阿姨 **āyí** also means a nursemaid or childcare worker in a nursery or kindergarten.

COUSINS

堂哥	**táng gē**	father's brother's son (older than you)
堂弟	**táng dì**	father's brother's son (younger)
堂姐	**táng jiě**	father's brother's daughter (older)
堂妹	**táng mèi**	father's brother's daughter (younger)

The above relations share the same surname as yourself. They are considered blood relations.

表哥	**biǎogē**	mother's brother/sister's son or
姑表哥、舅表哥	**gūbiǎogē, jiùbiǎogē**	father's sister's son
姨表哥	**yíbiǎogē**	(older than or yourself)

表弟	**biǎodì**	mother's brother/sister's son or
姑表弟、舅表弟	**gūbiǎodì, jiùbiǎodì**	father's sister's son
姨表弟	**yíbiǎodì**	(younger ythan yourself)

表姐	**biǎojiě**	mother's brother/sister's daughter or
姑表姐、舅表姐	**gūbiǎojiě, jiùbiǎojiě**	father's sister's daughter
姨表姐	**yíbiǎojiě**	(older than yourself)

表妹	**biǎomèi**	
姑表妹	**gūbiǎomèi**	mother's brother/sister's daughter or
舅表妹	**jiùbiǎomèi**	father's sister's daughter
姨表妹	**yíbiǎomèi**	(younger than yourself)

This group of cousins is different from the "**táng**" group in that they do not share the same surname as yourself.

Cousins who share the same surname are all related on your father's side—the children of his brothers. Cousins who have a different surname are related either on your mother's side—her brothers' and sister's children—or they are the children of your father's sister (whose children take the surname of her husband).

General terms for all cousins who do not share the same surname is 表哥 **biǎogē**, 表弟 **biǎodì**, 表姐 **biǎojiě**, 表妹 **biǎomèi**. However, it is also very common to specify if they are your mother's brother's children, your mother's sister's children, or your father's sister's children. The short term for your father's sister is 姑 **gū**, for your mother's brother is 舅 **jiù**, and for your mother's sister is 姨 **yí**. Combining all this together, we have the following possibilities:

姑表哥	**gūbiǎogē**	father's sister's son (older)
姑表弟	**gūbiǎodì**	father's sister's son (younger)

舅表哥	**jiùbiǎogē**	mother's brother's son (older)
舅表弟	**jiùbiǎodì**	mother's brother's son (younger)
姨表哥	**yíbiǎogē**	mother's sister's son (older)
姨表弟	**yíbiǎodì**	mother's sister's son (younger)

姑表姐	**gūbiǎojiě**	father's sister's daughter (older)
姑表妹	**gūbiǎomèi**	father's sister's daughter (younger)
舅表姐	**jiùbiǎojiě**	mother's brother's daughter (older)
舅表妹	**jiùbiǎomèi**	mother's brother's daughter (younger)
姨表姐	**yíbiǎojiě**	mother's sister's daughter (older)
姨表妹	**yíbiǎomèi**	mother's sister's daughter (younger)

That does still not exhaust the possibilities, because if your father's brother has several sons, they can be distinguished as 二堂哥 **èr tánggē** "second eldest male cousin (father's side)" or 三表妹 **sān biǎomèi** "third youngest female cousin (mother's side)," and so on through the system. Somehow being a member of a Chinese extended family seems a much more complicated business than being in a typical nuclear family you are probably more used to.

NIECES AND NEPHEWS

侄子	**zhízi**	brother's son
侄女	**zhínǚ**	brother's daughter
外甥	**wàishēng**	sister's son
外甥女	**wàishēngnǚ**	sister's daughter

RELATIONS BY MARRIAGE

公公	**gōnggong**	husband's father
婆婆	**pópo**	husband's mother
岳父	**yuèfù**	wife's father
岳母	**yuèmǔ**	wife's mother
内兄	**nèixiōng**	wife's elder brother
内弟	**nèidì**	wife's younger brother
大姨子	**dàyízi**	wife's elder sister
小姨子	**xiǎoyízi**	wife's younger sister
内侄女	**nèizhínǚ**	daughter of wife's brother
嫂子, 嫂嫂	**sǎozi, sǎosao**	elder brother's wife
姐夫	**jiěfū**	elder sister's husband
弟妇 / 弟媳妇	**dìfù / dìxífù**	younger brother's wife
妹夫	**mèifū**	younger sister's husband
女婿	**nǚxù**	son-in-law

媳妇	**xífù**	son's wife
儿媳妇	**érxífù**	daughter-in-law

As if this is not complicated enough, there are many variants of the above (third sister-in-law, fourth eldest uncle), and often different terms are used in different dialects. Many of these words have other meanings in different contexts. 婆婆 **pópo**, for example, means "husband's mother," but 老婆(儿) **lǎopó(r)** is a very common if not particularly polite word for "wife." 姨姨 **yíyi** is "mother's elder sister" and 太太 **tàitai** is a polite word for "wife," but 姨太太 **yítàitai** means "concubine," also called more colloquially 小老婆 **xiǎo lǎopó** "little wife." 姑 **gū** is "father's sister," but 三姑六婆 **sān gū liù pó** "three aunts and six mothers-in-law" refers to women engaged in not particularly reputable occupations: 尼姑 **nígu** "Buddhist nun," 道姑 **dàogu** "Taoist nun," 卦姑 **guàgu** "fortune-teller," 牙婆 **yápo** "an old woman trafficking in young girls," 媒婆 **méipo** "matchmaker," 师婆 **shīpo** "sorceress," 虔婆 **qiánpo** "madam [in a brothel]," 药婆 **yàopo** "peddler of quack medicines," and 稳婆 **wěnpo** "examiner of dead bodies." 太子 **tàizǐ** is a crown prince, 太医 **tàiyī** is an imperial physician, but 太监 **tàijiàn** "grand supervisor" is a court eunuch. The word 公公 **gōnggong**, which means "husband's father," or in some dialects, "grandfather," was also the polite form of address to a court eunuch in ancient China.

Foreigners do not really need to worry too much about all this unless they marry into a Chinese family, when they will (sooner or later) work out where they, and everyone else, fit into the overall scheme of things. It has recently been noted that with the advent of the one-child family in China, in the future one will have no brothers or sisters, either younger or older, so the whole elaborate system (except for the grandparents) might no longer have a role to play in Chinese society.

4.1.1 Other terms of address

During the cultural revolution practically everyone was addressed as 同志 **tóngzhì** "comrade." That word is definitely out of fashion nowadays, but one still hears it occasionally. As recently as 2005 I noticed an old soldier addressing a maid in a hotel as 服务员同志 **fúwùyuán tóngzhì** "comrade service person," but that would be unusual now. The term is also used in political meetings and amongst members of the communist party on formal occasions. The term 同志 **tóngzhì** "comrade" is now commonly used in the gay community in China, a usage which originated in Hong Kong and Taiwan. How times have changed!

The decline of 同志 **tóngzhì** as a term of address has left a gap. Young women are addressed as 小姐 **xiǎojiě** "little older sister." Male workers, such as taxi drivers, are usually addressed as 师傅 **shīfu** "master worker." The name of a well-known brand of instant noodles is 康师傅 **Kāng shīfu** "Master Cook Kang." Children you don't know are addressed as 小朋友 **xiǎopéngyou** "little friends," and someone in the street trying to sell you pirated CDs is likely to call you simply 朋友 **péngyou** "friend, buddy." Titles, reflecting one's profession, are also common terms of address: 老师 **lǎoshī** for "teacher," 教授 **jiàoshòu** for "professor," 大使 **dàshǐ** for "ambassador," and so on.

4.1.2 Family terms of address

After 1949 the term for both "husband" and "wife" was 爱人 **àirén** "lover," a term used much earlier by communists and left-wingers generally. Many Chinese outside Mainland China found this expression distasteful. Over recent years the older terms 先生 **xiānsheng** for "husband," and 太太 **tàitai** for "wife" have become more in vogue, though some people prefer the neutral terms 丈夫 **zhàngfu** and 妻子 **qīzi**, respectively. The wives of foreigners and other important people are sometimes referred to as 夫人 **fūren** "madame." Colloquial terms are 老婆(儿) **lǎopó(r)** for "wife," and 老头子 **lǎotóuzi** or 老头(儿) **lǎotóu(r)** ("old head") for "husband," but some people find these terms a bit vulgar, and avoid them. The term 老公 **lǎogōng** (for "husband") is from the south (especially Hong Kong), but is now commonly heard in Beijing.

Older people often refer to their husband or wife as 老伴儿 **lǎobànr** "my old partner." The term 爱人 **àirén** is sometimes still heard amongst Chinese officials of the older generation.

Many of these terms are used in extended senses. The term 小姐 **xiǎojie** is a perfectly respectable term of address for a young woman, but it can have derogatory connotations in certain circumstances, such as "there are ten **xiǎojie** waiting in the hotel lobby." When used as a term of address, this word is pronounced with a neutral tone on the second syllable, but elsewhere with a third tone. [In practice the use of the light tone in many words is a matter of stress, dialect and taste.] In previous decades in left wing circles 小姐 **xiǎojie** also implied the pampered spoilt daughter of a rich family, and 太太 **tàitai** suggested a tyrannical mistress of the household with a propensity for beating the maidservants. These words no longer carry such connotations, except perhaps in old movies. The term 大姐 **dàjiě** "big elder sister" can be used amongst women of approximately the same age, and is sometimes used as a title: 邓颖超 Deng Yingchao, the wife/widow of 周恩来 Zhou Enlai, was always referred to as 邓大姐 **Dèng Dàjiě**. 江青 Jiang Qing, the wife/widow of 毛泽东 Mao Zedong, was always 江青同志 **Jiāng Qīng tóngzhì**: Comrade Jiang Qing. 宋美龄 Song Meiling, the wife/widow of 蒋介石 Jiang Jieshi (Chiang Kai-shek) was never anything but 蒋夫人 **Jiǎng Fūren** "Madame Chiang." But 宋庆龄 Song Qingling, the wife/widow of 孙中山 **Sun Zhongshan** (Sun Yat-sen), was usually simply Song Qingling, or, surprisingly perhaps, 宋庆龄先生 **Sòng Qìnglíng xiānsheng**, the term 先生 **xiānsheng** (literally "first born"), almost exclusively used in reference to men, is an extremely respectful term for distinguished women. A female university professor, for example, may be addressed or referred to as 先生 **xiānsheng**.

Words for family members are also used in an extended sense: 的哥 **dígē** and 的妹 **dímèi** are slang words for male and female taxi drivers, for example. 北妹 **běimèi** "northern younger sister" is used in Hong Kong for a girl from Mainland China (usually derogatory). 菲妹 **fēimèi** are Filipino maids. In Beijing, 哥们儿 **gēmenr** meaning "buddy, mate" is widely used amongst young men. The female equivalent is 姐们儿 **jiěmenr**. Such terms are slang, but widely used.

Terms such as 康大哥 **Kāng dàgē** "elder brother Kang" are more at home in the world of martial arts novels, but are sometimes used jocularly among friends. Another common term from martial arts novels is 后会有期 **hòu huì yǒu qī** "afterwards there will certainly be a time," meaning "we are sure to meet each other again," sometimes used (in fun) as a pseudo-classical term for "goodbye." One might compare this to English speakers occasionally using terms like *au revoir* (French for "goodbye").

One occasionally hears old-fashioned honorific terms of address: 令尊大人 **lìng zūn dà rén** "your esteemed father"; 足下 **zú xià** "under your feet," a term of address amongst friends of the same age, especially in letters; 膝下 **xīxià** "under your knees," a respectful term of address for parents, especially in letters; 阁下 **géxià** "your excellency" used when formally addressing ambassadors, or 陛下 **bì xià** "your highness" which might be used in addressing the Queen of England. Needless to say, such words are hardly items of everyday speech, and need not bother the beginner, or even the advanced student of Chinese, unless he is perhaps a diplomat or moving in fairly elevated intellectual circles. These terms of honorific address, however, are commonly used in Chinese period movies.

4.2 Numerals

The "large forms" of the numerals, as shown by Figure 21, are used in receipts to avoid fraud. The "Suzhou figures" used to be used commonly in markets, and are sometimes still seen. The large figures are used in writing checks and receipts, to prevent fraud.

Western numerals	1	2	3	4	5	6	7	8	9	10
Standard numerals	一	二	三	四	五	六	七	八	九	十
Large numerals	壹	貳	參	肆	伍	陸	柒	捌	玖	拾
Suzhou numerals	〡	〢	〣	〤	〥	〦	〧	〨	〩	十

FIGURE 21 Chinese numerals. The "large numerals" are really independent characters which sound the same, or almost the same, as the standard numerals, and are used in writing checks, etc., to avoid fraud. The "Suzhou numerals" are sometimes seen in market places, but are quite uncommon nowadays. Nevertheless, they have recently been allocated Unicode numbers (the forms given above). Western numerals are probably just as common as Chinese ones nowadays. In traditional China zero was pronounced **líng** and written 零. So 0.5% is 百分之零点五 **bǎifēn zhī líng diǎn wǔ** "of a hundred parts, zero dot five," but nowadays it is more common to see zero written as ○: 2006 is written 二〇〇六.

Numerals in Chinese are quite simple, until you have to translate large numbers, when things become more complicated. The characters for the numerals are also among the easiest, and among the first you will learn. They are:

一	**yī**	"one"		六	**liù**	"six"
二	**èr**	"two"		七	**qī**	"seven"
三	**sān**	"three"		八	**bā**	"eight"
四	**sì**	"four"		九	**jiǔ**	"nine"
五	**wǔ**	"five"		十	**shí**	"ten"

In Beijing the word for "one" is usually pronounced **yāo** when it is used in a series of numbers, such as bus routes, telephone numbers, hotel rooms, house numbers etc. The date of the attack on the World Trade Center is called 九一一, read **jiǔ yāo yāo** "911." However, the 18th of September 1937, the date of the Marco Polo Bridge Incident which sparked off full-scale war with Japan, is called 九一八 **jiǔ yī bā** with **yī** for "one," rather than **yāo**. The use of **yāo** is common in Beijing, as well as in Singapore, but not elsewhere. The pronunciation **yāo** is not used for naming years: "1971" is still **yī jiǔ qī yī nián**.

The sound for "one," 一 **yī**, changes its tone depending on the tone of the word following it. Read in isolation it is **yī**. When followed by a fourth tone it becomes **yí**; followed by a second or third tone it becomes **yì**. In Beijing dialect, 七 **qī** and 八 **bā** are also pronounced with a rising tone when preceding a falling tone, so 七个 **qīge** "seven of them," and 八个 **bāge** "eight of them" (when counting people, etc.) are pronounced **qíge** and **báge**, but this is not standard, and is not common elsewhere.

The word for "two" when followed by a classifier is not 二 **èr** but 两 **liǎng**. This originally referred to things that came in pairs, but no longer necessarily so. One says 一本书 **yìběn shū**, 两本书 **liǎngběn shū**, 三本书 **sānběn shū** for "one book, two books, three books"; 两位老师 **liǎngwèi lǎoshī** "two teachers," 两个朋友 **liǎngge péngyou** "two friends," and so on. One can say 二百 **èrbǎi** or 两百 **liǎngbǎi** for "two hundred." There is also a colloquial term 俩 **liǎ**, from 两个 **liǎngge**, as in 你们俩 **nǐmen liǎ** "you two." Occasionally one sees expressions such as 二人 **èr rén** (as in 二人世界 **èr rén shì jiè** "a private world for two"), but this is really a classical expression used in the modern language.

The words for the "teens" are the same words preceded by 十 **shí** "ten":

十一	**shíyī**	"eleven"		十六	**shíliù**	"sixteen"
十二	**shí'èr**	"twelve"		十七	**shíqī**	"seventeen"
十三	**shísān**	"thirteen"		十八	**shíbā**	"eighteen"
十四	**shísì**	"fourteen"		十九	**shíjiǔ**	"nineteen"
十五	**shíwǔ**	"fifteen"		二十	**èrshí**	"twenty"

The word for "twenty" 二十 **èrshí** sets the pattern for thirty to one hundred:

二十	**èrshí**	"twenty"		七十	**qīshí**	"seventy"
三十	**sānshí**	"thirty"		八十	**bāshí**	"eighty"
四十	**sìshí**	"forty"		九十	**jiǔshí**	"ninety"
五十	**wǔshí**	"fifty"		一百	**yībǎi**	"one hundred"
六十	**liùshí**	"sixty"				

The hundreds are just as straightforward: 二百 **èrbǎi**, 三百 **sānbǎi**, 四百 **sìbǎi**, 五百 **wǔbǎi**, 六百 **liùbǎi**, 七百 **qībǎi**, 八百 **bābǎi**, 九百 **jiǔbǎi** and 一千 **yīqiān** for "a thousand." Similarly for the thousands. One occasionally sees the character 廿 **niàn** for "twenty," and even more rarely the character 卅 **sā** for "thirty," but they are very uncommon.

The problems start with the next order, because Chinese has a term for "ten thousand" (10,000) 万 [萬] **wàn**—which English and other European languages do not have. So "thirty thousand" is 三万 **sān wàn** "three ten thousands," and five hundred thousand is 五十万 **wǔshí wàn** "fifty ten thousands." A million is 一百万 **yìbǎi wàn** "a hundred ten thousands." The next numeral up in Chinese is 亿 **yì**, which means "ten thousand ten thousands," or "a hundred million." This term 亿 **yì** is very commonly used when discussing investments or real estate.

If all your calculations are done in either English or Chinese you can keep track, but once you start converting from one to the other, you will have problems. You will see many experienced interpreters who can confidently discuss all sorts of complicated matters, quickly grasping their pencils and some note paper whenever they have to translate higher numerals into Chinese.

For these reasons, speakers of Chinese in English-speaking countries sometimes use the term 百万 **bǎi wàn** "a hundred ten thousands" as the functional equivalent of "million," and say things like 二十七百万 **èrshí qībǎi wàn** for "twenty-seven million dollars" which in China would be expressed as 两千七百万 **liǎngqiān qībǎi wàn** "two thousand and seven hundred ten thousands."

The traditional character 萬 **wàn** is a pictograph of a scorpion. You can identify its feelers, back legs and sting. This character used to be classified under the radical 厶, which represents the scorpion's sting. More recent dictionaries also classify it under the grass radical 艹, which although etymologically unjustified, at least helps to locate it in the radical index.

FIGURE 23 The evolution of 萬 **wàn** from pictographs of a scorpion.

4.2.1 Ordinals
The Chinese words for "first," "second," "third" (that is, order of sequencing) could not be simpler: the numerals are preceded by 第 **dì**: 第一 **dìyī** "first," 第

五 **dìwǔ** "fifth," 第三百三十六 **dì sānbǎi sānshí liù** "the three hundred and thirty sixth." Colloquially one also hears 头 **tóu** for "first": 头一个问题 **tóu yī ge wènti** "the first question." The word 次 **cì** means "time" in modern Chinese, as in 第一次 **dì yī cì** "the first time," 第三次 **dì sān cì** "the third time"; 这是我第一次到中国来 **zhè shì wǒ dì yī cì dào Zhōngguó lái** "This is the first time I have been in China." In Classical Chinese 次 **cì** means "second" as in 次子 **cì zǐ** "second son," 次要 **cìyào** "of secondary importance," 次日 **cì rì** "the next day." The phrase for "the next day" in modern Chinese is 第二天 **dì èr tiān**.

4.2.2 Numbers as dates
The use of numbers to refer to dates is far more common in Chinese than in English. In English we now say 9/11; in Chinese one says 5/4 五四 **wǔ sì**, literally "five four," to refer to the May Fourth Incident of 1919, when rioting broke out to protest against the terms of the Treaty of Versailles. Numbers are used with other words in a bewildering number of proverbs, sayings and political slogans: 三反五反 **sān fǎn wǔ fǎn** "the three antis and the five antis"; 五讲四美 **wǔ jiǎng sì měi** "the five politenesses and the four beauties," which are similar to traditional expressions like 三纲五常 **sān gāng wǔ cháng** "the three cardinal guides and the five constant virtues." Even the expression 四人帮 **sì rén bāng** "the gang of four" reminds one of 四大美人 **sì dà měi rén** "the four classical beauties," 四大名著 **sì dà míng zhù** "the four great works of classical literature," and other similar expressions. There are also many proverbs and other sayings of this type: 乱七八糟 **luàn qī bā zāo** "in an awful mess" (literally "disorder seven, eight dregs"), or 三天打鱼，两天晒网 **sān tiān dǎ yú, liǎng tiān shài wǎng** ("three days go fishing, two days dry nets") meaning "to work in fits and starts"—often used in relation to one's efforts in learning Chinese.

4.2.3 Percentages
The standard Chinese way of expressing percentages is 百分之 **bǎifēn zhī** x "of one hundred parts, X." So 16% is 百分之十六 **bǎifēn zhī shíliù** "16 parts out of 100." In Hong Kong, Singapore and other overseas Chinese communities, the expression 巴仙 **bā xiān**, from English "percent," is common, so 16% is 十六巴仙 **shíliù bā xiān** (usually pronounced **bāsēn**). This way of expressing percentages is not accepted in the standard (formal) language—written or spoken.

4.3 Classifiers
One of the salient features of Chinese is the system of classifiers, or measure words. When a noun is preceded by a numeral, or by the demonstrative pronouns "this" and "that," a classifier or measure word is used to describe the shape, size or quantity of the noun.

For most nouns in English, when a numeral precedes a noun, we simply say "one dog, two dogs," and so on. There are some words, however, which we "measure." We do not say "one bread" or "one water," we say "a loaf/slice/crumb of bread," or "a glass of water," "a bucket of water." Sugar and salt are similarly treated: "one teaspoon of sugar," "a pinch of salt." We also have expressions like "five head of cattle," "a school of fish," "a herd of elephants," and so on.

Almost all Chinese nouns are treated like the English nouns for bread, sugar and salt: they are "measured" with appropriate measure words. Chinese measure words need not only refer to volume, they can describe the size or shape of the noun they are attached to. The classifier 条 **tiáo** is used with long and thin shaped things, for example: 一条蛇 **yī tiáo shé** "a snake," 一条河 **yī tiáo hé** "a river," 一条路 **yī tiáo lù** "a road." The classifier 张 **zhāng** is used for spread-out things, for example: 一张报 **yī zhāng bào** "a piece of paper," 一张桌子 **yī zhāng zhuōzi** "a table." 把 **bǎ** is used for things which can be grasped: 一把椅子 **yī bǎ yǐzi** "a chair," 一把刀 **yī bǎ dāo** "a knife," 一把雨伞 **yī bǎ yǔsǎn** "an umbrella." More examples of common classifiers are given on pages 121–123.

Does this mean you have to learn the appropriate classifier for every noun in the language? The short answer is yes, but it is not as hard as it might first seem. For a start, there is the "general classifier" 个 **gè** (usually pronounced unstressed as **ge**). This is generally used for people: 一个人 **yī ge rén** "one person," 一个小孩子 **yī ge xiǎo háizi** "one child," as well as widely used for nouns which do not have a particular classifier of their own: 一个国家 **yī ge guójiā** "one nation," 一个好主意 **yī ge hǎo zhúyi** "a good idea." You can also use this general classifier when you are not sure of the "correct" classifier, for example: 一个椅子 **yī ge yǐzi** "a chair" for 一把椅子 **yī bǎ yǐzi**; 一个电视机 **yī ge diànshìjī** "a television set" for 一台电视机 **yī tái diànshìjī**; 一个飞机 **yī ge fēijī** "one airplane" for 一架飞机 **yī jià fēijī**. This generalized use of **ge** is very common and certainly not incorrect. One always says 一本书 **yī běn shū** for "a book," but occasionally one hears 一个字典 **yī ge zìdiǎn** "a dictionary," as in 这是个很好的字典 **zhè shi ge hěn hǎo de zìdiǎn** "this is a very good dictionary." The use of 个 **ge** seems to have expanded in Modern Chinese, but careful speakers still prefer to use the correct classifier when possible.

There were no classifiers as such in Classical Chinese, and classical expressions absorbed into the modern language continue not to have classifiers: 三人行必有我师焉 **sān rén xíng bì yǒu wǒ shī yān** "three people walking, there must be my teacher among them" (a quote from Confucius). Modern Chinese has 三个人 **sān ge rén** with the classifer **ge**. The last word here, 焉 **yān**, is Classical Chinese for a preposition and a pronoun "in it, among them."

Classifiers are used after "this" and "that" as well as numerals: 这个人 **zhège rén** "this man," 那个朋友 **nèige péngyou** "that friend." Some nouns are not preceded by classifiers because they are considered classifiers themselves. These include 天 **tiān** "day" and 年 **nián** "year." So we have 一天 **yī tiān** "a day," 一个星期 **yī ge xīngqī** (or 一个礼拜 **yī ge lǐbài**) "a week," 一个月 **yī ge yuè** "a month," 一年 **yī nián** "a year," 一个世纪 **yī ge shìjì** "a century." Classifiers were not generally used in the classical period, but developed during the period of division between the Han and Tang dynasties.

Some other common classifiers are:

本 **běn**: for books: 一本书 **yī běn shū**. The word 本 **běn** means "root" (= "origin") as in the word 日本 **Rìběn** "Japan," the origin of the sun

笔 **bǐ**: for money: 一笔钱 **yī bǐ qián** "a sum of money"

部 **bù**: class, section; for books in more than one volume: 一部书 **yī bù shū** "one volume of a set of books," also 一部电影 **yī bù diànyǐng** "a movie"

道 **dào**: for rivers and bridges; courses of food: 一道河 **yī dào hé** "a river," 一道桥 **yī dào qiáo** "a bridge," 一道菜 **yī dào cài** "a course of dishes"

顶 **dǐng** "top": classifier for hats: 一顶帽子 **yī dǐng màozi**

朵 **duǒ**: for flowers: 一朵花 **yī duǒ huā**

封 **fēng** "to seal," classifier for letters: 一封信 **yī fēng xìn**

副 **fù**: used for things in pairs: 一副眼镜 **yī fù yǎnjìng** "a pair of glasses," 一副手套 **yī fù shǒutào** "a pair of gloves"

根 **gēn**: for long slender things: 一根棍子 **yī gēn gùnzi** "a stick"

盒 **hé**: for boxes and square containers, as in 一盒巧克力 **yī hé qiǎokèlì** "a box of chocolates"

间 **jiān**: used for rooms: 一间房子 **yī jiān fángzi** "a room"

件 **jiàn**: used for articles and things, also clothing: 一件事 **yī jiàn shì** "a matter," 一件衣服 **yī jiàn yīfu** "a piece of clothing," 一件东西 **yī jiàn dōngxi** "a thing"

句 **jù**: for words: 一句话 **yī jù huà** "a phrase, a sentence," as in 我们中国人有一句话 **wǒmen Zhōngguórén yǒu yī jù huà** "we Chinese have a saying..."

棵 **kē**: for trees: 一棵树 **yī kē shù** "a tree"

口 **kǒu** "mouth": for counting people: 我们家有八口人 **wǒmen jiā yǒu bā kǒu rén** "there are eight people in our family"; 人口 **rénkǒu** "population"

块 **kuài**: "piece, lump": 一块石头 **yī kuài shítou** "a rock," 一块木头 **yī kuài mùtou** "a piece of wood"; used for 元 *yuan* or dollar: 三块 (钱) **sān kuài (qián)** "three *yuan*" (in China), or "three dollars" (in Australia, the U.S. etc.). *Yuan* (Chinese dollar) by itself is not preceded by a classifier: we say **sān yuán** 三元 (without a classifier), or 三块钱 **sān kuài qián** to mean the same thing—"three *yuan*" or "three dollars." *Yuan* is more commonly (but by no means exclusively) used in the written language, whereas 块 **kuài** is the usual term in spoken Chinese.

辆 **liàng**: for cars and other land vehicles: 一辆汽车 **yī liàng qìchē** "a car," 一辆自行车 **yī liàng zìxíngchē** "a bicycle"

匹 **pǐ**: for horses: 一匹马 **yī pǐ mǎ** "a horse"

套 **tào**: for sets, such as books, clothes: 一套书 **yī tào shū** "a set of books," 一套衣服 **yī tào yīfu** "a suit of clothes"; also 套房 **tàofáng** "a suite of rooms in a hotel"

位 **wèi**: polite classifier for "human beings": 一位老师 **yī wèi lǎoshī** "a teacher," 一位客人 **yī wèi kèrén** "a guest"

盏 **zhǎn**: classifier for lamps: 一盏灯 **yī zhǎn dēng** "a lamp"

只 [隻] **zhī**: classifier for some animals, boats, some containers: 一只牛 **yī zhī niú** (also: 一头牛 **yī tóu niú**) "an ox," 一只狗 **yī zhī gǒu** "a dog," 一只猫 **yī zhī māo** "a cat," 一只鸡 **yī zhī jī** "a chicken"; also 一只船 **yī zhī chuán** "a boat." In the simplified script 只 is used for this classifier. The character 只, when not used as a classifier, is pronounced **zhǐ** and means "only."

支 **zhī** "branch of a tree": classifier for long, narrow things: 一支笔 **yī zhī bǐ** "a pen," 一支蜡烛 **yī zhī làzhú** (or 一根蜡烛 **yī gēn làzhú**) "a candle"

座 **zuò**: classifier for mountains, buildings, monuments and other immovable things: 一座山 **yī zuò shān** "a mountain," 一座楼 **yī zuò lóu** "an apartment block"

In these examples the word for 一 "one" is transcribed **yī**, as in standard *pinyin*. The actual tone of 一 depends on the tone of the following word. In some textbooks the numerals and their classifiers are written as one word, in others as two words. Here they are written separately for clarity.

Students get used to the idea of classifiers quickly, but it takes some time to know the correct ones to apply for particular groups of nouns, and when to use or not to use them.

4.4 Calendar events

4.4.1 Days of the week

There are currently two series in common use for listing days of the week. In the first—the "official" one you will find in your textbooks—"week" is 星期 **xīngqī**, literally "star period," and the days of the week are:

星期一	**xīngqīyī**	"Monday" (literally "week-one")
星期二	**xīngqī'er**	"Tuesday" (literally "week-two")
星期三	**xīngqīsan**	"Wednesday"
星期四	**xīngqīsì**	"Thursday"
星期五	**xīngqīwǔ**	"Friday"
星期六	**xīngqīliù**	"Saturday," and
星期日	**xīngqīrì**	"Sunday" (日 **rì** being the Classical Chinese word for "sun" and "day")

In the other series, "week" is 礼拜 **lǐbài** and the days of the week are:

礼拜一	**lǐbàiyī**	"Monday"
礼拜二	**lǐbài'èr**	"Tuesday"
礼拜三	**lǐbàisān**	"Wednesday"
礼拜四	**lǐbàisì**	"Thursday"
礼拜五	**lǐbàiwǔ**	"Friday"
礼拜六	**lǐbàiliù**	"Saturday"
礼拜天	**lǐbàitiān**	"Sunday"

天 **tiān** is Classical Chinese for "sky" and "heaven," as well as "day." The latter forms are of Christian origin: 礼拜 **lǐbài** means "worship," so 礼拜天 **lǐbàitiān** is "worshipping day" (Sunday), and the other days follow suit. The official system is probably more common in formal speech than the written language, but the "day" terms with 礼拜 **lǐbài** are also very commonly used.

Yet another word for 'week' is 周 [週 or 周] **zhōu**, which literally means "cycle." It is used in the words 周末 **zhōumò** "weekend" and 周刊 **zhōukān** "weekly [magazine]," and also in 周一 **zhōuyī**, 周二 **zhōuèr**, 周三 **zhōusān**, and so on for the days of the week, but more in the written language than the spoken.

4.4.2 Months of the year
The months of the year are also straightforward. "Month" is 月 **yuè**, also the Classical Chinese word for "moon." The months are:

一月	**yīyuè**	"January"	七月	**qīyuè**	"July"
二月	**èryuè**	"February"	八月	**bāyuè**	"August"
三月	**sānyuè**	"March"	九月	**jiǔyuè**	"September"
四月	**sìyuè**	"April"	十月	**shíyuè**	"October"
五月	**wǔyuè**	"May"	十一月	**shíyīyuè**	"November"
六月	**liùyuè**	"June"	十二月	**shí'èryuè**	"December"

The months are occasionally referred to as 月份 **yuèfèn**: 六月份 **liùyuèfèn** "June," and so on.

Before the modern period, these terms referred to lunar months, not the modern system based on solar months. The traditional year had twelve lunar months, with occasional "intercalary" months to maintain consistency with the seasons. The month was divided into three ten-day periods known as 旬 **xún**. This term is very ancient: it is common on the oracle bones of over 3,000 years ago. It is still used in an imprecise sense: early February is 二月上旬 **èryuè shàng xún**, mid April is 四月中旬 **sìyuè zhōng xún**, late June is 六月下旬 **liùyuè xià xún**. The words 初 **chū** "beginning" and 底 **dǐ** "end" are used to indicate the beginning and end of months: 八月初 **bāyuè chū** "beginning of August," 九月底 **jiǔyuè dǐ** "end of September."

4.4.3 The seasons
The terms for the seasons are 春 **chūn** "spring," 夏 **xià** "summer," 秋 **qiū** "autumn," 冬 **dōng** "winter," or in the spoken language, usually 春天 **chūntiān**,

夏天 **xiàtiān**, 秋天 **qiūtiān**, and 冬天 **dōngtiān**. In the old agricultural calendar, the year was divided into twenty-four periods, many of which are very evocative:

立春	**lìchūn**	"spring begins"	立秋	**lìqiū**	"autumn begins"
雨水	**yǔshuǐ**	"rain water"	处暑	**chǔshǔ**	"heat ceases"
惊蛰	**jīngzhé**	"insects awaken"	白露	**báilù**	"white dew"
春分	**chūnfēn**	"spring equinox"	秋分	**qiūfēn**	"autumn equinox"
清明	**qīngmíng**	"clear and bright"	寒露	**hánlù**	"cold dew"
谷雨	**gǔyǔ**	"grain rains"	霜降	**shuāngjiàng**	"frost falls"
立夏	**lìxià**	"summer begins"	立冬	**lìdōng**	"winter begins"
小满	**xiǎomǎn**	"small completion"	小雪	**xiǎoxuě**	"small snow"
芒种	**mángzhǒng**	"grain in ear"	大雪	**dàxuě**	"big snow"
夏至	**xiàzhì**	"summer solstice"	冬至	**dōngzhì**	"winter solstice"
小暑	**xiǎoshǔ**	"small heat"	小寒	**xiǎohán**	"small cold"
大暑	**dàshǔ**	"great heat"	大寒	**dàhán**	"great cold"

These words are still in quite common usage (or at least everyone knows them), especially 清明 **qīngmíng** "clear and bright," the day the Chinese traditionally sweep the graves of their ancestors.

4.4.4 Reign titles

The Chinese have now adopted the Western system of referring to years, but this dates back only to the beginning of the twentieth century. In imperial China, years were dated from the beginning of the reign of the emperor then in power, so 1776 was 乾隆四十年 **Qiánlóng 40 nián** "the 40th year of the reign of Emperor Qianlong," and 1840 was 道光十九年 **Dàoguāng 19 nián** "the 19th year of the reign of Emperor Daoguang." The terms 康熙 **Kāngxī**, 乾隆 **Qiánlóng**, 道光 **Dàoguāng** and so on were not the emperors' real names, but their "reign titles," and that is how they are usually referred to. The term 康乾盛世 **Kāng Qián shèng shì** is now commonly used in China to refer to the "golden years" of the Qing dynasty, when it was at the height of its power, and a potent symbol of China's prestige.

The Western expression "AD" (Anno Domini: the year of Our Lord) is translated into Chinese as 公元 **gōngyuán** "the common era," and BC (Before Christ) is translated as 公元前 **gōngyuánqián** "before the common era." The expressions CE for "common era" and BCE for "before the common era" are now becoming quite common in Western books about Chinese history.

Although this way of designating years may not greatly concern the beginner, it can be a trap for the more advanced student. The sixth day of the third month in the traditional Chinese calendar is certainly not the sixth of March in the Western one, and there are elaborate tables and reference works to help scholars equate the date in one system to the date in another.

4.4.5 Hexagenary stems

Another way of referring to years in traditional China was according to a sixty-year cycle, not a century (or hundred-year cycle), as in the West. The terms used to refer to the sixty years of the Chinese cycle were made up of two cycles: a cycle of ten, known as the "ten stems," and a cycle of twelve, "the twelve branches." The ten stems are:

甲	**jiǎ**	戊	**wù**	壬	**rén**
乙	**yǐ**	己	**jǐ**	癸	**guǐ**
丙	**bǐng**	庚	**gēng**		
丁	**dīng**	辛	**xǐn**		

The twelve branches are:

子	**zǐ**	辰	**chén**	申	**shēn**
丑	**chǒu**	巳	**sì**	酉	**yǒu**
寅	**yín**	午	**wǔ**	戌	**xū**
卯	**mǎo**	未	**wèi**	亥	**hài**

These were combined to form a series of sixty: 甲子 **jiǎzǐ**, 乙丑 **yǐchǒu**, 丙寅 **bǐngyín**, 丁卯 **dīngmǎo**, and so on. This system is also very ancient; it was in use since the time of the oracle bones, though in ancient times the terms referred to days rather than years.

In modern usage, certain historic events are often referred to according to the year in which they occurred: the 辛亥革命 **xīnhài gémìng** "the revolution of the **xīnhài** year (1911)," 甲午 **jiǎwǔ** was the year of a famous naval battle between China and Japan in 1894, the 庚子 **gēngzǐ** indemnity refers to the year it was paid, 1900. If you check any modern Chinese newspaper, you will see the date given in the traditional system as well as the modern one at the top of the paper. Practically all Chinese calendars give the traditional dates alongside the Western ones—particularly the almanacs which advise on auspicious and inauspicious days for such matters as getting married, moving house, and so on. The year 2003 was 癸未 **guǐwèi**; 2004 is 甲申 **jiǎshēn**, and

2005 is 乙酉 **yǐyǒu**. The same terms can also refer to 1943, 1944 and 1945, and for years 60 years before or after those years.

On today's newspaper the date is given as 二〇〇五年七月廿九日星期五, 夏历乙酉年六月廿四 **èr líng líng wǔ nián qīyuè niànjiǔrì xīngqīwǔ, xiàlì yǐyǒu nián liùyuè niànsì,** that is, Friday the 29th of July 2005, the 24th day of the 6th month of the year **yiyou** in the traditional lunar calendar. This date uses the character 廿 **niàn** for "twenty," but in *putonghua* people generally read it 二十 **èrshí** "two tens," the usual word for "twenty."

The system of referring to years by the animal cycle (the Chinese zodiac) seems to be of central Asian origin, but has been part of Chinese culture for more than a thousand years. The sequence of "animals" years is: 鼠 **shǔ** "rat," 牛 **niú** "ox," 虎 **hǔ** "tiger," 兔 **tù** "rabbit," 龙 **lóng** "dragon," 蛇 **shé** "snake," 马 **mǎ** "horse," 羊 **yáng** "sheep," 猴 **hóu** "monkey," 鸡 **jī** "chicken," 狗 **gǒu** "dog," and 猪 **zhū** "pig."

The animal cycle traditionally begins with "rat" and ends with "pig." Chinese frequently ask 你属什么? **nǐ shǔ shénme?** "what [animal] do you belong to?" to find out the age of the other person. The most recent year of the rat was 1996. So we have ox for 1997, tiger for 1998, rabbit for 1999, dragon for 2000, snake for 2001, horse for 2002, sheep for 2003, monkey for 2004, chicken for 2005, dog for 2006 and pig for 2007. Each of the animals is supposed to be associated with certain qualities: the ox is hard working, the rabbit timid, the monkey playful, the pig lazy, and so on. The most desirable year to be born in is said to be the year of the dragon, as dragons are both powerful and ethereal, and a distinct cut above the others. The snake is sometimes euphemistically referred to as a little dragon.

Chinese occasionally use classical allusions to refer to their age. Confucius said 三十而立, 四十而不惑 **sānshí ér lì, sìshí ér bù huò** "when I was thirty I could stand firm; when I was forty I was no longer confused," so 而立 **ér lì** means "thirty years old," and 不惑 **bù huò** means "forty years old." Other expressions on age commonly heard include: 年近半百 **nián jìn bànbǎi** "years close to half a hundred" to mean almost fifty; 花甲 **huājiǎ** for a cycle of 60 years, so 年逾花甲 **nián yú huā jiǎ** means "over 60 years old"; 八十高龄 **bāshí gāolíng** means "eighty years old."

You can ask a child 你几岁? **nǐ jǐ suì** "How old are you?," or a teenager 你多大? **nǐ duō dà?** "How big are you?," but the polite way of asking an adult's age is to ask 您多大岁数 **nín duō dà suìshù?** "May I ask your honorable age?" or even 贵庚多少 **guì gēng duōshao?** "What is your venerable age?"

4.5 Comparisons

Comparisons of two or more items in Chinese are quite straight-forward. To express the idea "I am taller than you," you say 我比你高 **wǒ bǐ nǐ gāo** "I compared to you am tall." The word 比 **bǐ** in Classical Chinese means "to stand next to," as is clear from the shape of the character. So one could understand this sentence as "I standing next to you am tall." You do not have to physically stand next to someone to be compared. Other examples of similar comparisons: 上海比北京热闹 **Shànghǎi bǐ Běijīng rènào** "Shanghai is noisier and more lively than Beijing"; 上海的温度比北京高六度 **Shànghǎi de wēndù bǐ Běijīng gāo liù dù** "the temperature in Shanghai is six degrees hotter than in Beijing."

To express "I am not as tall as you," you say 我没有你高 **wǒ méiyou nǐ gāo**, literally "I do not have your height." Similarly, 上海的公园没有北京这么多 **Shànghǎi de gōngyuán méiyou Běijīng zhème duō** "there are not so many parks in Shanghai as there are in Beijing." [Note: **zhème** is also pronounced **zèmme**.]

If you want to say "I am the same height as you," you say 我跟你一样高 **wǒ gēn nǐ yíyàng gāo**, literally "I and you the same height." "I am much taller than you" is 我比你高得多 **wǒ bǐ nǐ gāo de duō.**

Chinese like using the word 比较 **bǐjiào** (in Beijing pronounced **bǐjiǎo**) to mean "comparatively," in the sense of "fairly, pretty": 他的中文比较好 **tā de Zhōngwén bǐjiào hǎo** "his Chinese is pretty good," or 那个情况比较复杂 **nèige qíngkuàng bǐjiào fùzá** (in Beijing pronounced **fǔzá**) "that situation is fairly complicated."

4.6 Adjectives

Many linguists regard Chinese adjectives as a type of verb, which they call stative verbs. The word 高 **gāo** "tall, high," for example, really means "is tall, is high," especially when it follows a noun. So 那个人很高 **nèige rén hěn gāo** "that man is tall" does not contain a separate word for "is." The word 是 **shì** only equates to "is" when used with nouns: 孔子是中国人 **Kǒngzi shi Zhōngguó rén** "Confucius is a Chinese." If 是 **shì** is used with an adjective it is stressed and implies "but ..." as in 他是很聪明，但是特别懒惰 **tā shì hěn cōngmíng, dànshi tèbié lǎnduò** "he is intelligent, but ... he's really lazy." Adjectives (or stative verbs) can be turned into nouns by adding 的 **de**: 红 **hóng** "red, is red"; 红的 **hóng de** "the red one."

4.7 Particles

English uses changes in word order or intonation to ask a question, to stress a statement, or to express a certain doubt about something. In Chinese, tones change the meaning of words, and alterations in word order change the grammatical relationship between different components in a phrase/sentence. Chinese uses a number of "light tone" particles at the end of a statement to express a question, make a suggestion, etc. The most common such particles are 吗 **ma**, 呢 **ne**, 吧 **ba** and 啊 **a**.

4.7.1 Question particle 吗 *ma*

This is used to turn a statement into a question, as shown by the following examples:

他是中国人。
Tā shi Zhōngguó rén. } statement
"He is a Chinese."

他是中国人吗?
Tā shi Zhōngguó rén ma? } question
"Is he a Chinese?"

你会用毛笔写字。
Nǐ huì yòng máobǐ xiě zì. } statement
"You can use a Chinese brush to write characters."

你会用毛笔写字吗?
Nǐ huì yòng máobǐ xiě zì ma? } question
"Can you use a Chinese brush to write characters?"

Amongst overseas Chinese communities one often hears the expression 你好吗 **nǐ hǎo ma**? for "How are you?" However, the universal general greeting in Mainland China is 你好 **nǐ hǎo**, a statement rather than a question.

4.7.2 Question particle 呢 *ne*

This corresponds to English "what about..." in such sentences as 我喜欢吃辣的。你呢? **wǒ xǐhuan chī là de. Nǐ ne**? "I like hot food. What about you?" or 我想看电影, 你呢? **wǒ xiǎng kàn diànyǐng, nǐ ne**? "I feel like watching a movie; what about you?," or 日本人用筷子吃饭; 韩国人呢? **Rìběn rén yòng kuàizi chī fàn—Hánguó rén ne**? "Japanese use chopsticks to eat; what about Koreans?"

4.7.3 Polite suggestion 吧 *ba*

This is used as a sort of polite imperative: 走吧 **zǒu ba** "let's go," 你说吧 **nǐ shuō ba** "just tell me"; and to invite agreement 他大概二十多岁了吧 **tā dàigài èrshí duō suì le ba** "he must be in his 20s, I suppose," or 那就三点吧 **nà jiù sāndiǎn ba** "well, we'll make it three o'clock," the implication being that will be convenient for you.

4.7.4 Emphatic statement with 啊 *a*

This particle is mainly used to draw attention: 小心啊 **xiǎo xīn a**! "Be careful!," 救命啊 **jiù mìng a**! "Save my life: Help!"

4.8 Expression of time

If the action of a verb has not yet happened, Chinese tends to show this by means of appropriate adverbs of time: 他明天考试 **tā míngtiān kǎoshì** "he will sit for the examination tomorrow"; 我明年去美国 **wǒ míngnián qù Měiguó** "I'm going to America next year." If there is no appropriate adverb, the future is indicated by verbs as 想 **xiǎng** "think," as in 我想学日语 **wǒ xiǎng xué Rìyǔ** "I think I'll learn Japanese"; or 要 **yào** "to want" as in 我要减肥 **wǒ yào jiǎn féi** "I want to lose weight." In the written language 将 **jiāng** or 将要 **jiāngyào** "intend to" is also used. Note that 要 **yào** basically means "want," but the negative form, formed by adding 不 **bù** to 要 **yào**, becomes a negative imperative: 不要乱吃 **bù yào luàn chī** "you must not eat just any old thing," 不要害我 **bù yào hài wǒ** "don't harm me." In this sense it is often shortened to 别 **bié**: 别闹 **bié nào** "don't make such a ruckus!" If you want to say you don't want something, it is considered more polite to use 不想 **bù xiǎng** "have no desire" rather than 不要 **bù yào**.

4.9 Perfective aspect 了 *le*

Ask any learner of Chinese what the hardest thing about Chinese grammar is, and he'll almost certainly answer "the use of 了 **le**." Chinese grammarians write literally hundreds of articles on 了 **le** (and also on 把 **bǎ** and 被 **bèi**) and still have not worked out rules which explain all usages.

One basic problem is that Chinese does not have tense. That is, it does not explicitly distinguish past, present and future actions except by adverbs of time or auxiliary verbs. Chinese, however, does distinguish aspect, that is, whether an action has been completed or not. English speakers automatically equate the perfective aspect with the English past tense, and the imperfective aspect with the English present or future tenses. This gets them into trouble in trying to use the Chinese verbal system properly.

When 了 **le** is used after a verb, one of its uses is to indicate the perfect aspect, that is, to **show something has been completed**: 他看了一本书 **tā kànle yī běn shū** "he read a book." When 了 **le** is used at the *end* of a sentence, it implies a change of state: 他看书了 **tā kàn shū le** "he is reading a book now (but he wasn't doing so before)."

Some more examples of **le** after a verb, implying completion: 他昨天卖了他的 车子 **tā zuòtian màile tāde chēzi** "yesterday he sold his car," that is, the action of selling the car was completed. The negative form of this type of 了 **le** is to replace it with 没 **méi** or 没有 **méiyou** in front of the verb: 他昨天没有卖（他 的）车子 **tā zuótian méiyou mài (tāde) chēzi** "yesterday he didn't sell his car."

When a sentence has two verbs, the second of which can only be performed after the first one is completed, 了 **le** shows that the first verb is completed: 他请了一些朋友来吃饭 **tā qǐngle yīxie péngyou lái chī fàn** "he invited some friends over for a meal." Sometimes this is made clearer with the use of 才 **cái** "only then": 我的朋友们走了，我才有时间给你打电话 **wǒ de péng-youmen zǒule, wǒ cái yǒu shíjiān gěi nǐ dǎ diànhuà** "it wasn't until after my friends left that I had time to ring you" or "my friends have just left, so I have time to ring you."

了 **le** is also used after certain verbs to express the idea that something might happen, such as 想 **xiǎng** "to think," 希望 **xīwàng** "to hope," 恐怕 **kǒngpà** "to fear" (as in English "I fear he might not come"), etc. In such cases, 了 **le** is often found after the second verb: 我希望他已经离开了那个糟糕的地方 **wǒ xīwàng tā yǐjing líkāile nèi ge zāogāo de dìfang** "I hope he has already left that dreadful place."

了 **le** can also be used in an imperative sentence: 别扔了那本书 **bié rēngle nèiběn shū** "don't throw that book away"; 你穿了毛衣我们就可以走了 **nǐ chuānle maóyī wǒmen jiù kěyǐ zǒu le** "put on your pullover, then we can go." 了 **le** is also used to show an imminent action: 我走了 **wǒ zǒu le** "I'm off!" or 我 们马上就到北京了 **wǒmen mǎshang jiù dào Běijīng le** "we'll be arriving in Beijing any moment now."

4.9.1 Change of state 了 *le*

This is different from the **le** which indicates completedness. Modal 了 **le** implies a change of state: 他会说中国话 **tā huì shuō Zhōngguó huà** "he can speak Chinese"; 他会说中国话了 **tā huì shuō Zhōngguó huà le** "he can speak Chinese now (but he couldn't before)."

When 了 **le** is used after a stative verb, that is, an adjective with an implied verb "to be," such as 高 **gāo** "to be tall," it implies a change: 他高了 **tā gāo le** "he is taller now (previously he was not as tall)"; 他老了 **tā lǎo le** "he has become old (that is, he wasn't so old before)"; 我好了 **wǒ hǎo le** "I'm alright now (I wasn't alright before)." If I look out the window and say: 下雨 **xià yǔ**, this simply means it is raining. If I say 下雨了 **xià yǔ le**, I mean it is raining now (when it wasn't raining before). 不下了 **bù xià le** means "it is not raining any more (that is, it was raining before, but it isn't now)."

Generally speaking, if 了 **le** is found after a verb, it indicates the perfect aspect of an action, indicating something has been finished. When it is at the end of the sentence, it probably (but not necessarily) indicates a change of state. 我以前喜欢喝啤酒，现在喝可乐了 **wǒ yǐqián xǐhuan hē píjiǔ, xiànzài hē kělè le** "I used to like drinking beer, now I drink cola."

4.9.2 Double 了 *le*

So it should not surprise you that 了 **le** after a verb and 了 **le** at the end of the sentence can be used together, especially when a numeral is involved: 他已经卖了三本书了 **tā yǐjīng màile sān běn shū le** "he has already sold three books." The double 了 **le** can also indicate that the action of the verb lasted for a certain period of time: 他看了两个小时的书了 **tā kànle liǎng ge xiǎoshí de shū le** "he had been reading for two hours." When there are two verbs in the sentence, double 了 **le** indicates that both actions were completed at some time in the past: 他毕业了就出国了 **tā bìyè le jiù chū guó le** "he graduated, then left the country." This sentence could also mean if he ever manages to graduate, he will be able to go overseas. In that case, in English we would need to begin such a sentence with "if," or perhaps use a conditional, but Chinese does not need to do so.

4.10 Past experience with 过 *guò*

The Chinese equivalent of "have you ever...?" is a verb followed by 过 **guò**. Examples:

你去过中国了吗？
Nǐ qùguo Zhōngguó le ma?
"Have you ever been to China?"

你吃过四川菜吗？
Nǐ chīguo Sìchuān cài ma?
"Have you ever eaten Sichuan food?"

你看过这本书吗？
Nǐ kànguo zhèběn shū ma?
"Have you read this book before?"

我吃过兰州拉面。
Wǒ chīguo Lánzhōu lāmiàn.
"I have eaten Lanzhou-style noodles."

过 **guò** literally means "to pass through," and so is also the equivalent of "used to be": 他以前穷过，现在很有钱了 **tā yǐqián qióng guo, xiànzài hěn yǒu qián le** "he used to be poor; now he is very rich." 过 **guò** generally stresses an experience or a process: 我学过三年中文了 **wǒ xuéguo sān nián Zhōngwén le** "I have studied Chinese for three years."

4.11 Continuous action with 着 *zhe*

The particle 着 **zhe** shows that the action of a verb is continuous: 小姑娘躺着看小说儿 **xiǎo gūniáng tāngzhe kàn xiǎoshuōr** "the young girl is lying down and reading a novel"; 老头子喝着茶看戏 **lǎotóuzi hēzhe chá kàn xì** "the old man was drinking tea whilst watching the drama"; 我常常吃着饭看电视 **wǒ chángchang chīzhe fàn kàn diànshì** "I often eat while watching television."

It is often followed by 呢 **ne**: 我们说着话呢 **wǒmen shuōzhe huà ne** "we are talking," or more emphatically with 正 **zhèng** or 正在 **zhèngzài**: 我们正（正在）讨论这个问题呢 **wǒmen zhèng (zhèngzai) tǎolùn zhège wèntí ne** "we are just in the process of discussing this problem."

It is also used to show that something remains in the state indicated by the verb: 门关着呢 **mén guānzhe ne** "the door is closed"; 电视开着呢 **diànshì kāizhe ne** "the television is on." It can also show that two actions are going on at the same time: 他坐着看电视呢 **tā zuòzhe kàn diànshì ne** "he is sitting and watching television"; 他看着电视吃晚饭 **tā kànzhe diànshì chī wǎnfàn** "he is watching television and eating his dinner at the same time"; 出租汽车在外面停着 **chūzūqìchē zài wàimian tíngzhe** "the taxi has stopped outside (and is still there)"; 胶卷儿在桌子上放着 **jiāojuǎnr zài zhuōzi shang fàngzhe** "the film has been put on the table (and it is still there)."

4.12 The three *de* particles: 的, 地 and 得

These are three quite separate particles, all pronounced **de** in the spoken language. In earlier written vernacular Chinese all three were written as 的 **de** or 底 **di**, which are now clearly distinguished in modern written Chinese. 的 **de** is used for possessives and adjectives, 地 **de** for adverbs, and 得 **de** in verbal complements. These uses are discussed below.

4.12.1 Possessive particle 的 *de*

When we first discussed the pronouns we saw that the possessive forms are derived from the personal pronouns followed by 的 **de**: 我 **wǒ** "I," 我的 **wǒde** "mine"; 你 **nǐ** "you," 你的 **nǐde** "yours." The same 的 **de** can be used to indicate any possessive form: 中国的国旗 **Zhōngguó de guóqí** "China's national flag," 我母亲的朋友 **wǒ mǔqīn de péngyou** "my mother's friend."

The same 的 **de** is also used in what in English are called subordinate constructions, or constructions with relative pronouns. For example: 她最喜欢的电影 **tā zuì xǐhuan de diànyǐng** "the movie she likes most," the phrase 最喜欢 **zuì xǐhuan** "likes the most" describes the movie. These forms with 的 **de** can sometimes get quite long: what precedes 的 **de** is like a lengthy adjectival phrase describing what follows 的 **de**. This is usually rendered in English by words such as *who* or *which*. Some examples follow:

那个坐在屋子里的老人
Nèige zuò zài wūzi li de lǎorén
"That old man who is sitting in the room"

昨天下午离开香港前往悉尼的飞机还没到
Zuótian xiàwǔ líkāi Xiānggǎng qiánwǎng Xīní de fēijī hái méi dào
"The plane which left Hong Kong yesterday afternoon bound for Sydney still hasn't arrived"

In the second example 昨天下午离开香港前往悉尼 **Zuótian xiàwǔ líkāi Xiānggǎng qiánwǎng Xīní** is a lengthy adjectival phrase describing 飞机 **fēijī** "the plane," and is separated from it by 的 **de**.

4.12.2 Adverbial particle 地 *de*

In 她很快 **tā hěn kuài** "she is very fast," 快 **kuài** is a stative verb: "to be fast." In 她很快地吃完了早饭 **tā hěn kuài de chīwán le zǎofàn** "she finished her breakfast quickly," 快 **kuài** is an adverb, describing the way she finished her breakfast. In Chinese, such adverbs are marked with 地 **de**. If an adjective is preceded by an adverb, such as 很 **hěn**, 地 **de** is always used. It is not used with monosyllabic adjectives without such a preceding adverb: 你快去 **nǐ kuài qù** "go quickly." If duplicated, however, it is: 你慢慢儿地说吧 **nǐ mànmānrde shuō ba** "explain it slowly." Note that 慢慢儿地 **mànmānrde**, with a final 儿 **r** and a first tone on the second syllable, is Beijing dialect. You will often hear the expression 慢慢来 **mànmànlái**, or in Beijing 慢慢儿来 **mànmānrlái** (note: the first tone on the second syllable is pronounced **mār**), in relation to your efforts to learn Chinese.

You can also add 地 **de** to any adjective to make an adverb: 高高兴兴地 **gāogāoxìngxìng de** "joyfully"; 匆忙地 **cōngmáng de** or 匆匆忙忙地 **cōngcōng mángmáng de** "in a hurry"; 很客气地 **hěn kèqì de** "very politely"; 相当舒服地 **xiāngdāng shūfú de** "quite comfortably"; 随便地 **suíbiàn de** "in a casual fashion." Note that 随便 **suíbiàn** means "casual, informal," but can also mean "careless, slipshod," especially if one says 太随便 **tài suíbiàn**. Similarly 老实 **lǎoshí** means "honest, frank," but can also mean "simple-minded, easily cheated," especially if one says 他太老实了 **tǎ tài lǎoshí le** "he is too simple-minded (naive)."

Note too that 很 **hěn**, despite what your textbooks may say, does not really mean "very." It is mainly used with monosyllabic adjectives to form disyllables. Chinese do not say 他高 **tā gāo** for "he is tall"; they say 他很高 **tā hěn gāo**. 很 **hěn** can mean "very," but then it is strongly stressed: 我很生气 **wǒ hěn shēngqì** "I'm **really** angry." Usually people prefer adverbs such as 实在 **shízài** "really," or 非常 **fēicháng** "extremely" when they want to stress an adjective. 真 **zhēn** "truly" is another possibility: 她真漂亮 **tā zhēn piàoliang** "she's **truly** beautiful." You will also hear the suffix 不得了 **bùdéliǎo**, as in 他生气得不得了 **tā shēngqì de bùdéliǎo** "he was really angry." In a few words 了 is pronounced **liǎo**, such as in 不得了 **bùdéliǎo**, 了解 **liǎojiě** "to understand," and some classical expressions like 不了了之 **bù liǎo liǎo zhī** "to settle a matter by leaving it unsettled." Words with more than one pronunciation are known as 双音字 **shuāng yīn zì**.

4.12.3 The structural particle 得 *de* with complements
A verb provides simple information: 他跑 **tā pǎo** "he runs." A complement adds to the meaning: 他跑得快 **tā pǎo de kuài** "he runs fast." The complement is joined to the verb by the particle 得 **de**.

When certain verbs are joined, the second shows the result of the first: 写完 **xiěwán** "to write with the result that it is finished," that is, to finish writing; 听懂 **tīngdǒng** "to listen with the result that you understand," that is, to understand what you are listening to.

In Chinese the potential complement indicates that you are able to do something: 写得完 **xiědewán** "possible to finish writing," as in 我的论文，大概明年年底就写得完 **wǒde lùnwén, dàgài míngnián niándǐ jiù xiědewán** "I should be able to finish writing my thesis by the end of next year"; 爬得上 **pá de shàng** "possible to climb (up)" as in 那座山不特别高，我想我一定爬得上(去) **nèizuò shān bù tèbiè gāo, wǒ xiǎng wǒ yīdìng pá de shàng (qù)** "that mountain is not particularly high; I think I can certainly manage to climb it."

These are rather complicated structures, and are generally introduced in the later sections of a textbook. They are, however, extremely common. One of my favorites is 挤掉 **jǐdiào** "jostle–fall off," used to describe the buttons of your overcoat being torn off when you try to struggle your way out of an overcrowded Beijing bus. The same word can also mean to have one's place taken in a queue, or quota, by someone with more powerful connections.

If you want to say "I can't speak Chinese very well," you cannot say 我不会说中文 (汉语) 很好 **wǒ bù huì shuō Zhōngwén (Hànyǔ) hěn hǎo** (which practically every beginner does). That means "I cannot speak Chinese—that's very good," meaning that it is a very good thing that you cannot speak Chinese. What you should say is 我的中文 (汉语) 说得不好 **wǒde Zhōngwén (Hànyǔ) shuō de bù hǎo**, literally "as for my Chinese, I speak it with the result that it is no good." A typical use of a potential complement.

4.13 The disposal form (the 把 *bǎ* construction)
The basic word order in Chinese is the same as English: 我爱我的狗 **wǒ aì wǒde gǒu** "I love my dog." However, when the verb is more complex, as in the various complement constructions, the object of the verb is placed in front of the verb, and this unusual word order is marked by placing 把 **bǎ** in front of the transposed object. 把 **bǎ** both brings the object to the front of the verb and emphasizes disposal of or influence on the object. 他们把车票交给列车员 **tāmen bǎ chēpiào jiāo gěi lièchēyuán** "they gave the ticket to the conductor"; 你把钱包递给我吧 **nǐ bǎ qiánbāo dì gěi wǒ ba** "hand over your wallet."

把 **bǎ** is usually used when the verb is a "resultative complement." So to say "bring it in," we have to say "take it and bring it in": 把它拿进来 **bǎ tā nájìnlái**. Other examples are: 我把照相机拿出来 **wǒ bǎ zhàoxiàngjī náchūlái** "I took the camera out"; 我把毛衣脱下来 **wǒ bǎ máoyì tuōxiàlái** "I took my pullover off"; 我把扣子扣好了 **wǒ bǎ kòuzi kòuhǎo le** "I took the buttons and buttoned them up."

4.14 Negatives

The negatives in modern Chinese are straightforward. Verbs are negated by 不 **bù**: 他来，他不来 **tā lái, tā bùlái** "he is coming, he is not coming." The verb 有 **yǒu** "to have" is negated with 没 **méi**, as in one of the commonest words in the language 没有 **méiyǒu** "we don't have any." 没 **méi** is also used to negate the perfective aspect of verbs: 他没来 **tā méi lái** "he didn't come."

There are also a number of classical negatives used in the modern language. In Classical Chinese, 没有 **méiyǒu** is 无 **wú**. This appears in modern Chinese in such words as 无产阶级 **wúchǎnjiējí** (not have property class) "proletariat"; 无政府主义 **wúzhèngfǔzhǔyì** (not have government ideology) "anarchism"; 无神论 **wúshénlùn** (no spirit/God theory) "atheism"; the common expression 无可奈何 **wú kě nài hé** "nothing can be done about it," for which the modern equivalent is 没有办法 **méiyǒu bànfǎ**, and 一无所有 **yī wú suǒ yǒu** "I have nothing," the title of a popular song a few years ago.

The classical negative 未 **wèi** "not yet" appears in words like 未婚 **wèihūn** "not yet married, engaged," so 未婚夫 **wèihūnfū** and 未婚妻 **wèihūnqī** for "fiancé" and "fiancée," 未老先衰 **wèi lǎo xiān shuāi** "not yet old but already in decline," so prematurely senile; and 未来 **wèilái**, that which has not yet come, "the future."

You will also often see the classical negative imperative 勿 **wù** "do not [do something]," as in 请勿吸烟 **qǐng wù xī yān** "please do not smoke."

Nouns are negated in Classical Chinese with 非 **fēi**, which appears in modern words such as 非官方 **fēi guānfāng** "unofficial," 非法 **fēi fǎ** "illegal," and 非典 **fēidiǎn** "atypical [pneumonia]," that is SARS. 非卖品 **fēimàipǐn** "not-for-sale product" is a free sample. Note that the common adverb 非常 **fēicháng** "extremely" literally means "not ordinary."

4.15 The 被 *bèi* construction and the passive

Generally speaking, Chinese does not use the passive as much as English. One cannot say "the book was stolen" without saying who did it, though one can be vague: 我的字典被人偷走了 **wǒ de zìdiǎn bèi rén tōuzǒu le** "my dictionary was stolen by somebody." The usual marker for the passive was traditionally only used when something unpleasant was happening: 肉被狗抢走了 **ròu bèi gǒu qiángzǒule** "the meat was snatched away by the dog"; 老王被老婆儿骂了一顿 **Lǎo Wáng bèi lǎopór màle yī dùn** "Old Wang was scolded by his wife"; 收音机被小孩子弄坏了 **shōuyīnjī bèi xiǎoháizi nònghuài le** "the radio was broken by the child."

Mainly due to the volume of material translated into Chinese, particularly the Marxist classics from German and Russian, 被 **bèi** came to translate the passive form of European languages without any unfortunate implications, so one can see expressions such as 被赞扬 **bèi zànyǎng** "was praised," 被选举 **bèi xuǎnjǔ** "was elected." The more common way of expressing such things however would still be something like 他受到了观众的好评 **tā shòudàole guānzhòng de hǎopíng** "he received a good evaluation from the audience."

Although 被 **bèi** is quite common in spoken Chinese, more colloquial ways of expressing the passive are with 让 **ràng**, 叫 **jiào** and 给 **gěi**: 他让人摇醒了 **tā ràng rén yáoxǐng le** "he was shaken by someone with the result that he woke up"; 衣服让油漆弄脏了 **yìfú ràng yóuqī nòng zāng le** "the clothes were made dirty by the paint"; 逃跑了的狗叫 (给) 邻居看见了 **táopǎole de gǒu jiào (gěi) línjū kànjian le** "the dog that ran away was seen by the neighbors"; 老李怕叫人(被人)发现 **Lǎo Lǐ pà jiào rén (bèi rén) fāxiàn** "Old Li was afraid he would be found out by people." Chinese often does not make the passive explicit. The famous sentence 鸡吃了 **jī chī le** can either mean "the chicken has eaten" or "the chicken has been eaten." One has to rely on context and common sense.

In the early twentieth century Western sinologists would debate the issue: "does the Chinese language have parts of speech?" In more recent times linguists have concluded Chinese definitely does have a "grammar," but just exactly how one divides up a Chinese sentence and how one describes it is still a matter of controversy. The Chinese grammar presented in textbooks from China is "school grammar," approved for teaching "proper Chinese" in schools. Textbooks published outside China frequently use their own systems and their own terminology, though there is more uniformity now than there used to be. Linguists and grammarians are still working out ways to adequately explain the uses of 了 **le**, 把 **bǎ** and 被 **bèi**. All in all, however, Chinese grammar is still much more straightforward than that of many other languages you might have learned or might want to learn.

CHAPTER FIVE

Pronunciation

Chinese pronunciation looks deceptively simple. There are only 405 simple syllables, and only four tones. But Chinese pronunciation is one aspect of Chinese you will have to work on constantly, trying all the time to approximate the ideal, and often falling short.

The Chinese phonological system differs quite a lot from the English way of pronouncing vowels and consonants. If you are unaware of these differences you will be speaking Chinese of the "flied lice" variety, which ranges from the ludicrous to the incomprehensible. The famous linguist Y. R. Chao advocated spending the first six weeks of a language course learning to pronounce Chinese syllables correctly before attempting to string them together into sentences. In these days of "communicative competence" and instant results it is unlikely Chao's advice would be followed, but the fact remains: you will have to spend a lot of time and effort training your vocal organs to pronounce Chinese in an understandable way. Of course you want to be able to "speak Chinese" from Lesson One. However, if you don't pay a lot of attention to pronunciation right from the beginning, even if you can be understood, you will almost certainly "zound gweer," as Chao put it.

As you are no doubt aware, tones distinguish words. Taking **shi** as a case in point:

First tone:	诗 **shī** means "poem"	
	师 **shī** means "teacher"	
	尸 **shī** means "corpse"	
Second tone:	十 **shí** means "ten"	
	时 **shí** means "time"	
	石 **shí** means "stone"	
Third tone:	史 **shǐ** means "history"	
	使 **shǐ** means "to send"	
	屎 **shǐ** means "excrement"	
Fourth tone:	市 **shì** means "market"	
	事 **shì** means "a matter"	

Another example with **qing**: 青 **qīng** means "blue," 情 **qíng** means "feelings," 请 **qǐng** means "to invite," 庆 **qìng** means "to congratulate." And so it is throughout the language. Hundreds of other examples could be given.

Even when the 405 syllables of Chinese are distinguished by tone there are still only about 1,200 of them. This is less than 4 x 400, because quite a few syllables do not have all four tones: there is only 兰 **lán**, 懒 **lǎn** and 烂 **làn**, for example, no **lān**. **Gei** has only the third tone: **gěi**—for one word 给. There is 肝 **gān**, 敢 **gǎn** and 干 **gàn**, but no **gán**. Textbooks give a complete inventory of syllables and tones, but this information is of not much use unless you use the tones in actual words.

All textbooks have an introductory chapter on pronunciation. Many use technical terms like *voiceless*, *aspirated*, *retroflex* and *palatal* without telling you what these terms mean. Others will give diagrams showing where your tongue and teeth should be, but do not give any practical hints on just how to achieve these oral gymnastics.

One initial problem is the *pinyin* system of romanization itself. It uses the same 26 letters of the alphabet as English (actually it adds **ü** and omits **v**), and some of the letters are pronounced more or less the same as in English (**l**, **m**, **n**). However, the majority of them are not. Some *pinyin* letters (**b**, **d**, **g**) sound almost the same as the English ones to beginners, but they are really quite different. When we learn French, we take it for granted that some letters represent quite different sounds in French from the sounds the same letters represent in English. However, some learners tend to pronounce the *pinyin* letters as if these represented the same sounds as in English. This derives from confusing a romanization system with a sort of "imitated pronunciation"—that one might find in a phrase book. *Pinyin*, like any orthography, has its own conventions.

5.1 Terminology

5.1.1 Voiced and voiceless

Let us first look at some of the terminology. Your textbook will probably tell you that *voiced* means the vocal chords vibrate. But what does that mean? How do you make your vocal chords vibrate? How do you stop them? To make these concepts real you can do some simple experiments on your own vocal chords. Some of these might seem ridiculous, and are best practiced in private.

(1) Put your hands over your ears. Say *car, car, car, gar, gar, gar* (the first syllable in <u>gar</u>*den*). When you say *gar* you should hear a sort of "boom" coming from your throat, which is not there when you say *car*. The effect you hear comes from the vibration of the vocal chords which automatically happens when you pronounce **g** in English. In Chinese, however, when you pronounce **g**, the vocal chords do *not* vibrate.

(2) Put your hands over your ears. Say *sa, sa, sa*. Now say *za, za, za*. You will hear a buzz when you say **za** which you do not hear when you say **sa**. This is because **z** is voiced and **s** is not.

(3) Put your hands around your neck covering your voicebox with your palms. Say *ba, ba, ba*. Now say *pa, pa, pa*. You will hear a similar sort of boom coming from your voicebox (where your vocal chords are) when you say **ba**, and not when you say **pa**. In English, your vocal chords vibrate automatically when you say **b** and not when you say **p**. In Chinese, however, when you pronounce **b**, the vocal chords do *not* vibrate.

(4) Try the same experiments with **d** and **t**. Put your hands over your ears: *da, da, da, ta, ta, ta*. Put your palms over your voicebox: *da, da, da, ta, ta, ta*. Again, you will hear the same vibration with **da** as you did with **ga** and **ba**.

The important thing to understand here is that the letters represented by **b**, **d** and **g** in English are voiced. In Chinese they are *not* voiced. If you voice them you will "zound gweer," as if you used voiced consonants in "sound queer" instead of unvoiced ones.

This is automatic in English. Your vocal chords have been trained from an early age to voice **b**, **d** and **g**. How can you train them not to? It can be done— but first we must discuss another pair of terms: *aspirated* and *unaspirated*.

5.1.2 Aspirated and unaspirated

Again, let us do some exercises to understand exactly what these terms mean. Find a piece of thin, light tissue paper. Hold it about 10 cm from your lips. Say *kate, gate, kate, gate* (or any other words beginning with **k** and **g**). Now say *pay, bay, pay, bay* (or any other words beginning with **p** and **b**). Now say *tee, dee, tee, dee* (or any other words beginning with **t** and **d**). You will notice that when you say **ka**, **pa**, **ta** the paper will move. When you say **ga**, **ba**, **da** the paper will not (or move only very slightly). You can feel the same effect by putting your hand 10 cm in front of your mouth and repeating the exercise. The paper moves, or you can feel a puff of breath on your hand, because initial **k**, **p** and **t** in English are aspirated, that is, they are followed by a slight puff of breath. The paper does not move when you say **g**, **b** and **d**, because in English they are not aspirated—there is no puff of breath.

In Chinese, the aspirated initials **k**, **t**, **p** (as well as **ch**, **q** and **c**) are aspirated more strongly than in English. If you ask a person who pronounces both Chinese and English well, to say the Chinese word 怕 **pà** "to fear," followed by English words such as *path* and *bath*, you will see the paper jump when **pà** is pronounced, move less when English *path* is pronounced and not at all when English *bath* is pronounced. The same applies for the others: Chinese 他 **tā** "he," English **ta**, English **da** and so on. Chinese words written in the Wade-Giles romanization show this strong aspiration with an apostrophe: 邓 小平 **Dèng Xiǎopíng** is written *Têng Hsiao-p'ing*, or with tones indicated, *Têng⁴ Hsiao³-p'ing²*. *Pinyin* writes **k**, **t**, **p**, **q**, and **c** for the sounds written in Wade-Giles *k'*, *t'*, *p'*, *ch'*, and *ts'*. With *pinyin*, you have to remember to aspirate strongly without the apostrophe there to remind you.

Actually, the aspirated consonants are little trouble for native speakers of English, though they are for speakers of languages which do not have automatic aspiration after voiceless consonants. The real problem for English speakers is with the unaspirated consonants, because these are automatically voiced in English, but are not voiced in Chinese. If you use English **g**, **d**, **b**, to pronounce the Chinese initials written **g**, **d**, and **b** in *pinyin*, you will "zound gweer." Luckily, English does possess unaspirated, unvoiced consonants, but only after **s**, and most native speakers of English are unaware of them.

Let us try our exercises again. With your piece of tissue paper 10 cm in front of your mouth, say *kill, skill, kill, skill*. You will notice that the paper moves when you say *kill*, but not when you say *skill*. Now say *tar, star, tar, star*. Same thing. Now say *par, spar, par, spar*. Same thing. What you have discovered is that English unvoiced initials **k**, **t**, **p** are *aspirated* when not preceded by **s**, but are *unaspirated* when preceded by **s**. Say *kill, skill, gill, tart, start, dart, par, spar, bar*. You will hear distinct voicing when you say **g**, **d**, and **b**, but not when you say **p**, **t**, **k** (where you will notice aspiration), or when you say **sp**, **st**, **sk**, where you will notice neither voicing nor aspiration. The point of all this is that *pinyin* **b**, **d**, **g** are not like English **b**, **d**, **g**, but are like English **(s)p**, **(s)t**, **(s)k**. The trick is to isolate the voiceless unaspirated **p**, **t**, **k** from the preceding **s**.

This is not easy, but you can try the following exercises. Say *kill, skill, skill, skill, s-kill, s-kill, -kill*, where the dash in front of the **k** represents the suppressed, or separated (**s**). The **k** sound you are making is the *pinyin* **g**. Say *kill, kill, skill, skill, -kill, -kill, gill, gill*. You should immediately notice the voicing in *gill* immediately following the voicelessness of **-k** in (s)-*kill*. If you can hear no difference between -*kill* and *gill*, you are pronouncing the Chinese **g** as the English **g**, not as the English **-k**. This is not good. You can try the same exercises with *tart, start, dart, tart, tart, start, start, s-tart, s-tart, -tart, -tart, dart, dart*. You should be able to hear a strong voicing in *dart* which should not be present in -*tart*. Similarly for *par, par, spar, spar, s-par, s-par, -par, -par, bar, bar*. You should hear a clear difference between -*par* and *bar*. If you do not, you need more practice.

So what you need to remember is that *pinyin* **p, t** and **k** are like English **p, t,** and **k** but are more aspirated. If you are a native speaker of English this will cause no problem; if you are a native speaker of French or Indonesian, for example, you will have to pay special attention in aspirating these initials. When you see *pinyin* **b, d,** and **g** you must remember these are pronounced as (**s**)**p**, (**s**)**t**, and (**s**)**k** respectively, that is, like English **sp, st, sk** without the initial (**s**).

5.1.3 Palatals and retroflexes

These initials cause trouble because we do not have retroflexes in English, and although we have palatalization after some initial consonants, it is generally restricted to those occurring before long **u**. In English we have "hush consonants" like **sh** in <u>sh</u>*ip* or **ch** as in <u>ch</u>*ap*, which do not occur in Chinese, but which sound very similar to both the palatals and retroflexes. So we have to remember that *pinyin* **sh, ch,** and **zh** represent *retroflex* initials in Chinese, which sound a bit like the English *hush* consonants written <u>sh</u> and <u>ch</u>, but are really quite different. We also have to remember that *pinyin* **j** and **q** are not the same as English **j** as in *jam* or **ch** in <u>ch</u>*eese*, and that **x** represents a consonant which does not occur in English at all.

5.1.4 Palatals

Do the following exercise: say *do, due*; *fool, fuel*; *cool, cue*. After the second word in each of these series you will hear a distinct **y** sound between the initial consonant and the vowel. You can also hear this difference in varieties of English: *new* has the **y** sound in England but not generally in United States.

In Chinese, **j** and **q** have a **y** between them and the following vowel, which is always **i** or **ü**. So 七 **qī** "seven" sounds rather like <u>ch</u>*ee* (as in <u>ch</u>*eese*), except it has stronger aspiration and a noticeable **y** glide: *ch+h+y+ee...*; 鸡 **jī** "chicken" sounds a bit like *jea-* in *jeans*, except it is *not voiced* and has a noticeable **y** glide: *j+y+ee...* .

The other palatal initial is written in *pinyin* as **x**. It was written in the Wade-Giles system as **hs**, and in the Yale system as **sy**. It does indeed sound like a combination of **h** and **s**, or a combination of **s** and **y**. The Chinese word 西 **xī** "west" is pronounced neither *he, she* nor *see*. Say *see ya, see ya, see ya* very quickly until you are making one syllable *s-ya*, then *sya*. This is very close to the Chinese word 夏 **xià** "summer." Another way of making this sound is to place the end of a toothpick (or the tip of your fingernail) between your top and lower front teeth, and say *see*. There will be a hushing sound followed by *ee*. This is very close to the Chinese word 西 **xī** "west." Etymologically **x** derives both from palatalized **h** and palatalized **s**, and phonologically it is the unaffricated, unaspirated form of **q** and **j**. This information, however, may not help you very much.

When you have managed to imitate these sounds, you can repeat them: 鸡 **jī** "chicken," 七 **qī** "seven," 西 **xī** "west." Note the differences between them. All are unvoiced. All are followed by a distinct **y** glide. All are followed by the vowel **i**. As mentioned above, the palatals are followed only by **i** and **ü**, which may also be followed by final **n**, **ng** or a vowel.

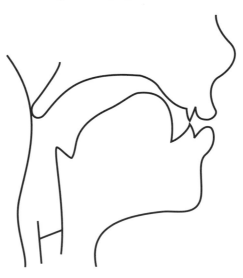

FIGURE 24 Diagram indicating the position of the tongue for the palatal consonants **j** and **q**. Note that the top part of the tongue presses against the hard palate. With x, there is a slight space between the tongue and the palate, which gives it a "hushing" sound.

The vowel **i** presents few difficulties for English speakers. After palatals, it is much the same as **ee** as in *see*. After retroflexes and sibilants, it has a "retracted" quality, which is discussed below. The vowel **ü** only occurs after the palatal initials: **jü**, **qü** and **xü**, and occasionally after **n** and **l**. After **n** and **l** it is always written with the two dots to distinguish it from the vowel **u**: 女 **nǚ** "woman," 怒 **nù** "anger"; 绿 **lǜ** "green," 路 **lù** "road." After the palatal initials, the vowel **u** does not occur: only **ü** does. This being the case, it is a convention in *pinyin* not to write the two dots: **ju** is really pronounced **jü**; **qu** is really pronounced **qü**; and **xu** is really pronounced **xü**. The problem is that we do not have the vowel **ü** in English—not in standard English at least, but it is common in Scottish English. It is common in French, as in the word *lune* "moon" and in German, where it is also written **ü**. Learning to pronounce it properly presents a bit of a challenge if you do not have that vowel in your present inventory of sounds. Probably the easiest way to acquire it is to say *ee-oo ee-oo ee-oo* quickly until the *ee* and the *oo* have merged into one sound: this is the sound you need to learn to make whenever you see Chinese words with **ü** (or **u** after **j**, **q**, **x**). Other vowels are described below.

5.1.5 Retroflexes

In English we have palatal consonants, though their distribution (and degree of palatalization) is different from Chinese. However, in English we do not have retroflex consonants at all. The closest one is likely to hear is in words like *shirt*, or the American pronunciation of *sure*. The sound is not the same as English **sh** as in <u>ship</u> or <u>shape</u>. To pronounce it you need to curl your tongue backwards until the lower tip of it is touching the top of your mouth. You can imagine you are trying to dislodge a crumb of bread caught on the top of your mouth with the front part of your tongue. Then say *sharp, sharp, sharp, sha, sha, sha chart, chart, chart cha cha cha*. The sounds you are making will be close to the Chinese 杀 **shā** "kill," and 茶 **chá** "tea." Now lower your tongue to its normal position: *sharp, sharp, chart, chart*. The latter are the normal English sounds. You will notice they are very different from the Chinese sounds. (Refer to Figure 25.)

There are four retroflex initials in Chinese: **sh**, **zh**, **ch**, and **r**. The first three are relatively easy once you have learned to curl the tip of your tongue backwards: they sound like the initials in <u>sharp</u>, <u>jar</u>, and <u>chart</u> respectively, except that **j** is unvoiced and **ch** is aspirated and, of course, the tongue is curled backwards. The initial **r** is generally considered a voiced version of **sh**, and certainly it is articulated in the same part of the mouth as **sh**, **ch**, and **zh**. For English speakers, it sounds rather like the **r** in <u>run</u> or <u>ran</u>, but with more friction. Say *ran, ran, ran*—and try to put your tongue in the same position as when you say Chinese 杀 **shā** "to kill," or 茶 **chá** "tea." This should then give you the pronunciation of 然 **rán** "thus."

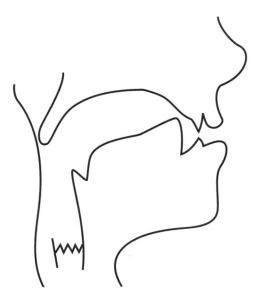

FIGURE 25 Diagram indicating the position of the tongue for the retroflex consonants **sh, ch, zh,** and **r.** Note there is a slight space between the tip of the tongue (curled slightly backwards) and the palate.

As well as **j, q, x** (the palatals), and **zh, ch, sh** (the retroflexed) Chinese also possesses a set of plain dentals: **z, c,** and **s.** Of these the only one which is not new is **s,** which sounds like English **s,** but to some people at least, it seems "sharper." The letters **z** and **c** represent combinations of **dz** and **ts** respectively. These sounds occur at the ends of words in English, such as *adze* or *cats,* but in Chinese *dz* is not voiced, and *ts* is strongly aspirated. However, in Chinese they appear at the *beginning* of a word. To learn the trick of reproducing these sounds at the beginning of a syllable, say *cats are..., cats are..., cats are...* Now leave off the initial syllable *ca* and you have *tsa... tsa... tsa...* Remember to aspirate this and you have the Chinese word 擦 **cā** "to rub." Now say *beds are... beds are... beds are... dsa... dsa... dsa...* As long as this is not voiced, you now have the Chinese word 杂 **zá** "mixed."

So you must learn to distinguish clearly between 三 **sān** "three," 山 **shān** "mountain," and 先 **xiān** "first"; 杂 **zá** "mixed," 炸 **zhà** "to bomb," and 加 **jiā** "to add"; and 擦 **cā** "to rub," 茶 **chá** "tea," and 恰 **qià** "coincidence."

The last consonant you need to pay attention to is that written **h** in *pinyin*. In standard Chinese, especially that spoken in the north of China (including Beijing) this is generally pronounced as a "rough" **h**, similar to the final **ch** in the German pronunciation of *Ba<u>ch</u>*. In the south, however, it is commonly pronounced much the same as English **h** as in <u>h</u>ard. Try to pronounce it as a "rough" **h**, as this is the standard pronunciation, even if a lot of Chinese don't pronounce it that way.

At the end of a syllable, only two consonants are to be found—**n** and **ng**—and both are pronounced much the same as in English.

5.2 Final *r*

One of the characteristics of the Beijing dialect is the use of the final **r**. It is applied to many nouns. It is often used with small things: 小孩儿 **xiǎoháir** for 小孩子 **xiǎoháizi** "child," 瓶儿 **píngr** "bottle," 刀儿 **dāor** "knife," 花儿 **huār** "flower," 画儿 **huàr** "picture," 单儿 **dānr** "list," 小猫儿 **xiǎomāor** "kitten." "Soft drink" is either 汽水 **qìshuǐ** or 汽水儿 **qìshuǐr**. 开门儿 **kāi ménr** is how one normally says "open the door." 天安门 **Tiānānmén** (the huge ceremonial gate overlooking Tiananmen Square in Beijing) is not a small door, and therefore it does not take the **r** suffix. 王府井 **Wángfujǐng**, the main shopping street, is however often called 王府井儿 **Wángfujǐngr**. The flea market of Beijing, which is hardly small, is called 潘家园儿 **Pānjiāyuánr**. 饭馆儿 **fànguǎnr** is a small restaurant; a more elaborate place is a 饭店 **fàndiān**. In 官儿 **guānr** "official" the **r** ending can show contempt. In some cases **r** can show familiarity, as in 老婆儿 **lǎopór** "wife." The **r** ending is not used with verbs, except 玩儿 **wánr** "to play." If this is pronounced without the final **r**, it is homophonous with 完 **wán** "to finish," which is one of the euphemisms for "to die." One finds both words in the expression 玩儿完了 **wánr wánle** "the playing is finished," meaning "the game's up" or "the party's over"—a somewhat disrespectful term meaning "he has passed away."

Many typical Beijing dialect expressions show the **r** suffix: 没门儿 **méi ménr** "no way, no chance," 没准儿 **méizhǔnr** "could be, maybe" (standard Chinese 也许 **yěxǔ**). In 明儿个 **míngrge** "tomorrow," pronounced **miě ge** (the ˜ on the ě indicates nasalization, from the loss of **ng** after **r**) (standard Chinese 明天 **míngtian**), the **r** is a vestige of 儿 **rì** "day," rather than 儿 **ér**. 一点儿 **yīdiǎnr** "a little bit" almost always has the **r** ending in Beijing. In Beijing the rapid pronunciation of words like 不知道 **bù zhīdào** "I don't know," and 告诉你 **gàosu ni** "I tell you," sounds like **bùrdào** and **gàùrni**. Listen for them.

As far as the pronunciation is concerned, after a vowel **r** is simply added: 花 儿 **huār** "flower." When added to a syllable ending in **i**, the **i** is elided: 小孩 儿 **xiāoháir** is pronounced **xiǎohár**. When added to a syllable ending in **n**, the **n** is not pronounced: 门儿 **ménr** "door" is pronounced **mér**. When added to a syllable ending in **ng**, the vowel is nasalized: 没空儿 **méi kòngr** "to have no spare time" sounds like **méi kũr**. The **ũ** indicates a nasalized **u**. Nasal vowels do not occur in English, or standard Mandarin, but are common in French, and occasionally occur in Beijing dialect.

The use or non-use of **r** is a delicate business, rather similar to *liaison* in French. As you can see from the above examples, it is rather complicated. Whole dictionaries are dedicated to the use of this word. Remember that the use of **r** is not compulsory. Many Chinese do not use it at all. Use it with 一 点儿 **yīdiǎnr** and **wánr** 玩儿, and maybe a few others, and follow your text-book and what you hear. If you go to Beijing you will certainly hear **r** all around you, but it might take you some time to know when to use it and when not to use it.

5.3 Vowels

Most English speakers seem to have little trouble with Chinese vowels. Most of them occur in English or are quite close to English vowels, but some of them do not. Most vowels have slightly different pronunciations if they are followed by another vowel or consonant.

The vowel written **a** in *pinyin* represents a back **a**—like the **a** in English *father*. The word 发 **fā** "to emit" rhymes with English *far*. When **a** is followed by **n**, it has a more central pronunciation: 饭 **fàn** "rice" more or less rhymes with English *fun*. When **a** follows **i** it still has the back variety: 家 **jiā** "family" more or less rhymes with English *jar*, but the initial is quite different. When following **i** but preceding **n**, however, **a** is more fronted: 电 **diàn** "electricity" sounds somewhat like English *den* (with a **y** sound after the **d**).

These variants are called allophones, varieties of the same vowel which occur in different phonetic environments.

The vowel written **e** in *pinyin* sounds like English **er** as in *her* when it is not followed by another vowel or consonant: 喝 **hē** "to drink" is similar in pronunciation to English *her*, but with a rough initial **h**. When followed by **i**, **e** is fronted: the combination **ei** rhymes with English *pay*, as in 黑 **hēi** "black." When followed by **n**, **e** is not like any English vowel. It is a central vowel which can be heard in the way some people pronounce *banana* or *tomorrow* with a very short, slurred vowel: *b'nana, t'morro*. The syllable *b'n* sounds very similar to the Chinese word 笨 **bèn** "stupid," except that the vowel is neither short nor slurred.

In *pinyin*, the symbol **i** represents a number of different vowels, and it takes some time to get used to these. After most consonants, including the palatals, **i** rhymes with English **ee** as in *see*: 你 **nǐ** "you" sounds like *knee*. When it precedes another vowel it is pronounced the same, only very short: 家 **jiā** "family" is one syllable: the vowel is **a**, and **i** is regarded as a *semivowel* or a *medial*.

However, when **i** follows the retroflexes **sh, ch, zh, r**, and the dental sibilants **s, c, z**, it is given a retracted pronunciation and prolongs the initial. So 是 **shì** "to be" does not rhyme with **nǐ** "you," but sounds rather like English *ssshhh*—retroflexed, of course. 四 **sì** "four" does not rhyme with 笔 **bǐ** "pen," but rather like English *sssss*. It is difficult, if not impossible, to pronounce this vowel by itself, but you can clearly hear it in the prolongation of the initial. Actually the timbre of the vowel following the retroflexes is slightly different from that following the dental sibilants. What *pinyin* writes as 是 **shì** "to be," 吃 **chī** "to eat," 纸 **zhǐ** "paper," and 日本 **Rìběn** "Japan" were written in the Wade-Giles system as 是 *shih⁴*, 吃 *ch'ih¹*, 纸 *chih³*, and 日本 *jih⁴-pên³*, while 四 **sì** "four," 刺 **cì** "to stab," and 字 **zì** "Chinese character," were written 四 *ssǔ*, 刺 *tsʻǔ⁴*, and 字 *tsǔ⁴* in Wade-Giles. The Wade-Giles system made the different qualities of the vowel more explicit, such as the accents over the **ê** and **ǔ**, and the apostrophe after the aspirated initials.

When you have learned to pronounce 是 **shì** "to be" and 四 **sì** "four" properly, you must be careful to distinguish them from 舍 **shè** "a shed" and 色 **sè** "color."

The vowel **o** does not cause much trouble, but one has to remember that after the labials **p, b**, and **m** there is a noticeable **w** between the initial and the vowel: 破 **pò** "to break" sounds like **pwò**; 墨 **mò** "ink" sounds like **mwò**.

The vowel **u** does not cause much trouble either, except that it does not occur in final position in English. The word 路 **lù** "road" does not sound like English *loo*. It is closer to the vowel in English *look* without the final **k**. When followed by another vowel **u** is very short: 国 **guó** "country" has only one vowel: **o**. The **u** is a semivowel, as **i** in the same position, as we saw above.

The problems with **u** come from the fact that the same letter is also used to represent a very different vowel: **ü**. It has this value when it follows the palatal initials **j**, **q**, **x**, and initial **y**. So **ju**, **qu**, **xu** and **yu** are pronounced **jü**, **qü**, **xü** and **yü** respectively. When **ü** follows **n** or **l**, the two dots are left on: **nü** and **lü**. This is because **n** and **l** can be followed by either **u** or **ü**, so they have to be distinguished. The Wade-Giles system made the pronunciation explicit: *pinyin* **ju**, **qu**, **xu** and **yu** were written *chü*, *ch'ü*, *hsü* and *yü*.

5.4 Tones

Chinese tones are the bugbear of every learner's life. It is very "counterintuitive" for English speakers to use tones the way they are used in Chinese, and even when one has got the knack of it, it is very difficult to remember which tone goes with each character. Various systems have been devised to make the process easier, but the task is still a frustrating one. Nevertheless, here are some tricks of the trade which might make mastering tones a little easier.

For a start, tones matter. Many students wish they did not, and some even manage to convince themselves that people can still understand you if you get your tones wrong. They are wrong. The centrality of tones in the Chinese system is like the importance of vowels in English, and a wrong tone is as puzzling as a wrong vowel in English. If you went into a shop and asked for a p'n, the salesperson would not know if you wanted a pen, a pin or a pan. They might guess right, or they might not. Even worse, if a non-native speaker of English uses a short vowel in English words such as *sheet* or *peace*, he will be (unwittingly) saying something quite different. This is what will happen to you in Chinese if you get your tones wrong.

You can only learn tones (or Chinese pronunciation generally) from a teacher. At the beginning you will find the tones hard to reproduce, and you may not even hear the difference between them. It might help you to reproduce the approximate shapes of Chinese tones by trying the following experiment. Imagine you are buying books, or cakes, or whatever. The salesperson asks if you want two or four. *Two? Or four. Two or four? Twó or fòur. Twó or fòur.* As your voice rises when you say *twó*, this is very close to the second tone. *Two* entoned like this sounds like the Chinese word 图 **tú** "chart."

As your voice falls when you say *four*, this is quite close (but not the same) as the fourth tone. Close but not the same—the Chinese tone falls much more sharply than when you say "four" in English in the context above. It falls sharply, more similar to when you make a sharp order in English, such as *sit!*

(if talking to a dog), or *no!* when saying "no!" to a child for the tenth time. So English-speaking learners instinctively avoid the falling tone in words when they are learning such basic words as 谢谢 **xièxie** "thank you," or 再见 **zàijiàn** "goodbye," because it sounds imperative, and somewhat rude, in English. In Chinese, however, this is simply the correct way to pronounce it, and 再见 **zàijiàn** pronounced any other way (**za-a-i je-e-e-n**, with no tones or tones all over the place) sounds dreadful.

Now to the third tone. In the early days of radio there was a drama about a Scottish doctor called Dr. Mac. Every episode began with the good doctor answering the phone: "Aye, it's me, Doctor Mac." The way he entoned *aye* sounds almost the same as Chinese 矮 **ǎi** "short (not tall)." The way he said *me* was much the same as the Chinese word 米 **mǐ** "uncooked rice."

The first tone is a long high tone which goes neither up nor down. Following our analogy about the books or the cakes above, you can imagine you are counting the books, perhaps making an inventory of them. As you count them "one, two, three, four," someone in the next room is noting down the numbers. If your voice is fairly high and neither rising nor falling, you are saying "one, two, three" in something like the Chinese first tone.

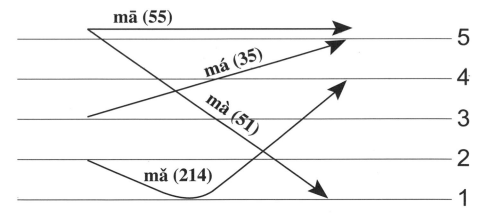

FIGURE 26 This diagram illustrates the Chao method for indicating tones. The *pinyin* tone marks ‐ ′ ˇ ˋ follow the tone contours in a typographically simplified way.

Another way of envisaging tones was devised by Y. R. Chao, with five levels ranging from the lowest (1) to the highest (5). The pattern of each tone can be indicated by a number indicating where it starts, and another where it ends. In this system, the first tone is indicated ⁵⁵, meaning it starts high and level, and ends high and level, as we tried to indicate with the counting of the books or cakes. The fourth tone is indicated ^{51}. It starts at the highest level and drops to the lowest level. The second tone is indicated ^{35}. It starts in the middle and rises to the top of the range. The third tone starts just below the middle of the range, drops a little, then rises to just below the top of the range: ^{214}. The third tone has a variant, when it is followed by a syllable with the first, second or fourth tone. This is called the "half third tone" and does not rise after the fall. It is denoted ^{21}. When a third tone is followed by another third tone, it sounds like the second tone: ^{35}. This phenomenon is known as *tone sandhi*.

In summary, the first tone is ^{55}, the second tone ^{35}, the third tone ^{214} (or ^{21} or ^{35}) and the fourth tone ^{51}. These tonal letters are also used in noting the tonal contours of the tones in Chinese dialects.

5.4.1 Tone sandhi

Tones in succession influence each other, as consonants and vowels do in English. When a word with a third tone is followed by another word with a third tone, the third tone on the first word sounds like a second tone: so 你好 **nǐ hǎo** "how are you" sounds like **ní hǎo**, and 很好 **hěn hǎo** "very good" sounds like **hén hǎo**—though this change is not shown in the *pinyin* spelling. When a third-tone word is pronounced in isolation, it falls, then rises: ^{214}. When it is followed by another word, it falls but does not rise. 很 **hěn** "very" is ^{214}, but in 很坏 **hěn huài** "very bad," 很 **hěn** is pronounced ^{21}. These changes are not explicitly shown in *pinyin*. The word 一 **yī** "one" has the first tone when read in isolation or followed by a first tone; the fourth tone when followed by a second or third tone; and a second tone when followed by a fourth tone. In standard *pinyin* only **yī** is written, and you have to remember that in 一碗米饭 **yī wǎn mǐfàn** "a bowl of rice," 一 **yī** is really pronounced **yì**.

Note too the tone sandhi, or changed tone, on 不 **bù**. Before words with the fourth tone it regularly changes to the second tone, so 不来 **bù lái** "don't come," but 不去 **bù qù** "don't go" is pronounced **bú qù**. So 不要 **bù yào** is pronounced **bú yào**. The changed tones are not indicated in standard *pinyin*, but some textbooks make them explicit, and write 不要 **bú yào**, which reflects the actual pronunciation, rather than **bù yào**. In rapid speech 不要 **bù yào**, or **bú yào**, when it is used as a negative imperative, is sometimes shortened to **bié**, written 别: 别闹 **bié: bié nào** "don't make such a dreadful noise!"

5.4.2 The light tone

A very important and very obvious difference between standard Chinese as it is spoken in Mainland China, modelled as it is on Beijing dialect, and that spoken outside Mainland China, including Taiwan, is the use of the 轻声 **qīngshēng** or light tone. For a start, all particles are toneless, or are pronounced with a light tone. 他来了吗 **tā lái le ma**? "Has he come?" This is shown in *pinyin* by simply not putting any tone marks on the word concerned—**ma** in the sentence above. The problem is with other unstressed syllables. 他是我的朋友 **tā shì wǒde péngyou** "he is my friend." You would not normally say 朋友 **péngyǒu** with a third tone on the second syllable, unless you wanted to stress that he really is your friend, or you are speaking very slowly, clearly or deliberately. Similarly 姑娘 **gūniang** "girl," not **gūniáng**; 漂亮 **piàoliang** "beautiful," not **piàoliàng**; 关系 **guānxi** "connections," not **guānxì** (or even **guānxī**, as some people pronounce it, as they try to imitate a neutral tone not very successfully). The correct use of the light tone is a tricky business, and textbooks, dictionaries and native speakers often differ. As in the case of the use or non-use of **r**, the light tone is very characteristic of Beijing dialect. Not all Chinese use it. Indeed, there are clear indications that the younger generation of educated Beijingers regard "the language of the hutongs" (which abounds in **r** endings and light tones) as distinctly downmarket, and prefer to speak standard *putonghua* "with a Beijing accent," which is quite a different matter from speaking Beijing dialect.

5.5 The importance of getting it right

There are many stories about the problems foreigners get into when they mispronounce Chinese. In a first-year oral exam a student was asked 你喜欢吃中国饭吗? **nǐ xǐhuan chī Zhōngguó fàn ma?** "do you like to eat Chinese food?," to which he replied: 我喜欢吃中国粪 **wǒ xǐhuan chī Zhōngguó fèn** "I like to eat Chinese shit." In a second-year exam, a student was asked if she had a weekend job. She replied: 我在妓院工作 **wǒ zài jìyuàn gōngzuò** "I work in a brothel." Further enquiries ascertained she worked in a 剧院 **jùyuàn** (theater). Another foreigner introduced his wife as his 车子 **chēzi** "motor car" instead of his 妻子 **qīzi** "wife." 严格 **yángé** means "strict." 阉割 **yāngē** means "to castrate." If you want to describe your teacher, make sure you get your tones right. Knowing when to use the suffix 子 **zi**, 儿 **r** or no suffix at all can also cause problems. Some words, such as 车 **chē** "car," can take the 子 **zi** suffix: 车子 **chēzi**. Others cannot. A foreigner visiting a doctor raised a smile when he referred to his gall bladder 胆 **dǎn** as his feather duster 掸子 **dǎnzi**. If you are trying to buy a fake Rolex in the night markets and add a 子 **zi** suffix to the word for wrist watch, 表 **biǎo** (which, despite being a small object, does not take a suffix), you will be unwittingly enquiring about the cost of a cheap prostitute (婊子 **biǎozi**).

A certain ambassador always addressed his opposite number in the Chinese Embassy, whose name was 林平 Lin Ping (**Lín Píng**), as 淋病 Mister Lin Bing (**Lín Bìng**), "Mr. Gonorrhea." The list goes on.

There is a story of a German missionary who had been preaching in Chinese for quite some time when a parishioner approached him asking if he would teach him German. The missionary said he would be delighted, but asked his convert why he wanted to learn German. "Well, we've been listening to your sermons in German for quite some time, and it doesn't seem too different from Chinese ..."

CHAPTER SIX

Beyond the Basics

6.1 Chinese in its social context

You can learn words and sentences, pronunciation and grammar from a book or in class. Learning to use the language appropriately in its social setting is another matter. If you are aiming at more than a smattering of Chinese, or if you are going to spend some time in a predominantly Chinese society, you will quickly find out that some words do not always really mean what they might appear to mean.

6.1.1 Greetings

The general greeting, as you know, is 你好! **Nǐ hǎo!** You cannot go far wrong there. However, if someone sees you leave your house, they might say 到哪儿去 **dào nǎr qù?** Or, more likely in Beijing, 上哪儿? **shàng nǎr?** "Where are you going?". Westerners might think this a strange thing to ask. After all, your neighbors at home probably wouldn't say anything like that. However, they are not asking you where you are going. They are again simply saying "hello" in another way. You can answer 出去了 **chū qù le** "I'm going out," and all is well.

6.1.2 Polite language — 客气话 kèqìhuà

There is no real equivalent in modern Chinese of the "polite language" of Japanese. A generation or two ago a man might have referred to another's wife as 太太 **tàitai** ("exceedingly exceedingly"), and his own wife as 内人 **nèirén** ("the inside person") or even 那口子 **nàkǒuzi** ("that mouth"); to another's daughter as 掌上明珠 **zhǎng shàng míng zhū** "the bright pearl in your palm," and his own son as 小犬 **xiǎo quǎn** "little doggie." When someone asked for his 贵姓 **guìxìng** "honorable surname," his reply would be his 敝姓 **bìxìng** "humble surname" was 王 **Wáng** "Wang." Generally speaking only the honorific terms like 太太 **tàitai** and 贵姓 **guìxìng** have survived, and have become neutral. One's own wife is one's 太太 **tàitai**, and one's own surname is neither honorable nor humble: the standard answer now is simply 我姓王 **wǒ xìng Wáng** "my surname is Wang."

There is, however, a large stock of words and expressions known as 客气话 **kèqìhuà** "polite language." Again, things are not what they seem. Polite language is used mainly among people who do not know each other well, but are seeking to make a good impression by a flow of excessive compliments or offers of hospitality. The unwary foreigner can be confused by all this. If you say more than three words of comprehensible Chinese, any Chinese will tell you your Chinese is just wonderful. This, of course, is not true. It is polite language.

One of the basic principles of **kèqìhuà** is to say things that are 好听 **hǎo tīng** "good to listen to," and to avoid saying things which are 不好听 **bù hǎo tīng** "not good to listen to," and/or to avoid saying things which are too brusque or too decisive. On the other hand, if 客气话 **kèqìhuà** is not called for, Chinese can seem far ruder than what one might expect in English. Westerners are constantly amazed at the rudeness of staff in department stores, post offices and so on. The staff have no 关系 **guānxi** "connections" with you, nor you with them. As such, you are simply a nuisance, and should be treated accordingly. It is nothing personal, and there is no point in getting angry. That's just the way it is.

6.1.3 Polite expressions

Other polite expressions you will constantly hear include the following: 久仰, 久仰 **jiǔ yǎng, jiǔ yǎng**, or 久仰大名 **jiǔ yǎng dà míng** "I have been looking up to your great name for a long time." This is what you say when being introduced to anyone, not necessarily famous. The reply might be 不敢当, 不敢当 **bù gǎn dāng, bù gǎn dāng** "how do I dare accept such a position," which can also be used if someone offers you an honorary position in a literary society or similar. A variety of this is 岂敢, 岂敢 **qǐ gǎn, qǐ gǎn** "how could I possibly dare?".

When people compliment you on your Chinese, you must feign humility and embarrassment; the appropriate **kèqìhuà** expression is 过奖, 过奖 **guò jiǎng, guò jiǎng** "excessive praise, excessive praise." Or you can say 哪里, 哪里 **nǎlǐ, nǎlǐ** "How could you say such a thing?"; 马马虎虎 **mǎmǎhūhū** "Horse horse tiger tiger"; 说得不好 **shuō de bù hǎo** "I speak very badly." "Horse horse tiger tiger," for obscure reasons, means sloppy or slovenly. Here it means something like "barely passable."

Scholars will refer to their own books as 拙作 **zhuō zuò** "clumsy work," and that of the person they are talking to as their 大作 **dà zuò** "great work." Other **kèqìhuà** expressions are 不敢冒昧 **bù gǎn màomèi** "I do not dare to presume" (when about to ask a favor), or 爱莫能助 **ài mò néng zhù** "I would love to help you, but I am unable to do so," when turning down such a request. Appropriate use of **kèqìhuà** is the mark of the accomplished speaker of Chinese, and if you pepper your speech with it, you will achieve instant recognition as a truly civilized individual.

Many foreigners get frustrated at "not being able to get a straight answer" because they have not mastered the art of deciphering the ambiguity and vagueness of much Chinese **kèqìhuà**, and sometimes someone familiar with both cultures needs to have a quiet word to explain what is really going on.

6.1.4 Lack of guānxi

On the other hand, conversations with people with whom you have no 关系 **guānxi** "connections" can be very frustrating. Any request will be met with a stream of negatives: 没有 **méi yǒu** "we don't have any"; 没有办法 **méi yǒu bànfǎ** "it cannot be done/helped"; 不行 **bù xíng** "no way"; or some dismissive phrase like 明天吧 **míngtiān ba** "try tomorrow"; 不知道 **bù zhīdào** "I don't know"; or 考虑考虑 **kǎolǜ, kǎolǜ** "I'll think about it." Or you will be simply ignored. There does not seem to be much you can do about such responses. 没有 **méi yǒu** does not necessarily mean they don't have any; it could mean they can't be bothered getting it for you. 没办法 **méi bànfǎ** does not necessarily mean "it cannot be done"; it might mean "why should I exert myself for you?". Of course, the more status or the more **guānxi** you have, the more likely you are to hear more polite turns of phrase. As with **kèqìhuà** above, the key point is that words do not always mean what they appear to mean if taken literally. It takes some practice to know when **méi yǒu** really means "there isn't any of whatever you want," and when **méi yǒu** really means that "they do have plenty of whatever it is, but not for you."

6.2 Culturally specific words

关系 **guānxi**, the dictionary will tell you, means "connections," but its role in Chinese society is far more important. With **guānxi** a relatively difficult matter can be solved fairly easily; without **guānxi** a very straightforward matter can take forever to get done. You might have **guānxi** because of your status, or you may have to cultivate it by invitations or doing favors. **Guānxi** is reciprocal. If you 拉关系 **lā guānxi** "pull connections" to get something done, you must expect that you owe a favor which you might well be expected to repay one day.

差不多 **chàbuduō** means literally "difference not much," and is a good term to use when you need to give a vague response, which can be quite often. 那

个饭馆儿怎么样? **nèige fànguǎnr zěnmeyàng?** "what is that restaurant like?". 哦，差不多 **O, chàbuduō** "oh, difference not much." This is hardly unrestrained praise. Another such expression is 不清楚 **bù qīngchǔ** "not clear," an appropriate response to a question like "does your sister have a boyfriend?".

麻烦 **máfan** (or **máfán** if stressed), the dictionary will tell you, means "trouble." The word literally means "tangled hemp." Chinese society, relationships and bureaucratic regulations can become a nightmare. After you have had your first involvement with a fully fledged **máfan**, you will know what I mean.

面子 **miànzi** literally means "face." However, for Chinese people, 面子 **miànzi** "face" has a more socio-cultural significance. It is rather the impression you project of yourself and to others in a given circumstance. 他给我很大的面子 **tā gěi wǒ hěn dà de miànzi** "he gave me a lot of face" is what you might say if an important person praises you in public, or accepts your invitation to dinner. Another word for "face" is 脸 **liǎn**. 那个人不要脸 **nèige rén bù yào liǎn** means "that fellow is shameless." To "lose face" is 丢脸 **diū liǎn** or 丢面子 **diū miànzi**.

不方便 **bù fāngbiàn** means "not convenient." Whenever you hear this phrase, you are being told, in a polite/oblique way, to go away for reasons no one wants to make specific. To explain things might be **bù hǎo tīng** "not good to listen to," or perhaps just too much trouble. Smile graciously and make other plans. Or you can 想办法 **xiǎng bànfǎ** "think of a way around things," which is what the Chinese do.

6.3 New words

Chinese society is changing so quickly, and there are many new words flooding the language. Many dictionaries have been updated with a listing of these new words. There are literally thousands of these, and they mostly refer to economic and social developments in China over the past couple of decades. The following is a very small selection, which nevertheless gives some idea of how Chinese uses its native word stock to express new ideas.

白色污染	**báisè wūrǎn**	"white pollution"—referring to disposable plastic bags which get caught in tree branches (a common sight)
病毒	**bìngdú**	"virus"; the term is also applied to computer viruses

宠物	**chǒngwù**	"pet" (cat or dog; also applied to people—a favorite of someone)
大款	**dàkuǎn**	"someone with lots of money"
倒爷	**dǎoyé**	(turn over grandpa) "someone who buys goods in one place and sells them at another"
电话磁卡	**diànhuà cíkǎ**	(electric words magnet card) "telephone card"
电视病	**diànshìbìng**	"television disease," an ailment characterized by aching legs, indigestion, backache, near sightedness etc.
电子邮件	**diànzǐ yóujiàn**	"e-mail"
电子游戏	**diànzǐ yóuxì**	"computer games"
打个的	**dǎ ge dī**	"take a cab"
迪斯科	**dísīkē**	"disco"
迪厅	**dítīng**	"discotheque" (厅 **tīng** means "hall")
地下人行道	**dìxià rénxíng dào**	"underground pedestrian walkways"
二手烟	**èrshǒuyān**	(second-hand smoke) "passive smoking"
肥皂剧	**féizào jù**	(soap drama) "soap opera, 'soapie'"
购物中心	**gòuwù zhōngxīn**	"shopping center"
汉字信息处理	**Hànzì xìnxī chǔlǐ**	"Chinese character coding," various systems for inputting characters into computer programs
核电	**hédiàn**	"electricity generated by nuclear energy." The basic meaning of 核 **hé** is "stone or pit in a fruit," such as peach-stone, peach-pit. It was extended to mean "atomic nucleus."
环保	**huánbǎo**	"environmental protection"
空气污染	**kōngqì wūrǎn**	"air pollution"
跨国公司	**kuàguó gōngsī**	"transnational company." 跨 **kuà** means "to stride, to straddle."
绿色食品	**lǜsè shípǐn**	(green colored food) "organic food"
麦当劳	**Màidāngláo**	"McDonalds"
肯德基	**Kěndéjī**	"Kentucky Fried Chicken"
美食街	**měishíjiē**	(beautiful food street) "food court (in a shopping center)"
牛仔裤	**niúzài kù**	(cowboy trousers) "jeans"
人工智能	**réngōng zhìnéng**	"artificial intelligence"

软件	**ruǎnjiàn**	"software"
天南海北	**tiān nán hǎi běi**	"heaven south sea north"—places considered desirable to find a job: 天津 *Tian*jin, 南京 *Nan*jing, 上海 Shang*hai*, and 北京 *Bei*jing.
新西兰	**Xīnxīlán**	"New west orchid"—This is the standard word for "New Zealand," but the three characters 新 **xīn**, 西 **xī** and 兰 **lán** also refer to 新疆 *Xin*jiang, 西藏 *Xi*zang (Tibet), and 兰州 *Lan*zhou, the capital of 甘肃 Gansu province. These three places are considered unpleasant places to work or live. Lanzhou is said to be the most polluted city in China.
网页	**wǎngyè**	"web page"
伟哥	**wěi gē**	(powerful elder brother) "Viagra"
下海	**xià hǎi**	"go into the sea," referring to people who leave their professions to get involved in business
写字楼	**xiězìlóu**	(write characters building) a Hong Kong expression for "an office building." The more formal expression is 办公楼 **bàngōnglóu**.
星战	**xīngzhàn**	"star wars"; more formally 星球大战计划 **xīngqiú dàzhàn jìhuà**
信用卡	**xìnyòngkǎ**	"credit cards"; note also 刷卡 **shuā kǎ** "swipe card" (when booking into a hotel)
易拉罐	**yìlāguàn**	(easy pull jar) "a can of soft drink, beer etc. which is easy to open." The classifier for a can of beer or soft drink is now 一听 **yī tīng**, from the English word "tin."
自助餐	**zìzhùcān**	(self help dinner) "buffet"
快餐	**kuàicān**	"fast food"
追星族	**zhuīxīngzú**	(chase stars tribe) "people who pursue movie stars and other celebrities"

The word for "paparazzi" is 狗仔队 **gǒuzǎiduì** "son of a bitch brigade," apparently confusing the *papa* in "paparazzi" with the English word "puppy." The use of the character 仔 **zǎi** in this word probably indicates it originated in Hong Kong, as this suffix is very common in Cantonese, but not *putonghua*. The standard word for "cur, whelp" is written 狗崽子 **gǒuzǎizi**, with a different character for **zǎi**. Over the past couple of years a new word for a pop singer's fans has emerged. They are called **fěnsī**, borrowed from English *fans*, but written with characters 粉丝 which otherwise mean "rice vermicelli." It remains to be seen how long this word will last.

6.4 Ancient loanwords

There are a few loanwords still in use which entered the language two thousand years ago, for example 葡萄 **pútáo** "grapes," possibly from Greek *botrys*, and 狮子 **shīzi** "lion," possibly from Persian *shir*, or a similar word in a related language. Neither grapes nor lions are native to China—in case you have ever wondered why Chinese lions do not look very much like lions. Other suggestions are that 蜜 **mì** "honey" might be related to the ancient Indo-European word for "honey," which appears in English as *mead*, or that 犬 **quǎn** "dog" is related to the ancient Indo-European word which appears in Latin as *canis* (cf. English *canine*), but there is no proof of these possible etymologies.

Buddhism brought many words into Chinese, but most of those which have survived were made up of Chinese elements, rather than transliterations, such as 世界 **shìjiè** "world." Some of the transliterated words still in common usage are 刹那 **chànà** "instant, split second" from Sanskrit *ksana*, 夜叉 **yèchā** "a malevolent spirit, a vengeful person" from Sanskrit *yaksha*, and 三昧 **sānmèi**, Sanskrit *samadhi*, "contemplation," which has now acquired the meaning of "to get the knack of something." The common word 僧 **sēng** "Buddhist monk," is from Sanskrit *sangha* "a community of monks"; 袈裟 **jiāshā** "a monk's robe" is from *kasaya*. In some words, only one part of the original has survived: the **ní** in 尼姑 **nígū** "Buddhist nun" is the last syllable of the Sanskrit *bhikkini* (the second syllable is Chinese 姑 **gū** "girl, woman"), and the **píng** in 苹果 **píngguǒ** "apple," is from Sanskrit *bimba* "apple" (the second syllable is Chinese 果 **guǒ** "fruit").

蘑菇 **mógu** "mushroom" is from Mongol *megu* (or a similar word in a related language). The modern word 站 **zhàn**, as in 火车站 **huǒchēzhàn** (fire vehicle station) "railway station" is from Mongol *jam*, the "post stops" at which Mongol horsemen exchanged horses on their long trips across the Mongol empire. The original Chinese word, 驿 **yì**, is no longer used (except in historical novels) but is preserved in the common Japanese word for "railway station," 駅 *eki*. One of the "musts" nowadays for tourists to Beijing is to go on a "*hutong* tour," a bicycle (or tricycle) ride through the back lanes and alleys of Old Beijing. The word 胡同(儿) **hútòng(r)**, with 同 here pronounced **tòng(r)**, not **tóng** as usual, is from Mongol *hoton* "town," which one can still see in Mongolian place names, such as Huhhot [呼和浩特 **Hūhéhàotè** in Chinese], the capital of Inner Mongolia. 萨其马 **sàqímǎ**, a common type of sticky candy available at any food shop in Beijing, is from Manchu.

Many early loanwords betray their origin by the prefix 胡 **hú** "barbarian." The word originally means "dewlap, the fold of skin under the neck of cattle," but may itself be a very old loanword derived from the Chinese name for the Huns. So we have 胡蜂 **húfēng** (barbarian bee) "wasp, hornet," and 胡萝卜 **húluóbo** (barbarian turnip) "carrot"—also, by popular etymology, 红萝卜 **hóngluóbo** (red turnip). Note also 狐臭 **húchòu** (fox smell) "body odor, B.O.," earlier 胡臭 **húchòu** "barbarian smell," and 胡说 **húshuō** (barbarian words) "nonsense."

Many loanwords in the nineteenth century were indicated by the prefix 洋 **yáng** "ocean, foreign." So we have 洋车 **yángchē** (foreign vehicle) "rickshaw." The rickshaw was an import from Japan; the English word derives from Japanese 人力车 *jinrikisha*, not Chinese. Others are 洋火 **yánghuǒ** (foreign fire) "matches" (now more formally 火柴 **huǒchái** "fire twigs"), and 洋鬼子 **yángguǐzi** "foreign devil." Foreigners are now generally referred to as 老外 **lǎowài**, a friendly version of the formal 外国人 **wàiguórén** (outside country person). 洋人 **yángrén** is a common and fairly neutral term. Older terms, such as 洋鬼子 **yángguǐzi** "foreign devil," 大鼻子 **dàbízi** "big nose," are still sometimes heard, but more as a joke.

6.5 Modern loanwords

Most loanwords used in Chinese in the early twentieth century, such as 得律风 **délǜfēng** "telephone," 德莫克拉西 **démòkèlāxī** "democracy," 赛恩斯 **sàiēnsī** "science" have not survived, replaced by words using basic Chinese elements: "telephone" is now 电话 **diànhuà** (electric words), "democracy" is 民主 **mínzhǔ** (people rule), and "science" is 科学 **kēxué** "the study of classification." Exceptions are 幽默 **yōumò** "humor," 逻辑 **luójī** "logic," 麦克风 **màikèfēng** "microphone," 沙龙 **shālóng** "salon," and 沙发 **shāfā** "armchair/settee." Some earlier loanwords survive alongside Chinese-based compounds: 盘尼西林 **pánníxīlín** "penicillin," more formally 青霉素 **qīngméisù** (green mildew element), and 维他命 **wéitāmìng** (support his life) "vitamin," now more formally 维生素 **wéishēngsù** (maintain life element). Some old loanwords have acquired new uses: the Tang dynasty loanword 塔 **tǎ**, from Sanskrit *stupa* "pagoda" is now used to translate "tower" as in 电视塔 **diànshìtǎ** "television tower."

Some foreign words have become assimilated and are readily used with Chinese words to form new combinations. The standard word for "bus," for example, is 公共汽车 **gōnggòng qìchē** "common altogether steam vehicle," but now part of the Hong Kong term 巴士 **bāshì** "bus" has become accepted in 小巴 **xiǎobā** (little **ba**) "minibus," and 大巴 **dàbā** "tour bus." Occasionally one sees the word 巴士 **bāshì** in company names, but this has not yet entered the spoken language. Not yet, but it might any day. The typical Cantonese expression 买单 **mǎidān** "bill" (in a restaurant), which was unknown a few years ago in China, has now more or less replaced the standard term 结账 **jiézhàng** (which remains the term for settling one's hotel bill).

The un-Chinese sounding syllable 卡 **kǎ-** has become accepted in 卡车 **kǎchē** "ka-vehicle" = cart (lorry, truck), 卡片 **kǎpiàn** ("ka-card") "greeting card," and even 圣诞卡 **shèngdànkǎ** (holy birthday ka) "Christmas card." 咖 is used for **kā** in 咖啡 **kāfēi** "coffee," but in 咖喱 **gālí** "curry" it is pronounced **gā**. 吧 **bā** is used for "bar," so we have 酒吧 **jiǔbā** ("wine **ba**") [bar], and now **wǎngbā** 网吧 (net **ba**) "internet café."

The greatest influence, however, has been from Taiwan and Hong Kong, and the speech of the younger generations is full of such expressions, much to the distress of their elders. So we hear 蛮好 **mǎn hǎo** "very good" from Taiwanese Mandarin, along the standard 很好 **hěn hǎo** or the Beijing dialect 挺好 **tǐng hǎo**; 拜拜 **bāibái** or **báibái** from the Hong Kong Cantonese loanword from English *bye-bye*, which can mean "goodbye," or "to split up from a girlfriend or boyfriend." 拜 is normally pronounced **bài** in Mandarin, but here the tone reflects Cantonese intonation. The word 宝贝 **bǎobèi or** 宝贝儿 **bǎobèir** is indirectly from English *baby*, a term some people might use to refer to their girlfriend, or to a small child. It happens, by coincidence, to be a perfectly good Chinese word meaning "precious." The use of 好 **hǎo**, as in 好惨 **hǎo cǎn** "really cruel" is a Cantonese expression, which is also common in Taiwanese romantic fiction, and is hence popular with teenage girls. Various swear words are, of course, used more commonly by men. Interestingly 酷 **kù**, the teenage expression of high approval, from English "cool," which was all the rage in the 1990s, is now being replaced by 爽 **shuǎng**, the Chinese word for "cool" (as in weather). Among teenagers the ubiquitous Cantonese expression 哗 **wà!** (*wow*) has become trendy, but mainly among the same set which would use "wow" in English.

Over the past few years several words have sometimes been used for a new concept, until one eventually wins out. The World Wide Web was first translated as 万围网 **wànwéiwǎng** "ten thousand interconnections web," later as 因特网 **yīntèwǎng**, the first two syllables transcribing English *inter*. Now it has settled as 网络 **wǎngluò**, 络 **luò** being another word for "net." We also have 网址 **wǎngzhǐ** "net address," and 网吧 **wàngbā** (net bar) "internet café."

The term for AIDS has settled as 艾滋病 **àizībìng**, after being called 爱滋病 **àizībìng** for some time. The word for "love" (爱) has been replaced by the word for "mugwort" (艾). 滋 **zī** can mean "to grow, to multiply, to nourish, to spurt out, moist or juicy." Take your pick.

When SARS first appeared it was called 非典型肺炎 **fēidiǎnxìng fēiyán** (non-typical-lung-inflammation), which was quickly shortened to 非典 **fēidiǎn** "atypical," but in speech practically everyone called it SARS. "Bird flu" is 禽流感 **qínliúgǎn**, 禽 **qín** being the classical word for bird, or more specifically fowl. 流感 **liúgǎn** is short for 流行性感冒 **liúxíngxìng gǎnmào** "epidemic influenza."

Chinese does not assimilate many loanwords. Those which have become part of the language can be divided into certain categories— words which refer to foreign foods, drinks, dances or other culturally-specific items. We can identify the following groups:

6.5.1 Drinks
The following are some commonly used loanwords for beverages: 啤酒 **píjiǔ** "beer," 白兰地 **báilándì** "brandy," 香槟酒 **xiāngbīnjiǔ** "champagne," 威士忌 **wēishìjì** "whisky," 咖啡 **kāfēi** "coffee," 伏特加 **fútèjiā** "vodka," 苏打水 **sūdǎshuǐ** "soda water," 可可 **kěkě** "cocoa," 可口可乐 **kěkǒu kělè** (can mouth can happy), so "delicious and exhilarating" a brilliant translation of "Coca Cola" dating from the 1930s. Now 可乐 **kělè** "cola" is used for a variety of drinks, including 百事可乐 **bǎishì kělè** (hundred things cola) "Pepsi Cola," and even 蜜茶可乐 **mìchá kělè** "honey tea cola."

6.5.2 Foods
The loanwords for food items include the following: 巧克力 **qiǎokèlì** "chocolate," 三明治 **sānmíngzhì** "sandwich" and 汉堡包 **hànbǎobāo** (Hamburg-bun) "hamburger" are loanwords, but 热狗 **règǒu** (hot dog) is a direct translation. 冰淇淋 **bīngqílín** "ice cream" is a hybrid: 冰 **bīng** is "ice" and 淇淋 **qílín** is a transcription of "cream." The word for "ice cream" is also written as 冰激凌 **bīngjílíng**. "Pie" is 排 **pái**, as in 苹果排 **píngguǒpái** "apple pie."

Earlier imported foods have good Chinese names. "Tomato" is 番茄 **fānqié** "barbarian eggplant" in the south, and 西红柿 **xīhóngshì** "western red persimmon" in the north. Pineapple is 凤梨 **fènglí** "phoenix pear." Potato is 土豆 **tǔdòu** "earth bean." Maize is 玉米 **yùmǐ** "jade rice."

6.5.3 Dances and music

Common loanwords that come to mind: 芭蕾舞 **bāléiwǔ** "ballet," 迪斯科 **dísīkē** "disco," 探戈舞 **tàngēwǔ** "tango" but 狐步舞 **húbùwǔ** (fox step dance) "foxtrot." The name of the opera *La Traviata* is 茶花女 **cháhuānǔ** (tea flower woman), 茶花 **cháhuā** meaning "camellia," from the original French *La dame aux Camilles*. It was once famously mistranslated as *The Tea Lady*. 爵士乐 **juéshì yuè** or 爵士音乐 **juéshì yīnyuè** is "jazz." 爵士 **juéshì** by itself translates the British terms of nobility "Lord, Sir."

"Rock and roll" is 摇滚音乐 **yáogǔn yīnyuè** (shaking and rolling music); "heavy metal" is 重金属 **zhòng jīnshǔ**, a direct translation. 萨克管 **sàkèguǎn** "saxophone," and 巴松管 **bāsōngguǎn** "bassoon" are loanwords, though made clearer by adding the Chinese 管 **guǎn** "pipe, tube, wind instrument." Most Western musical instruments are compounds with the word for the ancient Chinese instrument 琴 **qín** "zither": 钢琴 **gāngqín** (steel **qín**) "piano," 风琴 **fēngqín** (wind **qín**) "organ," 小提琴 **xiǎotíqín** (small lifted **qín**) "violin," 中提琴 **zhōngtíqín** (middle lifted **qín**) "viola," 大提琴 **dà tíqín** (large lifted **qín**) "cello," 口琴 **kǒuqín** (mouth **qín**) "mouth organ," 竖琴 **shùqín** (upright **qín**) "harp," and so on.

Note also the words 嬉皮士 **xīpíshì**, a transcription of "hippie" which is a reference to the ancient expression 嬉皮笑脸 **xīpí xiàoliǎn** "grinning cheekily, smiling and grimacing." The more recent "yuppie" is 雅痞 **yǎpǐ** "elegant riff-raff."

6.5.4 Animals

Most words for animals are, of course, native Chinese words. 狮子 **shīzi** "lion" and 骆驼 **luòtuo** "camel" are ancient loanwords from central Asia. Some particularly fierce animals are used with the familiar prefix 老 **lǎo**, such as 老虎 **lǎohǔ**, which does not mean "old tiger," simply "tiger"; 老鼠 **lǎoshǔ** "rat," and 老鹰 **lǎoyīng** "eagle." In some dialects we find 老鸹 **lǎoguā** "crow" (an evil bird to the Chinese) and 老蛇 **lǎoshé** "snake," but these words are not in *putonghua*. The idea is that by using the familiar prefix 老 **lǎo** it makes them less fearsome. Some students think the word 老师 **lǎoshī** "teacher" should be part of this series.

Animals unfamiliar to traditional China are given Chinese sounding names: "turkey," from the Americas, is 火鸡 **huǒjī** (fire chicken). From Africa, 河马 **hémǎ** (river horse) is "hippopotamus," and 长颈鹿 **chángjǐnglù** (long neck deer) is "giraffe." Other non-native animals are 海象 **hǎixiàng** (sea elephant) "walrus" and 海豹 **hǎibào** (sea leopard) "seal." 变色龙 **biànsèlóng** "change color dragon" is a "chameleon." From Australia, "kangaroo" is 袋鼠 **dàishǔ** (bag rat); "koala" is 树熊 **shùxióng** (tree bear), though 考拉 **kǎolā** is also common. 鸭嘴兽 **yāzuǐshòu** (duck mouth animal) is "platypus." My favorite is 丁狗 **dīnggǒu** (*ding* dog) for "dingo," where the second syllable in "dingo" happens to sound the same as the Chinese word for "dog," 狗 **gǒu**.

6.5.5 Games
保龄球 **bǎolíngqiú** "bowling," and 高尔夫球 **gāo'érfūqiú** "golf" are loanwords, but most Western sports are formed from Chinese elements: 足球 **zúqiú** "football," 网球 **wǎngqiú** (net ball) "tennis," 台球 **táiqiú** (table ball) "billiards," 羽毛球 **yǔmáoqiú** (feather ball) "badminton," and so on. Note too 奥林匹克 **Aòlínpǐkè** "Olympics," now usually referred to as 奥运会 **Aòyùnhuì** (**Aò** sports meeting).

6.5.6 Clothing
Not many loanwords here; the common ones in use are 夹克 **jiákè** "jacket," 迷你裙 **mínǐqún** (fascinate you skirt) "miniskirt." A suit is 西装 **xīzhuāng** "Western-style clothing." Note also the use of 的确良 **díquèliáng** (which literally means "really good") for "dacron, terelyne" and 尼龙 **nílóng** for "nylon."

6.5.7 Vehicles and weapons
Loanwords uder this category include: 摩托车 **mótuōchē** "motorbike," 坦克车 **tǎnkèchē** "tank," **kǎchē** "truck (from "cart")," 吉普车 **jípǔchē** "jeep," 雷达 **léidá** "radar," 来复枪 **láifùqiāng** (coming-returning gun; 枪 **qiāng** in pre-modern Chinese meant "spear") "rifle."

6.6 Chinese words in English
We mentioned in the introduction that there are few loanwords in Chinese. Similarly, there are few Chinese loanwords in English. Most of these are quite old, and from non-Mandarin dialects. Examples are *tea* from Hokkien *te*, and *kumquat* from Cantonese (金桔). More recent borrowings are in their Mandarin form, such as 功夫 *gongfu* (also written *kung-fu*), 太极 **tàijí** (also written *tai-chi* or *t'ai-chi*), 阴阳 **yīnyáng**, and 气 **qì** (also written *chi* or *ch'i*). *Yam-cha* is a fairly recent borrowing from Cantonese (饮茶 *yam cha* "drink tea"). *Ketchup* is from Hokkien *khe-chiap* (茄汁), via Malay, via U.S. English.

The word literally means "eggplant juice," but here refers to the "barbarian eggplant," the tomato. Some words in English borrowed from Japanese are themselves old loanwords from Chinese, such as *Zen* "a type of Buddhism (Chinese 禅 **Chán**)," *bonzai* (Chinese 盆景 **pénjǐng**) "miniature trees and rockery," and *tofu* (Chinese 豆腐 **dòufu**) "bean curd."

6.7 Acronyms

During the twentieth century a small number of words containing letters of the English alphabet entered Chinese: X光 **X-guāng** "X-rays," 三K党 **Sān K Dǎng** "the three K party" (meaning the Ku Klux Klan), B-52 (pronounced **B-wǔshíēr**) "a type of bomber" (Lin Biao's nickname for Mao Zedong), AB型血 **AB xíng xuè** "A-B blood type," and 阿Q **Ah Q**, which is not English at all, but the name of Lu Xun's anti-hero in his famous novel. The Russian acronym KGB was adopted into Chinese as 克格勃 **kè-gé-bó**, using characters instead of letters of the Russian alphabet. Generally, however, words were translated: the UN was (and still is) 联合国 **Liánhéguó**, a literal translation of "united nations."

The world of the twenty-first century, however, has brought a huge number of internationally used acronyms to China, and they are accepted more and more in their foreign alphabetic form—in many cases becoming far more common than the official, literal translations. A sampling of such words in common use in modern China would include:

Acronyms	Full Term	Chinese Term
AI	"artificial intelligence"	人工智能 **réngōng zhìnéng**
ATM	"automated teller machine"	自动柜员机 **zìdòng guìyuán jī**
CCTV	"China Central Television"	中央电视台 **Zhōngyáng diànshìtái**. The acronym CCTV, based on the English name of the station, is on their official logo.
CEO	"chief executive officer"	首席执行官 **shǒuxí zhíxíngguān**
CIA	"Central Intelligence Agency"	中央情报局 **Zhōngyáng qíngbàojú**
FAQ	"frequently asked questions"	常见问题 **chángjiàn wèntí**
GNP	"gross national product"	国民生产总值 **guómín shēngchǎn zǒngzhí**
GM	"genetically modified"	基因改性的 **jīyīn gǎixìngde**; 基因 **jīyīn** is itself a loanword from English *gene*

Acronyms	Full Term	Chinese Term
IMF	"International Monetary Fund"	世界货币基金组织 **Shìjiè huòbì jijin zǔzhī**
ISBN	"International Standard Book Number"	国际标准图书编号 **guójì biāozhǔn túshū biānhào**
IT	"information technology"	信息技术 **xìnxí jìshù**
NGO	"non-government organizations"	非政府组织 **fēizhèngfǔ zǔzhī**
PC	"personal computer"	个人电脑 **gèrén diànnǎo**
PR	"public relations"	公共关系 **gōnggòng guānxì** or often shortened to 公关 **gōngguān**
SOHO	"small office, home office"	家庭办公室 **jiātíng bàngōngshì**
WTO	"World Trade Organization"	世界贸易组织 **Shìjiè màoyì zǔzhī**, or 世贸组织 **Shìmào zǔzhī**

There are, of course, many more of these: APEC, BBC, CD, DNA, DOS, DVD, EU, GMT, IBM, LCD, MBA, NATO, OPEC, RAM, ROM, UNICEF, UFO, VCR, VIP, WHO...

In most of these words the letters are read as they are in English. X in **X-guāng** is read *ex* or **àikèsī**. IELTS (International English Language Testing System) is spelled out as IELTS, or is pronounced [aielts], and also has a Chinese name: 雅思 **Yǎsī** "elegant thoughts." TOEFL (Test of English as a Foreign Language) is generally called by its Chinese name 托福 **Tuōfú**, derived from the polite expression (**kèqìhuà**) 托福 **tuōfú** "my good fortune is due to you" (used when replying positively to an enquiry about your health). 托派 **Tuōpài** (派 **pài** means a political sect) used to mean "Trotskyite"; now it is a slang word for people who work day and night to pass the TOEFL exam which enables them to study overseas.

Each of the acronyms above is spelled out in English; the more formal Chinese terms are generally a direct translation of the English, and are more common in newspapers than in conversation. For some unknown reason, the Chinese tend to read English letters in the first tone, which makes them sound a bit peculiar to native speakers of English.

There are also some interesting hybrids of this type. X光 **X-guāng** "X-rays" is part alphabet, part character, as is BP 机 **BP-jī** "beeper," where BP sounds like beeper and 机 **jī** "machine" is tacked on; IP 卡 **IP-kǎ**, in which the first two letters are from the English acronym for "internet phone," followed by **kǎ**, which is a transcription of the English word *card*; 卡拉 OK **kǎlā-OK**, from Japanese *karaoke*, in which the first two syllables are transcribed with characters, and the second two with the English letters *OK*, and T恤 **T-xù**, where the T is English, and the **xù** from Cantonese *shuet*, which sounds a bit like *shirt*. MP-3 is pronounced MP **sān**, but F-1 ("formula one motor racing") is pronounced *F-one*. In the case of DJ, the Chinese don't even attempt a translation.

6.8 Conversation fillers

The most common equivalent of "hum, hum" or "er, er" in English—that is, what you would say when you can't think of the right word—is 这个, 这个 **zhège, zhège** (in Beijing **zhèige, zhèige**). Another very common filler is 就是说, 就是说 **jiù shi shuō, jiù shi shuō**, which one can sometimes hear repeated many times in rapid succession until the speaker has found the word he wants. Other common expressions are 就是, 就是 **jiù shì, jiù shì** "that's right, that's it" (said rather slowly) when listening to someone's long list of complaints, and 可不是吗 **kě bù shì ma**, literally "how could it be that is not so," which corresponds to "you can say that again!"

6.9 Euphemisms

Sometimes people avoid something unpleasant or embarrassing by using euphemisms, which can be misleading if you do not know what is meant. 她有了 **tā yǒu le** "she has it," for example, may mean "she is pregnant." 他不在了 **tā bù zài le** "he is not here" may mean "he is dead." For this reason many people in Beijing substitute the grammatically irregular 没在 **méi zài** when they really do mean "he is not here." 老了 **lǎo le**, or 太老了 **tài lǎo le** "he is too old," can also mean "he is dead." Or it may just mean he is very old. 过去 **guòqù** "to pass away," 去世 **qù shì** "to leave the world," and 逝世 **shì shì**, a more respectful way of saying the same thing, are fairly obvious. Mao Zedong used to say he would sooner or later 见马克思 **jiàn Mǎkèsī** "go and see Marx." A classical expression is 呜呼哀哉 **wūhū āi zāi** "alas, how sad it is." A rather rude expression is 翘辫子了 **qiào biānzi le** "to hold up the pigtail," this being the position assumed for decapitation in the old days. The English equivalent would be "to kick the bucket." 炒鱿鱼 **chǎo yóuyú** "fried squid" means "to be fired." Many Chinese consider the number 4 unlucky, because 四 **sì** "four" sounds like 死 **sǐ** "death." In elevators one sometimes sees 1, 2, 3, 3A, 5 in the same way that 13 is avoided in elevators in the West. On the other hand, 8 is a lucky number, because both in *putonghua* and Cantonese, 八 **bā** / *bat* rhymes with 发 **fā**/ *fat*, which is the first character in the expression 发财 **fācái** / *fat choi* "to grow rich." For this reason, the numeral 8 is highly valued in telephone numbers or car registration plates. The traditional greeting at Chinese New Year is 恭喜发财 **gōngxǐ fācái** / *kung hee fat choi* "Congratulations! May you grow rich!" This expression was out of favor for many years, of course, but recently has returned with a vengeance.

Amongst the many gifts Chinese give each other clocks are avoided, because 送钟 **sòng zhōng** "to give someone a clock as a present" is homophonous with 送终 **sòng zhōng**, which means "to escort a coffin to the graveside." And many Chinese avoid using a red pen, especially to write names. The use of red ink was, in traditional China, the prerogative of the emperor. The only time anyone's name would be written in red was on an execution warrant. So if you see Chinese people looking for a black or blue pen to write someone's name when a red one is available, that is why.

6.10 Exclamations

The quintessential Chinese exclamation is 哎呀 **āiyā**, or its variants 哎哟 **āiyō** or simply 哎 **āi**, which is extremely common and extremely catching. Many foreigners who live in Chinese-speaking communities for a while pick it up and pepper their English with it. It is an exclamation of surprise, complaint, disgust or horror. It corresponds to anything ranging from "oh dear" to "oh shit!" 好家伙 **hǎo jiāhuo**, literally "good fellow," means "good lord, goodness gracious." 天啊 **tiān ā** is "good heavens."

6.11 Rude language

The following are some mild swear words you will hear in everyday conversation.

糟糕 **zāo gāo** (rotten cake) "damn it!"
糟了 **zāo le** (oh, dregs!) "what a mess"
该死了 **gāi sǐ le** (ought to die) "damn thing," as in 该死的狗 **gāisǐ de gǒu** "that bloody dog"
死老头子 **sǐ lǎo tóuzi** (dead old head) "silly old fool"
傻瓜 **shǎguā** (silly melon) "you idiot!"
蠢猪 **chǔn zhū** "stupid pig"
倒霉鬼 **dǎoméiguǐ** (fall in mildew ghost) is "poor wretch." To fall in the mildew means "to be down on one's luck"
破鞋(子) **pòxié(zi)** (worn out shoe) is "a loose woman, a slut."

A common Beijing expression is 臭娘儿们 **chòu niángrmen** (pronounced **niǎr men**) "stinking bitch" which despite its plural ending, is singular. Another, pronounced **yāoting**, is a slurred version of 丫头养的 **yātou yǎng de** "brought up by a concubine (servant girl)."

An expression somewhat stronger, but very common, is 他妈的 **tā mā de**, or just 妈的 **mā de**, literally "his mother's." The famous writer Lu Xun dubbed this 国骂 **guómà** "the national swear word." The word 王八 **wángba** is a slang word for "turtle." The character 王 **wáng** is supposed to look like the markings on the back of the turtle, and 八 **bā** are its back legs. The Chinese, for obscure reasons, think the turtle is promiscuous. A common swear word is 王八蛋 **wángba dàn** "bastard, son of a bitch." The textbooks will tell you that 蛋 **dàn** means "egg," but here it is a Beijing slang word for "testicle," adding insult to injury. The standard word for "hen's egg" is 鸡蛋 **jīdàn**, but many older people in Beijing avoid this word and say 鸡子儿 **jīzǐr** "hen's son" instead, much in the way that some English speakers avoid the word "cock." The word for "cock" in this sense is 鸡巴 **jība**, the suffix 巴 **ba** referring to an appendage, such as 尾巴 **wěiba** "tail," or 锅巴 **guōba** "the crust of cooked rice stuck to the bottom of a pot." 鸡 **jī** by itself means "chicken, cock." "Buggery" is 鸡奸 **jījiān** (chicken rape), but **yějī** (wild chicken) means "streetwalker."

Other quaint but fairly harmless "rude expressions" are 狗屁 **gǒupì** "dog's fart" (something worthless), or 马尿 **mǎniào** "horse piss" (watered down or otherwise undrinkable beer). 滚蛋 **gǔndàn** "roll over, bollocks" is "bugger off." A milder version is 滚开 **gǔnkāi** "roll away" which can be used by young ladies being pestered by admirers. An even milder expression is just 去你的 **qùnǐde** "get lost." 放屁 **fàng pì** "fart" means something like "bullshit." Or you may prefer to say 胡说八道 **hú shuō bā dào** "stuff and nonsense." 拍马屁 **pāi mǎ pì** (to pat the horse's arse) means "to flatter, to crawl."

大便 **dàbiàn** (big convenience) and 小便 **xiǎobiàn** (little convenience) are the standard words for "defecate" and "urinate" respectively. The ruder versions are 拉屎 **lā shǐ** "pull shit," and 撒尿 **sā niào** "splash piss." The characters for 屎 **shǐ** "shit" and 尿 **niào** "piss" show rice (米) under a body (尸) and water (水) under a body (尸) respectively. A common expression is 站着茅坑不拉屎 **zhàn zhe máo kēng bù lā shǐ** "occupy thatched pit not pull shit," meaning to occupy an important position but not do any work. The standard word for "toilet bowl" is 马桶 **mǎtǒng** "horse bucket." A "bedpan" is a 尿壶 **niào hú** (piss pot). The standard word for "toilet" is 厕所 **cèsuǒ**, which is what you will find on toilet doors: 男厕 **náncè** and 女厕 **nǔcè** for male and female toilets respectively. The current euphemism is 洗手间 **xǐshǒujiān** (wash hands room). The expression 洗脚 **xǐjiǎo** (wash feet), however, means to visit a massage parlor, pedicure apparently being one of the services offered.

Such scatalogical references sometimes turn up in the most unexpected places. A recent article in the *People's Daily* referred to the Japanese Prime Minister's visits to the Yasukuni shrine as being "a pellet of rat shit spoiling a bowl of congee," quoting the old proverb 一粒老鼠屎坏了一锅粥 **yīlì lǎoshǔ shǐ huàile yī guō zhōu**. The Japanese were not impressed with their shrine to the war dead being compared to rat shit, but the Chinese explained that the shrine was the congee, the shit was the Prime Minister. I do not know if the Japanese could draw on their ancient literature to answer in kind.

There are of course many quainter and ruder expressions than these, but you need to know which ones can be used and which ones are utterly taboo. This will take time and probably a few raised eyebrows until you get a sense of what is appropriate and what is not.

6.12 Proverbs and sayings

There are literally thousands of Chinese proverbs and other sayings, and hundreds are in everyday use. Once students discover these they provide an endless source of amusement and interest. The more of them you learn, the more you hear and see them in books, magazines, movie subtitles and even advertisements all around you. Vivid and pithy, they are very characteristic of everyday Chinese.

There are many Chinese proverb dictionaries available, some of which are very large indeed. A pocket-sized one, which its preface says is suitable for people with a primary school education, contains more than 3,000 成语 **chéngyǔ**, mainly expressions with four characters. A larger, but by no means exhaustive, dictionary contains 18,000. You will meet with such sayings very early in your studies, and many more of them as your studies advance.

Most of the "Chinese proverbs" most commonly quoted in the West, such as "May you live in interesting times," are not Chinese proverbs at all. Any saying which sounds abstruse but somehow meaningful is said to be a Chinese proverb. Real Chinese proverbs and turns of phrase are far more fascinating, and can be as abstruse or meaningful as any of the fabricated ones. Below are some examples:

- 不见棺材不落泪 **bù jiàn guāncái bù luò lèi** (not weep until you have seen the coffin) "refuse to believe something unpleasant until proof is given"

- 非驴非马 **fēi lǘ fēi mǎ** (neither ass nor horse) "nondescript, neither this nor that"

- 不翼而飞 **bù yì ér fēi** (no wings but fly) "to vanish mysteriously"

- 指鹿为马 **zhǐ lù wéi mǎ** (point at deer and call it horse).
  A test of loyalty devised by the First Emperor of the Qin dynasty to see how far his officials would go to support his views, even if clearly ridiculous. To agree with whatever your boss says, no matter how ridiculous. Also, "deliberate misrepresentation," or, to use another Chinese saying, 颠倒黑白 **diāndǎo hēibái** "juggling black and white."

- 得意忘形 **dé yì wàng xíng** (get intention forget surroundings) "so excited one forgets about the appropriateness of one's behavior"

- 对牛弹琴 **duì niú tán qín** (towards ox strum lute) "to play a lute to an ox"—casting pearls before swine

- 放下屠刀，立地成佛 **fàng xià tú dāo, lì dì chéng Fó** (put down your butcher's knife and immediately achieve Buddhahood) "to turn over a new leaf"

- 废寝忘食 **fèi qín wàng shí** (neglect sleep forget eat) "so preoccupied one forgets to eat and sleep"

- 高枕无忧 **gāo zhěn wú yōu** (high pillow no worries) "peace of mind"

- 狐群狗党 **hú qún gǒu dǎng** (fox crowd dog pack) "a group of scoundrels." Note that the word 党 **dǎng**, which now means a "political party," was a derogatory term in traditional China.

- 一丘之貉 **yī qiū zhī hé** "raccoons from the same lair"—partners in crime

- 狼狈为奸 **láng bèi wéi jiàn** "to act in collusion." 狼 **láng** is said to be a wolf with long forelegs and short hind legs. 狈 **bèi** is a sort of wolf with short forelegs and long hind legs. They can only get around by cooperating in a ridiculous and awkward manner. So 狼狈 **lángbèi** means "to be in an extremely awkward position, in a sorry plight, in dire straits."

- 虎头蛇尾 **hǔ tóu shé wěi** (tiger's head snake's tail) "to start something with great enthusiasm but end up not achieving much." Applicable to the learning of Chinese.

- 浑水摸鱼 **hún shuǐ mò yú** (muddy water grope fish) "to take advantage of a chaotic situation"

- 狼心狗肺 **láng xīn gǒu fèi** (wolf's heart, dog's lungs) "cold blooded, ungrateful." Compare 没心没肺 **méi xīn méi fèi** (no heart no lungs) "gormless"

- 老虎屁股摸不得 **lǎohǔ pìgu mòbudé** (one should not pat the backside of a tiger) "do not provoke an influential person"

- 力不从心 **lì bù cóng xīn** (strength not follow heart) "lack of energy frustrates one's ambitions"

- 未老先衰 **wèi lǎo xiān shuāi** "not yet old, already in decline" — prematurely senile

- 僧多粥少 **sēng duō zhōu shǎo** (monks many, gruel little) "too many applicants for a job; not enough to go around." Also phrased as 粥少僧多 **zhōu shǎo sēng duō.**

- 上有政策, 下有对策 **shàng yǒu zhèngcè, xià yǒu duìcè** "the superiors have a policy, and the inferiors have a counter policy"
  A common expression in China. When the government announces a new policy which is not popular, some people think of ways to seemly implement it while actually doing nothing, or even going the opposite way.

- 树倒猢狲散 **shù dǎo húsūn sàn** "when the tree falls the monkeys scatter"— to desert an influential person when he is in trouble

- 水落石出 **shuǐ luò shí chū** (water falls stones emerge) "the truth will emerge in the end"

- 似是而非 **sì shì ér fēi** (seems to be but is not) "appearances can deceive"

- 口是心非 **kǒu shì xīn fēi** (mouth yes heart no) "to say one thing but mean another"

- 同床异梦 **tóng chuáng yì mèng** (same bed different dreams) "strange bedfellows"

- 天高皇帝远 **tiān gāo huáng dì yuǎn** "the sky is high and the emperor is far away" Officials in the provinces can get away with ignoring directions from the central government, particularly in reference to injustice and local corruption, safe in the knowledge that Beijing is a long, long way away.

- 小巫见大巫 **xiǎo wū jiàn dà wū** (a little shaman meets a big shaman) "to meet someone with far greater powers or abilities than yourself"

- 难得糊涂 **nán dé hú tú** "stupidity is hard to obtain" The motto of 郑板桥 Zheng Banqiao, one of the Eight Eccentrics of Yangzhou. This famous inscription in Zheng's distinctive calligraphy can be found in any art shop. The text continues: "to be intelligent is hard; to be stupid is hard; to change from intelligence to stupidity is even harder." The idea is that in difficult times you will be less likely to get into trouble if you feign stupidity. Zheng was also famous for his paintings of bamboo, a symbol of flexibility but strength under pressure.

- 无法无天 **wú fǎ wú tiān** (no law no heaven) "to act without restraint"

- 行尸走肉 **xíng shī zǒu ròu** (walking corpse, running meat) "a worthless person"

- 前门拒虎, 后门进狼 **qián mén jù hǔ, hòu mén jìn láng** (front door resist tiger, back door enter wolf) "to fend off danger from one quarter only to fall victim to another"

- 阎王好见, 小鬼难缠 **yánwáng hǎojiàn, xiǎoguǐ nánchán** "the King of Hell is easy to see, the little demons are difficult to get around"—it's easier to go straight to the boss rather than try to deal with his underlings. The word 阎 **Yán** in 阎王 **Yánwáng** is an old loanword, from the Hindu word for the King of Hell, Yama.

- 癞蛤蟆想吃天鹅肉 **lài háma xiǎng chī tiān é ròu** "an ugly toad wants to eat swan flesh"—an ugly man lusting after a beautiful girl (with no hope of success). The word for "swan" is 天鹅 **tiān é** "heavenly goose." The word 蛤蟆 **háma** is a Beijing dialect word for "frog"; the standard word is 青蛙 **qīngwā**. Note also 田鸡 **tiánjī** "field chicken" for "frog (as a meal)."

- 岂有此理 **qǐ yǒu cǐ lǐ** "how could it be that there is such a principle?": "outrageous"

- 挂羊头，卖狗肉 **guà yáng tóu, mài gǒu ròu** "hang up sheep's head, sell dog meat"—false advertising

- 一人得道，鸡犬升天 **yī rén dé dào, jī quǎn shēng tiān** (when a man reaches enlightenment, his chickens and dogs ascend to Heaven)—"when someone is appointed to an important position, his relatives and hangers on enjoy the same benefits"

- 莫名其妙 **mò míng qí miào** (no one can explain its mystery) "unfathomable, incomprehensible, perplexing"

- 玄而又玄 **xuán ér yòu xuán** (mysterious and more mysterious) "curiouser and curiouser"

6.13 Classical allusions

The meanings of the idioms above are more or less understandable from their component parts. Another type of Chinese saying is the "classical allusion," which refers to a story in Classical Chinese literature to describe a certain situation. If you know the story, well and good, otherwise these sayings can appear very obscure indeed. These following classical allusions are all very common in modern spoken Chinese: they are also more than 2,000 years old.

- 自相矛盾 **zì xiāng máo dùn** (mutual reciprocal spear shield)
  A man wanted to sell his spear and shield by claiming that the spear was so sharp no shield could resist it, and his shield was so hard no spear could pierce it. This expression now means "mutually contradictory." 矛盾 **máo dùn** "spear and shield" was used to translate the Marxist term "contradiction." It is now commonly used to describe any sort of argument, such as marital discord: 他们两个人有矛盾 **tāmen liǎngge rén yǒu máodùn** "those two have a contradiction." A famous left-wing writer in the 1930s adopted the nom-de-plume 茅盾 **Máo Dùn**, using the homophonous character 茅 (with the grass radical: "thatching") as this is a recognized surname, whereas 矛 **máo** "spear" is not.

- 杞人忧天 **Qǐ rén yōu tiān** (Qi man worry sky)
  A man of the ancient state of Qi was always worried that the sky might fall down. This expression now means "to have groundless fears."

- 守株待兔 **shǒu zhū dài tù** (guard stump wait hare)
  A man saw a hare bump into a tree stump, break its neck and die. Happy at getting something for nothing, he sat by the tree day after day, waiting for another hare to come by and do the same thing. The expression is used to warn against hoping for an unexpected windfall, or to expect that just because something has happened before, it will happen again.

- 朝三暮四 **zhāo sān mù sì** (morning three evening four)
  A man offered his monkeys three chestnuts in the morning, and four in the evening, but they complained this was too little. So he offered them four in the morning, and three in the evening, which they were happy to accept. This expression is used to express the ease with which monkeys (and certain people) can be hoodwinked.

- 画蛇添足 **huà shé tiān zú** (draw snake add feet)
  A pot of wine was given to a group of friends. There was not enough wine for all of them, so they decided to have a competition: whoever was first to finish drawing a snake would win the wine. One man did so more quickly than the others, but being a bit too smart for his own good (as the Chinese would say, 太聪明了 **tài cōngmíng le**) he added some legs. He lost the competition because what he had drawn was no longer a snake. This expression means "to ruin something by adding superfluous details."

- 狐假虎威 **hú jiǎ hǔ wēi** (fox borrows tiger fearsomeness)
  A fox wanted to establish his leadership of the pack by claiming that the animals of the forest were all afraid of him. The fox followed a tiger (at a distance). When the foxes saw the other animals all running away they thought it was because of the fox. This expression refers to a small but smart creature (or person) using powerful connections to get his way.

- 鹬蚌相争, 渔人得利 **yù bàng xiāng zhēng, yú rén dé lì** (snipe clam mutually struggle, fisherman receives benefit)
  A snipe saw a clam on the beach and tried to peck at it, but the clam snapped shut, catching the snipe's beak. Neither could give way, and both were finally caught by a passing fisherman. This expression now refers to a stalemate, especially one in which a third party could benefit.

- 井底之蛙 **jǐng dī zhī wā** (well bottom frog)
  A frog spent all his life sitting at the bottom of the well, but thought he could see the whole sky from his vantage point. This expression is used to

describe people of limited experience or outlook, especially those who think they know a lot.

- 刻舟求剑 **kè zhōu qiú jiàn** (carve boat search sword)
  On a boat journey a man accidentally dropped his sword into a river. He decided to make a mark on the side of the boat at the place where the sword had fallen, so that he could find it later. Later when the boat landed, he was surprised that he could not locate the fallen sword. This expression is used to describe people who act in the same old way, who are unimaginative in coping with changed circumstances. It is in general use, and was commonly used during the first few years after the end of the Cultural Revolution, to describe the inability of some officials to realize that times indeed had changed.

- 塞翁失马 **sài wēng shī mǎ** (frontier old man lose horse)
  An old frontierman's horse ran away but returned later, bringing other horses with it. In another incident his son broke his leg, but was then found unfit for military service. This expression means "a blessing in disguise."

- 五十步笑百步 **wǔ shí bù xiào bǎi bù** (fifty steps laugh hundred steps)
  Soldiers who fled fifty paces from the field of battle laughed at those who fled a hundred paces: a case of "the pot calling the kettle black."

- 四面楚歌 **sì miàn Chǔ gē** (four sides Chu songs)
  In the final battle for the empire after the fall of the Qin dynasty, the leader of the Chu armies heard the Songs of Chu in the camp of the opposing forces. He realized his troops had deserted him, and that he had lost the campaign. He then killed his horse, his concubine and himself. The story runs through the film *Farewell My Concubine*. The expression means "to be besieged on all sides; to be under fire from all sides without any hope of rescue."

- 世外桃源 **shì wài táo yuán** (world outside peach source)
  A fisherman followed a grove of peach blossoms to its source, which led him to an ideal world. This expression refers to a refuge beyond the world of everyday cares, a utopia, Shangri-la. Often used of Australia.

- 一枕黄粱 **yī zhěn huáng liáng** (one pillow yellow millet)
  A man went to sleep while cooking some millet. He dreamt he became a

famous scholar, married a beautiful woman, had five sons, became a powerful official ... then he woke up and realized that the millet had not yet been cooked. This expression refers to the transitory nature or delusions of success and glory. *Sic transit gloria mundi.*

- 名落孙山 **míng luò Sūn Shān** (name below Sun Shan)
  When asked about the results of an examination, a candidate told people his name was "just below that of Sun Shan." He did not mention that Sun Shan was last on the list of successful examination candidates. A euphemism for failing an examination. I have often reflected on the unfortunate Sun Shan, whose name has gone down in Chinese history as the man who just scraped in.

6.14 歇后语 xiēhòuyǔ

There is yet another type of Chinese idiom, the 歇后语 **xiēhòuyǔ** "wait for the next word." You need say only the first part of a saying, knowing that your listener will know the second part. So we have:

- 屎壳郎戴花 **shǐkeláng dài huā** "a dung beetle wearing flowers" = 臭美 **chòuměi** "smelly and beautiful" = "unctuous, supercilious"

- 泥菩萨过江 **ní púsà guò jiāng** "a mud bodhisattva crossing the river" = 自身难保 **zì shēn nán bǎo** "I'm in no position to help you, I have enough problems looking after myself."

- 外甥打灯笼 **wài shēng dǎ dēnglóng** "the sister's son is carrying a lantern" = 照舅 **zhào jiù** "to shed light on his maternal uncle," which has the same pronunciation as 照旧 **zhào jiù** "as usual, just the same."

- 懒婆娘的裹脚 **lǎn póniáng de guǒjiǎo** "a lazy old hag's foot bindings," which are said to be 又长又臭 **yòu cháng yòu chòu** "both long and smelly," said of a long boring speech.

- 小葱拌豆腐 **xiǎo cōng bàn dòufu** "spring onions mixed in beancurd," which can be described as 一青二白 **yī qīng èr bái** "one green two white," which is homophonous with 一清二白 **yī qīng èr bái** "one clear two white," meaning "very obvious."

The Beijing dialect word for frog, 蛤蟆 **háma**, mentioned above in the word-for "toad" (癞蛤蟆 **làiháma** "ugly frog") also appears in the **xiēhòuyǔ** 蛤蟆跳

井 **háma tiào jǐng** "frog jumping into a well," which makes the sound 扑通 **pūtōng** "splash," which sounds like 不懂 **bùdǒng** "I can't understand."

These are relatively straightforward examples. Guessing the meaning of **xiēhòuyǔ** is a sort of parlor game, like trying to work out the answer to a riddle. A recent dictionary of 歇后语 **xiēhòuyǔ** lists 9,000 of them.

6.15 Illogical expressions

Some Chinese expressions, if taken literally, do not seem to make any sense at all. Examples:

- 救火 **jiù huǒ** "save fire" means to save someone from a fire, or to put out the fire

- 养病 **yǎng bìng** "nurture a disease" means to look after yourself when you are sick

- 生前 **shēngqián** "before he was born" means "before he died"

- 好容易 **hǎo róngyi**, which seems to mean "very easy," in fact means "with great difficulty"

- 手足之情 **shǒuzú zhī qíng** "the emotion of hands and feet" means "brotherly love"

- 裹足 **guǒzú** "bound feet" means "to hesitate to move forward," and is an abbreviation of the *chengyu* 裹足不前 **guǒzú bù qián** (bound feet not go forward)

- 终身大事 **zhōng shēn dà shì** (end body big affair) looks as if it might mean "funeral," when in fact it means "wedding."

My favorite example of the perversity of Chinese is 年方二八 **nián fāng èr bā**, literally "years only two eight," which, one might think, means "she was twenty eight years old." In fact it means "she was only sixteen." The classical expression 破瓜 **pò guā** (break the melon) means "to deflower a virgin." The character for "melon," 瓜 **guā**, if split into two, gives two 八 **bā** "eight." So 破瓜 **pò guā** or 二八 **èr bā** also means "to reach sixteen years of age." It is at such times one feels like giving up. Chinese is not for the faint-hearted. On the other hand, it could be said that, like China itself, it provides an endless source of amazement and fun for discovery of the unexpected. You never know what tricks the language is going to play on you next.

6.16 Quotations

In addition to the various types of proverbs and idioms listed above, Chinese are also fond of quoting various philosophers, poets, writers and politicians. These quotations are also very common in everyday speech. So from Confucius we have:

- 己所不欲, 勿施于人 **jǐ suǒ bù yù, wù shī yú rén** "that which you do not like yourself, do not inflict on other people" (do unto others as you would have them do unto you)

- 有朋自远方来, 不亦乐乎 **yǒupéng zì yuǎn fāng lái, bù yì lè hū** "to have friends come from faraway places, is this not a pleasure" (as a foreigner you will hear this quotation from Confucius very often)

- 三人行, 必有我师焉 **sān rén xíng, bì yǒu wǒ shī yān** "three people walking, there will certainly be my teacher among them" (I can always learn something from other people)

- 昼闻道, 夕死可矣 **zhòu wén dào, xī sǐ kě yǐ** "if in the morning I hear the Way [of Heaven], it is alright if I die in the evening."

And many, many others.

The *Quotations of Mao Zedong* was compulsory reading during the Cultural Revolution, and some of his more pithy sayings are still common:

- 搬起石头打自己的脚 **bānqǐ shítou dǎ zìjǐ de jiǎo** "to lift up a rock only to drop it on your own feet"

- 树欲静而风不止 **shù yù jìng ér fēng bù zhǐ** "the tree wants peace but the wind won't stop"

- 天下大乱, 形势大好 **tiānxià dàluàn, xíngshì dà hǎo** "there is great disorder under Heaven, and the situation is excellent," and

- 一切反动派都是纸老虎 **yīqiè fǎndòngpài dōu shi zhǐ lǎohǔ** "all reactionaries are paper tigers."

The Tang poet Du Fu was often quoted after the Cultural Revolution: 国破山河在 **guó pò shān hé zài** "the country is in ruins, only the mountains and rivers remain." The epitome of villainy is summed up in a quotation from the Ming novel *The Romance of the Three Kingdoms*. After having killed an innkeeper and his wife whom he suspected were plotting to kill him (in fact they were planning to kill a pig for his supper) Cao Cao's comment was: 宁可我负天下人，不可天下人负我 **nìng kě wǒ fù tiānxià rén, bù kě tiānxià rén fù wǒ** "I would rather betray the whole world than to allow the world to betray me." Another common quotation from the *Romance of the Three Kingdoms* is 三十六计，走为上计 **sānshíliù jì, zǒu wéi shàng jì** "of the thirty six stratagems, running away is the best."

Chinese intellectuals concerned about the future of China often quote the Song statesman Fan Zhongyan: 先天下之忧而忧，后天下之乐而乐 **xiān tiānxià zhī yōu ér yōu, hòu tiānxià zhī lè ér lè** "worry about the world before anyone else, and be happy only after everyone else is happy." Or they might quote the motto of the Donglin Academy, 东林书院 **Dōnglín Shūyuàn**, a group of reformist scholars in the late Ming who were massacred by court eunuchs for their cause: 风声，雨声，读书声，声声入耳。家事，国事，天下事，事事关心 **fēng shēng, yǔ shēng, dú shū shēng, shēng shēng rù ěr. Jiā shì, guó shì, tiānxià shì, shì shì guān xīn** "the sound of wind, the sound of rain, the sound of books read aloud: all these sounds enter our ears. Family matters, national matters, all matters under heaven, all these matters concern our hearts."

When they are drinking people might say 三碗不过岗 **sānwǎn bù guò gǎng** "three cups and you can't cross the mountain ridge," referring to a famous drinking scene in the Ming dynasty novel *The Men of the Marshes*. In referring to the difficulty of reforming the bureaucracy, they might say 百足之虫，死而不僵 **bǎi zú zhī chóng, sǐ ér bù jiāng** "an insect with a hundred legs might die but it doesn't get stiff," quoting from the Qing dynasty novel *The Dream of the Red Chamber*. Or if they want to make a really obscure (and whimsical) comment on the modern world, they might quote from the first chapter of the same book: 假作真时真亦假，无为有处有还无 **jiǎ zuò zhēn shí zhēn yì jiǎ, wú wéi yǒu chù yǒu huán wú** "when false is true, truth is also false; when nothing becomes something, something also becomes nothing." A saying as abstruse but somehow as meaningful as you would find anywhere.

By this stage in your studies you will have realized you are not just learning a language, you are learning a complete civilization. Such complications are best left to more advanced studies, but you can see some of the delights Chinese yet has in stock for you!

6.17 Conclusion

So there we are. Such is the Chinese language. We leave you with a few Chinese proverbs:

- 天不怕, 地不怕, 只怕洋鬼子说中国话 **tiān bù pà, dì bù pà, zhǐ pà yángguǐzi shuō Zhōngguóhuà** "Heaven is not to be feared, earth is not to be feared. The only thing to be feared is a foreign devil speaking Chinese."

- 不怕慢, 只怕站 **bù pà màn, zhǐ pà zhàn** "do not fear slowness, only fear stopping."

- 学如逆水行舟 **xué rú nì shuǐ xíng zhōu** "studying is like rowing a boat against the tide." If you relax your efforts, you will go backwards.

- 不入虎穴, 焉得虎子 **bù rù hǔ xuè, yān dé hǔ zǐ** "if you do not enter the tiger's cave, you cannot expect to catch a tiger cub." Nothing ventured, nothing gained.

Or to quote Chairman Mao,

- 下定决心, 不怕牺牲, 排除万难, 去争取胜利 **xiàdìng juéxīn, bù pà xīshēng, páichú wànnàn, qù zhēngqǔ shènglì** "be resolute, fear no sacrifice, surmount every difficulty, grasp victory!"

Finally, a quote from the spiritual founder of Daoism, 老子 Lao Zi:

- 千里之行, 始于足下 **qiān lǐ zhī xíng, shǐ yú zú xià** "a thousand *lǐ* journey is started by taking the first step."

And a modern farewell: 一路平安 **yīlù píng ān**! "Have a great trip!"

Sources of Illustrations
and Quotations

Figure 1 (p. 16): Herbert A. Giles, A *Chinese-English Dictionary*, First edition, Shanghai, 1892; Second edition, revised and enlarged, Shanghai 1912; reprinted Ch'eng-wen, Taiwan, 1978

Figure 3 (p. 31): Qiu Xigui, *Chinese Writing* (Translated by Gilbert L. Mattos and Jerry Norman), The Society for the Study of Early China, Institute of East Asian Studies, University of California, Berkeley, 2000

Figure 6 (p. 56): *Chinese Character Exercise Book for Practical Chinese Reader, Book 1* ,The Commercial Press, Beijing, 1981

Figure 10 (p. 70): *The Kangxi Dictionary* was first published in 1716

Figure 13 (p. 74): *The Thousand Character Classic* dates from the Liang dynasty, 502–557

Figures 14, 15 (pp. 79, 80): Oracle bone texts from Li Pu, *Jiaguwen xuan zhu* [Selected oracle bone inscriptions with notes], Shanghai, Guji, reprint 1993

Figure 17 (p. 82): Modern calligraphy based on the oracle bone script: Liu Xinglong, *Jiaguwen jilian* [Couplets in the oracle bone script]. Beijing Ribao,1989

Figures 18, 19 (pp. 83, 84): Bronze inscriptions from Qin Yonglong, *Xi Zhou Jinwen Xuanzhu* [Bronze inscriptions from the Western Zhou, with notes], Beijing Shifan Daxue Chubanshe, 1992

Figure 20 (p. 86): Calligraphy in the small seal style from *Wu zhuan Lunyu* [The Analects written in the Wu style of the small seal script], reprinted Taiwan, 1967

Middle Chinese (p. 88): Transcribed form of Middle Chinese based on William Baxter, *An Etymological Dictionary of Common Chinese Characters* (with modifications).

Figure 21 (p. 91): hP'ags-pa script from: Junast (ed), *Xinbian Yuandai Basiba zi Baijiaxing* [Newly edited Yuan dynasty hP'ags-pa script Hundred Family Surnames], Wenwu Chubanshe, Beijing 2003

"A Conversation in Shanghaiese" (p. 97): from Lance Eccles, *Shanghai Dialect, An Introduction to Speaking the Contemporary Language*, Dunwoody Press, 1993

"A Conversation in Cantonese" (p. 99): from Sidney Lau, *Cantonese—A Crash Course,* Hongkong, 1979

"A Conversation in Hakka" (p. 100): adapted from *Hakka One*, Maryknoll Language School, Taiwan, 1975

"A Conversation in Hokkien" (p. 101): adapted from N. C. Bodman, *Spoken Amoy Hokkien*, Kuala Lumpur, 1955

"A Conversation in Fuzhou (Foochow)" (p. 101): Examples of Fuzhou (Foochow) from teaching material from Ma-tsu.

"A Conversation in Chaozhou" (p. 103): Examples of Chaozhou conversation from Lin Lunlun, *Cháozhöuhuà yïyuè töng,* Guangdong, 1997.

Tables of dialect readings (pp. 104–105); adapted from Forrest, *The Chinese Language*, pp. 325–339, Faber and Faber, 1965.

Figures 24, 25 (pp. 144, 146): adapted from *Practical Chinese Reader, Book 1*, The Commercial Press, Beijing, 1981

p. 172: reference to *People's Daily* commentary under the name of Wu Ming, Feb. 2, 2006.

Suggestions for Further Reading

It is possible to learn a lot about Chinese from a book like this, and it is possible to *improve* your Chinese by guided readings with notes and vocabulary lists, but it is not possible to actually *learn* Chinese without a teacher. This even applies if your aim is purely to learn to read Classical Poetry—you need to acquire a reasonable command of modern Chinese before you can even begin an elementary textbook on Classical Chinese.

If you intend to learn some conversational Chinese in an evening class, you will be guided in your choice of textbook by your teacher. If you are studying in an English-speaking country, this will very likely be one of the books in the *Teach Yourself* series, the *Colloquial* series or Hugo's *Three Month* series. These books teach the basic vocabulary and grammatical structure of simple modern spoken Chinese, but they need to be studied thoroughly through to the last lesson to be effective. Chinese being what it is, this is likely to take you more than three months, especially at the rate of a couple of hours a week. Sometimes these books have some characters in them, but they do not teach characters in a regular fashion.

Phrase books are not a substitute for such a course, but they have their uses. They often contain lists of everyday items which textbooks do not have room to include. To use them on your travels, you still need to be able to pronounce the *pinyin* or imitated pronunciation acceptably. Many of them have accompanying tapes. As a supplementary language learning tool, they can be very helpful. The *Lonely Planet* and *Berlitz* phrasebooks are reliable, up-to-date and more than adequate for this purpose.

If you are studying Chinese at a tertiary institution, you will probably use a textbook which teaches characters right from Lesson One. For decades a succession of books from the Beijing Language Institute (now the Beijing Language University) have been used in something like 70% of university courses in English-speaking countries, at least for the first year or so. Over the past four or five years the National Office for the Teaching of Chinese as a Foreign

Language has been developing its own series of up-to-date, authoritative text-books. The current one is called the *New Practical Chinese Reader* (新实用汉语课本 *Xin Shiyong Hanyu Keben*). This course is designed to be covered in the first year of an intensive Chinese language course in Beijing, and comes in three volumes, each of which has its own workbook, teacher's guide and tapes. After having finished this course, a student can confidently expect to pass the basic level of the *HSK Chinese Proficiency Examination*. This course presumes 4 hours per day, five days a week, for ten months. At the rate Chinese is studied at most universities in the west, the course would take three years—though at most universities there would also be lectures on Chinese literature, history, civilization and so on from the second year onwards.

There are other language courses used in some universities (particularly the United States), but my own preference is to use the most recent textbooks from China. Some of the language in some textbooks published elsewhere is quaint, weird or just plain wrong.

You will need a dictionary, or rather a series of dictionaries, during your studies. The *Oxford Starter Chinese Dictionary* (Oxford, 2000) is a very useful dictionary for the modern beginner. The most recent dictionary of this type is the new *Collins Chinese Dictionary* (2006). For many years the *Times English-Chinese (Pinyin) Dictionary*, also known as *The Pocket English-Chinese (Pinyin) Dictionary* (Commercial Press) and the *Concise English-Chinese Chinese-English Dictionary* (Oxford University Press) were widely used by beginning and intermediate level students, but are now perhaps a little dated. In these dictionaries characters are transcribed into *pinyin*, and examples of usage, also in characters and *pinyin*, are also given. Many students use them as vocabulary builders as well as reference works. Sooner or later you will need to know all the characters and words in dictionaries of this level, so you may as well start early in your studies.

There are a number of dictionaries published in China which are guides to the HSK examination, and as such can be considered intermediate level dictionaries. The HSK 词语用法详解 *HSK Ciyu Yongfa Xiangjie* [A Guide to the Usage of HSK Vocabulary], published by the Beijing Language and Culture University, lists the prescribed characters at each level with a brief English gloss, and gives examples of correct usage.

For many years the standard dictionary for all serious students of Chinese was the 汉英词典 *Han-Ying Cidian* [Chinese-English Dictionary], edited by

吴景荣 Wu Jingrong, published in 1978. It was superceded by the 汉英词典 (修订版)*Han-Ying Cidian* (*Xiudingban*) [Chinese-English Dictionary (Revised)], published in 1995 and again in 1997. In both of these editions, all the headwords and compounds are given in characters and *pinyin*, but the examples only in characters. The latest edition is called the 现代汉英词典 *Xiandai Hanyu Cidian* [A Modern Chinese-English Dictionary] (2001), which contains 53,000 entries, of which 10,000 are newly added, reflecting the changes in the language over the past few years. A similar number of rare or obsolete characters and expressions were deleted. In this edition, however, *pinyin* is only given for the headwords, not for sub-entries or examples, and so is really only suitable for advanced foreign students. If your aim is to read modern Chinese, however, it is invaluable, and you had better become an advanced student as soon as you can. In the meantime, however, you will find the earlier edition (1997) much more useful, and which will probably meet most of your needs.

If you are reading Chinese of the pre-liberation period, sooner or later you will need to become acquainted with Matthew's *Chinese-English Dictionary*. This is a work of great sinological erudition, full of the most amazing information, but it can also be infuriatingly difficult to use. Its continued usefulness, however, is indicated by the fact that it has recently been republished, and beautifully reproduced editions are readily available. A must-have for the budding sinologist.

Another very important dictionary is 梁實秋 Liang Shih-ch'iu's *A New Practical Chinese-English Dictionary*. This was published in Taiwan in 1972, and is in traditional characters. All the headwords and compounds are given in the National Phonetic Alphabet, which is a major incentive to the serious student to learn the system. The latest (abridged) edition, under the title *Far East Chinese-English Dictionary* (2000), edited by Zhang Fangjie, has indices in the 国语罗马字 *Gwoyeu Romatzyh* romanization as well as *pinyin*, which it calls the "UN Mandarin Phonetic Symbols." This dictionary was also published in the Mainland in 1994, under the same title, but compounds and expressions are given in *pinyin*, and characters are given in both simplified and traditional scripts.

Another dictionary which is very valuable for reading pre-liberation Chinese, or Chinese as it is used outside Mainland China, is 林语堂 Lin Yutang's 當代 漢英詞典 *Chinese-English Dictionary of Modern Usage* (Chinese University of Hong Kong, 1972). This contains many words not listed elsewhere, especially from vernacular literature. Lin invented his own romanization system and his own method of classifying characters, neither of which has caught on. Most students get the hang of it after a while, and can generally locate a character in the index, romanized according to Lin's system, which refers to a page number.

Interestingly enough, the biggest and most comprehensive dictionaries of Chinese are in Japanese, Russian and French. Until recently most sinologists relied on Morohashi's 大漢和詞典 *Dai Kan-Wa Jiten* [Great Chinese-Japanese Dictionary] to locate really difficult words or obscure references. It was translated and adapted into Chinese in Taiwan in the 1960s, under the title 中文大辭典 *Zhongwen Da Cidian*. The *Bolshoi Kitaĭsko-Russkiĭ Slovar'* of Oshanin (1980) is in four volumes. *Le Grand Dictionnaire Ricci de la Langue Chinoise* (2002) is in six volumes, plus a further volume of indices and supplements; it contains 13,500 characters and over 300,000 expressions, all translated into French. The new three-volume *Comprehensive Chinese-English Dictionary* published in Liaoning (2004) includes a large number of specialist, scientific and technical terms, as well as being a comprehensive dictionary of the modern and pre-modern forms of Chinese. A project now underway in Norway, the *Thesaurus Linguae Sericae*, under the editorship of Christoph Harbsmeier, is a web-based resource which aims to include practically everything written in Chinese, including oracle bone texts, bronze inscriptions, the classical corpus, Buddhist texts, vernacular literature, modern Chinese—with interlinear translations into English and links to dictionary entries. You can find more information on the TLS on the web.

Most sinologists nowadays rely on Chinese encyclopedic dictionaries, but there are still many occasions when one needs a direct translation rather than a definition, and this is when Matthews or the *Grande Dictionnaire Ricci* is invaluable. A very useful dictionary recently published is the 汉字英释大字典 *Hanzi Yingshi Da Zidian* [Chinese Character Dictionary with English Annotations], which gives an English equivalent of 29,000 characters, far more than the 7,000 or so one would find in Matthews, Liang Shih-ch'iu or Lin Yutang. There are also a large number of specialized dictionaries available. Examples taken more or less at random would include *A Chinese-English Glossary of Cultural Relics and Archeology* (2005), *A Chinese-English Dictionary of Buddhist Terms* (2005), *Tibetological Terminology Chinese-English, English-Chinese* (1997), *Chinese-English Dictionary of Traditional Chinese Medicine* (1988), *A Chinese-English Dictionary of the Historical Archives in the Ming and Qing* (1999) and any number of similar dictionaries for specialists. Of course you will not need any of these for a long time, but it may be reassuring to know that such dictionaries exist.

The advanced student of Chinese also has a number of Chinese-only dictionaries on his bookshelf. There are six basic ones: the 新华字典 *Xinhua Zidian*, the 现代汉语词典 *Xiandai Hanyu Cidian*, 辞海 *Cihai*, 词源 *Ciyuan*, 汉语大字典 *Hanyu Da Zidian* and the 汉语大词典 *Hanyu Da Cidian*. The difference between a 字典 **zìdiǎn** and a 词典 **cídiǎn** is that the former is a dictionary of characters (字 **zì**) and the latter is a dictionary of words (词 **cí**). 词 **cí** is also written 辞 [辭] , so you occasionally see this word written 辞典 [辭典].

The 新华字典 *Xinhua Zidian* is a modern dictionary of characters—standard, simplified and "alternate" of the modern Chinese language, with standard (and alternate) readings. The most recent edition was 2004.

The 现代汉语词典 *Xiandai Hanyu Cidian* is a dictionary of words. The most recent edition is 2005. It is the equivalent of a desk dictionary such as *The Concise Oxford*.

The 词源 *Ciyuan* is an encyclopedic dictionary in four volumes which essentially concentrates on the language prior to 1840 (the Opium War). The 辞海 *Cihai*, in three volumes, concentrates on the language from 1840 to 1949, though there is of course a lot of overlap, and many pre-Opium War expressions are still in common use. The 汉语大字典 *Hanyu Da Zidian* is a dictionary, in eight volumes, of practically every character ever used in Chinese.

If all else fails (as often happens), you can consult the twelve volume 汉语大词典 *Hanyu Da Cidian*. Generally speaking, you can find practically anything in this dictionary. But the definitions, of course, are in Chinese, and the examples are often in Classical Chinese (without translation). It is not very helpful if you need an English equivalent.

These dictionaries are always available in any medium-sized bookshop which sells Chinese books, or which specializes in foreign languages. Any university library will have most of them, as will many non-university reference libraries. Most serious students of Chinese start buying dictionaries and other reference material early in their studies, and keep buying during their lives. New dictionaries appear constantly, and older ones quickly become out of date—and no one dictionary is likely to meet every need you might have.

Most books on the history of the Chinese language are highly technical, but if you are interested in this aspect of Chinese you can consult Jerry Norman's *Chinese* (Cambridge 1988) or S. Robert Ramsey's The *Languages of China* (Princeton 1987). Older books, such as R. A. D. Forrest's *The Chinese Language* (Faber and Faber, 1965), are now dated, but contain much information which is still of interest. A more recent reliable book about the development of Modern Chinese over the past hundred years or so is Ping Chen's *Modern Chinese—History and Sociolinguistics* (Cambridge 1999).

If you are interested in the etymologies of Chinese characters, you could start with 谢光辉 Xie Guanghui's 常用汉字图解 *Changyong Hanzi Tujie* [The Composition of Common Chinese Characters—An Illustrated Account] (Peking University Press, 1997). This (and similar books) give examples from the oracle bone and bronze forms of characters, and traditional etymologies (not all of which are accepted by specialists nowadays). An attractive book for learners is Edoardo Fazzioli's *Understanding Chinese Characters—A Beginner's Guide to the Chinese Language*, originally published in Italian in 1986. There are many books of this type on the market, but some are fanciful from a scholarly point of view. A scholarly but very technical book on the development of the Chinese script is Qiu Xigui's *Chinese Writing* (Berkeley 2000), an English translation by Gilbert Mattos and Jerry Norman of a standard Chinese work.

If you would like to learn some Classical Chinese, books published overseas are more helpful than books published in China, which are aimed at advanced students. Jeannette L. Faurot's *Gateway to the Chinese Classics—A Practical Guide to Literary Chinese* (1995) is an excellent introduction for students who have barely begun Modern Chinese. If you would like to have some first hand acquaintance with Tang poetry relatively early in your studies, you could start with Faurot's supplementary volume *Drinking With The Moon—Selections of Classical Chinese Poetry* (1998). You can then move on to textbooks of Classical Chinese published in China, such as 徐宗才 Xu Zongcai's 古代汉语课本 *Gudai Hanyu Keben* [Textbook of Classical Chinese] (Beijing Language and Culture University, 3 vols, 1998) which contains much the same texts as the Chinese high school syllabus, and which derives ultimately from the 古文观止 *Guwen Guanzhi* [Anthology of Classical Chinese], first published in 1695.